LIVING *the* WORD

**Scripture Reflections and Commentaries
for Sundays and Holy Days**

MW00413305

**Dennis D. Sylva and
Rev. James A. Wallace, C.Ss.R**

NOVEMBER 29, 2009 THROUGH NOVEMBER 21, 2010   YEAR C

LIVING *the* WORD

Scripture Reflections and Commentaries
for Sundays and Holy Days

Vol. 25   November 29, 2009–November 21, 2010

Published annually

Individual copy: $14.95
(2-9 copies: $10.95 per copy;
10-24 copies: $9.95 per copy;
25-99 copies: $8.95 per copy;
100 or more copies: $6.95 per copy)

Scripture readings are taken from the *Lectionary for Mass*, copyright © 1970, 1997, 1998, Confraternity of Christian Doctrine, Washington, DC. All rights reserved. Used by permission.

The English translation of some psalm responses from *Lectionary for Mass*, © 1969, 1981, 1997, International Committee on English in the Liturgy, Inc. (ICEL); excerpts from the English translation of *The Roman Missal*, © 1973, ICEL. All rights reserved. Used by permission.

Excerpt from the English translation of the sequence *Lauda Sion* is taken from *The Roman Missal* approved by the National Conference of Catholic Bishops of the United States © 1964 by the National Catholic Welfare Conference, Inc. All rights reserved.

Excerpt from *Deus Caritas Est*, ©2005, *Libreria Editrice Vaticana*. Used with permission.

Excerpt from *Mother Teresa: Come Be My Light*, © 2007, Doubleday Books, New York, NY. All rights reserved. Used by permission.

Editor: Michael E. Novak
Copy Editor: Marcia T. Lucey
Typesetter: Tejal Patel
Cover Design: Jane Pitz and Tejal Patel
Director of Publications: Mary Beth Kunde-Anderson

Copyright © 2009 by World Library Publications,
the music and liturgy division of J. S. Paluch Company, Inc.
3708 River Road, Suite 400, Franklin Park, IL 60131-2158
800 566-6150 • fax 888 957-3291
wlpcs@jspaluch.com • www.wlpmusic.com
All rights reserved.

Printed in the United States of America
WLP 006774 • (ISSN) 1079-4670 • (ISBN) 978-1-58459-443-7

Our renewed liturgy has generated a great deal of interest in sacred scripture. In turn, a richer appreciation of the readings for Mass has done much for participation in our liturgical celebrations. *Living the Word* is designed to help facilitate this twofold deepening of the Christian life. It is our hope that individuals, homilists, catechumens, candidates, discussion groups, religious education classes, and similar gatherings will all benefit from the commentaries and reflections found on these pages.

The readings for each Sunday, holy day, and major celebration from November 2009 through November 2010, Year C of the Lectionary cycle, are presented here, along with a brief passage intended to suggest a focus or approach to consider while reading them. Following the readings is a commentary that provides a context for understanding them, incorporating both biblical scholarship and the Church's age-old wisdom. A reflection section develops the initial focus and ties it together with the commentary. The discussion questions and suggestions for responses that follow offer help in moving from reflection to action, inviting those who use this volume to go about truly "Living the Word."

Whether reflecting on the scriptures in a group setting or individually, it is best to do so in the context of prayer. Consider creating an atmosphere that will foster prayerful reflection when you are using this book. In a quiet space, perhaps with lit candles and simple seasonal decoration (incense or soft music may also be appropriate), begin with a prayer and read aloud the scriptures for that day, even if you are alone. Groups can encourage members to focus on one word or idea that speaks to them from each reading. Participants might want to share these ideas with one another before continuing.

After listening to the readings, ask yourself how they have changed you, enlightened you, moved you. Proceed to the commentary, reflection, and response. Use the discussion questions to shape your conversation or as a springboard for your own questions. How does the brief "Responding to the Word" reflection invite you to "live the word" in your relationship with God, with family and friends, at work, school, or church, or in the broader community?

Having started with prayer, perhaps once you have spent time in reflection or discussion it will be appropriate to lift up someone or something in a prayer that is related to the readings or your reflections. Pray spontaneously as you think about the texts' meaning for you, or invite people in the group to offer prayers informally.

Finally, what action will you take this week that grows out of your prayerful reflection on this week's scriptures? You may propose your own prayer for help to do something in response to the readings or simply stand and pray the Lord's Prayer. If you are in a group, offer one another a sign of peace before departing. If alone, extend yourself to another in a gesture of peace later in the day or week, in person, by phone, or by offering a simple prayer.

Repeating this pattern over time can help your prayerful reflection to deepen your appreciation for and commitment to God's word every day of your life.

Table of Contents

Prayers Before Reading Scripture

Lord Jesus,
we give you praise.
Speak to us as we read your word,
and send your Spirit into our hearts.
Guide us today and each day in your service,
for you are our way, our truth, our life.

Lord Jesus, we love you:
keep us in your love for ever and ever. *Amen!*

or

Blessed are you, Lord God,
king of all creation:
you have taught us by your word.
Open our hearts to your Spirit,
and lead us on the paths of Christ your Son.

All praise and glory be yours for ever. *Amen!*

or

Lord, open our hearts:
let your Spirit speak to us
as we read your word. *Amen!*

or

Lord Jesus,
to whom shall we go?
You have the words of eternal life.

Speak, Lord,
your servants are listening:
here we are, Lord,
ready to do your will. *Amen!*

Prayers After Reading Scripture

Blessed are you, Lord God,
maker of heaven and earth,
ruler of the universe:
you have sent your Holy Spirit
to teach your truth to your holy people.
We praise you for letting us read your word today.

Grant that we may continue to think and pray
over the words we have read,
and to share your thoughts with others
throughout this day.

Loving God, we praise you
and thank you in Jesus' name. *Amen!*

or

God of all graciousness, we thank you
for speaking to us today
through your holy word. *Amen!*

In Year C of the Lectionary the Advent and Christmas Gospels come largely from the Gospel of Luke. These readings, as well as those that accompany them, provide rich perspectives on living in ways that welcome God into our lives by welcoming others.

On the First Sunday of Advent we hear Paul inform the Thessalonian Christians about what the love that welcomes others implies. He then inspires them to love by showing how doing so transforms a person's character.

The next three Sundays the Gospel of Luke builds on this theme of welcoming God through welcoming others. On the Second Sunday of Advent the Lukan passage shows how the reign of God comes through the willingness of people to serve others even when such service is not easy for them. For the solemnity of the Immaculate Conception, Luke's Gospel reading suggests how receiving God means helping others in practical ways. It also means speaking plainly about God's actions, even in the face of accepted cultural modes of speech that deny God's movement in the world. Luke's message for the Third Sunday of Advent is that welcome is shown most truly in whether or not we use our wealth for the good of those who are in need.

The Fourth Sunday of Advent and the Christmas Mass at Midnight feature readings that highlight God's presence to those who are in difficult situations. For the Fourth Sunday of Advent we go back to the prophet Micah, who expands our horizons with vivid poetic images of God transforming the lives of those whose options seem to be limited. The Gospel for Christmas Mass at Midnight describes the beautiful nativity scene. What we may not notice, however, is how difficult it is for Mary and Joseph when they are displaced from their home at the time that Mary is about to give birth.

The feast of the Holy Family features a Lukan perspective on how family remains rooted in God's life by actively seeking God's will. The Year C reading for the feast of Mary the Mother of God shows how profoundly and powerfully God is present to those who find themselves in situations in which the larger society is of little help.

Finally, on the Sundays of the Epiphany and the Baptism of the Lord two readings from the prophet Isaiah guide us. In the first reading for Epiphany, Isaiah provides resources to counter the spiritual shortsightedness that often afflicts people who are suffering. The passage from Isaiah chosen for the Baptism of the Lord dovetails with the other two readings for this day, both from Luke's writings, to show that the purpose of Jesus' baptism was to do good for people—good that culminates in the restoration of their relationship with God.

7

November 29, 2009

FIRST SUNDAY OF ADVENT

Today's Focus: Interior Decorating

Advent invites us to begin the new church year by doing some interior decorating as we prepare for Christmas. Just as many of us will be pulling out the boxes to decorate our houses or apartments or perhaps just a particular corner of the room sometime before Christmas, we can think of Advent as a time to engage in some interior decorating of our hearts.

FIRST READING
Jeremiah 3:14–16

The days are coming, says the LORD, when I will fulfill the promise I made to the house of Israel and Judah. In those days, in that time, I will raise up for David a just shoot; he shall do what is right and just in the land. In those days Judah shall be safe and Jerusalem shall dwell secure; this is what they shall call her: "The LORD our justice."

PSALM RESPONSE
Psalm 25:1b

To you, O Lord, I lift my soul.

SECOND READING
1 Thessalonians 3:12 — 4:2

Brothers and sisters: May the Lord make you increase and abound in love for one another and for all, just as we have for you, so as to strengthen your hearts, to be blameless in holiness before our God and Father at the coming of our Lord Jesus with all his holy ones. Amen.

Finally, brothers and sisters, we earnestly ask and exhort you in the Lord Jesus that, as you received from us how you should conduct yourselves to please God—and as you are conducting yourselves —you do so even more. For you know what instructions we gave you through the Lord Jesus.

GOSPEL
Luke 21:25–28, 34–36

Jesus said to his disciples: "There will be signs in the sun, the moon, and the stars, and on earth nations will be in dismay, perplexed by the roaring of the sea and the waves. People will die of fright in anticipation of what is coming upon the world, for the powers of the heavens will be shaken. And then they will see the Son of Man coming in a cloud with power and great glory. But when these signs begin to happen, stand erect and raise your heads because your redemption is at hand.

"Beware that your hearts do not become drowsy from carousing and drunkenness and the anxieties of daily life, and that day catch you by surprise like a trap. For that day will assault everyone who lives on the face of the earth. Be vigilant at all times and pray that you have the strength to escape the tribulations that are imminent and to stand before the Son of Man.

The first Sunday of Advent features an exhortation by Paul to the Thessalonian Christians on how to prepare for the coming of Christ (1 Thessalonians 3:12 — 4:2). In a nutshell, Paul claims that nothing provides welcome like a loving environment.

This is the advice and help that Paul gives, then, in order for the Thessalonians to create such an atmosphere. First, Paul prays for their love, showing that love is foremost a gift for which people do well to look to God to provide. Prayer for others should not neglect the appeal for this special virtue in their lives.

Second, Paul provides himself as an example of love; people learn by emulation. Throughout this letter Paul has indicated the extent of his love for the Thessalonians. Thus, he and his companions took care of the spiritual needs of the Thessalonians without imposing on them. Rather, they worked night and day to support themselves while establishing the Thessalonian church (2:9). Moreover, Paul and his coworkers gave as unstintingly of themselves as a mother nursing a child or a father caring for his children (2:7, 11).

Third, the apostle claims that love transforms character. If people wish to enter into a relationship with Christ, their characters need to be reformed. The interpersonal is the engine that drives the intrapersonal; love remakes and renews people (3:12–13).

Finally, Paul clarifies for the Thessalonians how love is expressed. He takes pains to make clear that this virtue is expansive; it attempts always to do more (3:12; 4:1). This largesse of love is shown by what one does and does not do. Love attempts to grow both in refraining from immoral acts and in concentrating on the work each has been given to do (4:3–12). Love is the generous and focused attempt to do what a person has been given to do for others rather than exploiting them or being a busybody.

✛ Reflecting on the Word

How do you prepare a heart for Christmas? It is not all that different from how we prepare any room for the season. We move some things out and bring others in: lights, candles, and appropriate decorations. We can also apply this to our hearts, both our individual heart and our community heart. Today four voices offer direction.

Jeremiah calls us to remember God who worked on the house of Israel and Judah, bringing "a just shoot" (Jeremiah 33:15) to flower from the old stump that Israel had become, replacing lifeless leadership with a new branch of the house of David. Justice would flourish for all the people. Jeremiah calls us to trust God's designs that go beyond the surface.

Jesus' words, however, seem to contradict all this, predicting signs that will dismay and perplex, with people dying of fright. What happened to security and justice? But all this frightening activity is not for those waiting on the Lord. Jesus' words are strong: Don't cower; stand erect. Don't let your heart sink into sleep, dive into drink, or be corrupted by carousing. Redemption is in the room, a heartbeat away.

Paul reminds us that we best renovate our hearts by filling them with God's love for others. We do this by how we treat each other. A new year offers time to bring healing to damaged relationships, to reach out to someone we have neglected. And God works along with us, pouring the Holy Spirit into our hearts.

✥ Consider/Discuss:

- With almost four full weeks of Advent ahead, what are some ways to open your heart to others?
- What needs to be taken out to make more space for God's love?

✥ Responding to the Word

Advent is a time to enter more deeply into conversation with God. Pray with the words of the psalmist, who encourages us to turn to God, who will make known the way, teach us the right paths, and draw us into divine kindness, constancy, and friendship.

December 6, 2009

SECOND SUNDAY OF ADVENT

Today's Focus: Change the Terrain

John the Baptist was a man of God's word, both receiving and proclaiming it. While others operated from the centers of power, John was moving about "the whole region of the Jordan" (Luke 3:3), calling for people to change the terrain so that God could move easily through the world. The work's not done yet.

FIRST
READING
Baruch 5:1–9

Jerusalem, take off your robe of mourning and misery;
   put on the splendor of glory from God forever:
wrapped in the cloak of justice from God,
   bear on your head the mitre
   that displays the glory of the eternal name.
For God will show all the earth your splendor:
   you will be named by God forever
   the peace of justice, the glory of God's worship.

Up, Jerusalem! stand upon the heights;
   look to the east and see your children
gathered from the east and the west
   at the word of the Holy One,
   rejoicing that they are remembered by God.
Led away on foot by their enemies they left you:
   but God will bring them back to you
   borne aloft in glory as on royal thrones.
For God has commanded
   that every lofty mountain be made low,
and that the age–old depths and gorges
   be filled to level ground,
   that Israel may advance secure in the glory of God.
The forests and every fragrant kind of tree
   have overshadowed Israel at God's command;
for God is leading Israel in joy
   by the light of his glory,
   with his mercy and justice for company.

PSALM
RESPONSE
Psalm 126:3

The Lord has done great things for us; we are filled with joy.

SECOND READING
Philippians 1: 4–6, 8–11

Brothers and sisters: I pray always with joy in my every prayer for all of you, because of your partnership for the gospel from the first day until now. I am confident of this, that the one who began a good work in you will continue to complete it until the day of Christ Jesus. God is my witness, how I long for all of you with the affection of Christ Jesus. And this is my prayer: that your love may increase ever more and more in knowledge and every kind of perception, to discern what is of value, so that you may be pure and blameless for the day of Christ, filled with the fruit of righteousness that comes through Jesus Christ for the glory and praise of God.

GOSPEL
Luke 3:1–6

In the fifteenth year of the reign of Tiberius Caesar, when Pontius Pilate was governor of Judea, and Herod was tetrarch of Galilee, and his brother Philip tetrarch of the region of Ituraea and Trachonitis, and Lysanias was tetrarch of Abilene, during the high priesthood of Annas and Caiaphas, the word of God came to John the son of Zechariah in the desert. John went throughout the whole region of the Jordan, proclaiming a baptism of repentance for the forgiveness of sins, as it is written in the book of the words of the prophet Isaiah:

A *voice of one crying out in the desert:*
"Prepare the way of the Lord,
make straight his paths.
Every valley shall be filled
and every mountain and hill shall be made low.
The winding roads shall be made straight,
and the rough ways made smooth,
and all flesh shall see the salvation of God."

❖ Understanding the Word

Luke's account of the ministry of John the Baptist continues to provide preparation for the celebration of the birth of Christ. In Luke's Gospel, John the Baptist, as an emissary of the heavenly King, demonstrates by way of contrast to more worldly representatives how to live as an agent of God's rule.

Only Luke situates the coming of John in relation to the political and religious leaders of the day. Luke tells us in what year of the reign of the Emperor Tiberius John began preaching, who were the various regional government leaders, and who were the high priests (Luke 3:1–2). Matthew, Mark, and John do not provide this background against which to show the significance of the Baptist. Only Luke claims that "the word of God came to John" at this time (3:2). In other words, John is portrayed as a prophet who acts as a representative for God in a manner similar to the way the regional political leaders represent the emperor.

Unlike these governmental functionaries who preside over particular areas, however, John journeys "throughout the whole region of the Jordan" proclaiming baptism and repentance (3:3). This is the only place in the Gospels where we see John taking the message out to different areas instead of staying in one neighborhood. John not only preaches that people should "prepare the way of the Lord" but also goes out on the way to aid in this preparation. Later, the Lukan Jesus will contrast those who live richly in royal palaces with John, whom Jesus calls the greatest person "born of woman" (7:25, 28).

By these similarities and contrasts between John and political representatives of the emperor, Luke shows that the reign of God comes through people who are willing to engage in the rigors of moving out beyond their comfort zones for the sake of preparing "the way of the Lord" in others (3:4).

❖ Reflecting on the Word

"[T]he word of God came to John . . . in the desert. John went throughout the whole region of the Jordan, proclaiming a baptism of repentance" (Luke 3:2, 3). The word of God came to John, who then went out and proclaimed it. The important people were doing what they thought were the important things: governing, "tetrarching," high priesting. But who now remembers Philip, the tetrarch of Ituraea and Trachonitis, or Lysanias, tetrarch of Abilene? And who remembers Herod and Pilate, apart from their connection with John and Jesus?

But we continue to remember John each year at this time. He stands before us so we can hear and heed his call: "Prepare the way of the Lord, / make straight his paths" (3:4). He is the morning star of the Christmas season, the cock that signals the dawn of a new age then and a new church year now. And he calls to us now, we who live near the close of the first year of the presidency of Barack Obama, with Adrian Fenty as mayor of Washington, D.C., and Tim Kaine as governor of Virginia, and Martin O'Malley governor of Maryland, and during the pontificate of Benedict XVI and the episcopacy of Donald Wuerl as archbishop of Washington, D.C. Now, in our day, John continues to speak a word to us.

One could hear his message as the "same old same old." We heard it last year and the year before and the year before, and on and on, and a worthwhile question could be what did it mean then, and what did we do then? But Advent is a time to look forward, so we ask ourselves, what does it mean now and what are we going to do now? What needs changing?

❖ Consider/Discuss:

- What valleys need to be filled in, what mountains made low, what paths made straight, so that God can enter our world, our lives?
- What does it mean to "see the salvation of God"? How will I recognize it?

❖ Responding to the Word

We pray that God will find a way into our world this new year of grace, so that our love "may increase ever more and more in knowledge and every kind of perception, to discern what is of value, so that [we] may be pure and blameless for the day of Christ" (Philippians 1:10–11).

December 8, 2009

THE IMMACULATE CONCEPTION OF THE BLESSED VIRGIN MARY

Today's Focus: Full of Grace, Fully Alive

Today's solemnity draws our attention to what God has done in, for, and through Mary in preparing her for her unique role as the mother of God's Son: God "let her share beforehand in the salvation Christ would bring by his death, and kept her sinless from the first moment of her conception" (Sacramentary, Opening Prayer, Solemnity of the Immaculate Conception).

FIRST READING
Genesis 3: 9–15, 20

After the man, Adam, had eaten of the tree, the LORD God called to the man and asked him, "Where are you?" He answered, "I heard you in the garden; but I was afraid, because I was naked, so I hid myself." Then he asked, "Who told you that you were naked? You have eaten, then, from the tree of which I had forbidden you to eat!" The man replied, "The woman whom you put here with me — she gave me fruit from the tree, and so I ate it." The LORD God then asked the woman, "Why did you do such a thing?" The woman answered, "The serpent tricked me into it, so I ate it."

Then the LORD God said to the serpent:
"Because you have done this, you shall be banned
   from all the animals
   and from all the wild creatures;
on your belly shall you crawl,
   and dirt shall you eat
   all the days of your life.
I will put enmity between you and the woman,
   and between your offspring and hers;
he will strike at your head,
   while you strike at his heel."
The man called his wife Eve, because she became the mother of all the living.

PSALM RESPONSE
Psalm 98:1a

Sing to the Lord a new song, for he has done marvelous deeds.

SECOND READING
Ephesians 1: 3–6, 11–12

Brothers and sisters: Blessed be the God and Father of our Lord Jesus Christ, who has blessed us in Christ with every spiritual blessing in the heavens, as he chose us in him, before the foundation of the world, to be holy and without blemish before him. In love he destined us for adoption to himself through Jesus Christ, in accord with the favor of his will, for the praise of the glory of his grace that he granted us in the beloved.

In him we were also chosen, destined in accord with the purpose of the One who accomplishes all things according to the intention of his will, so that we might exist for the praise of his glory, we who first hoped in Christ.

GOSPEL
Luke 1:26–38

The angel Gabriel was sent from God to a town of Galilee called Nazareth, to a virgin betrothed to a man named Joseph, of the house of David, and the virgin's name was Mary. And coming to her, he said, "Hail, full of grace! The Lord is with you." But she was greatly troubled at what was said and pondered what sort of greeting this might be. Then the angel said to her, "Do not be afraid, Mary, for you have found favor with God. Behold, you will conceive in your womb and bear a son, and you shall name him Jesus. He will be great and will be called Son of the Most High, and the Lord God will give him the throne of David his father, and he will rule over the house of Jacob forever, and of his kingdom there will be no end." But Mary said to the angel, "How can this be, since I have no relations with a man?" And the angel said to her in reply, "The Holy Spirit will come upon you, and the power of the Most High will overshadow you. Therefore the child to be born will be called holy, the Son of God. And behold, Elizabeth, your relative, has also conceived a son in her old age, and this is the sixth month for her who was called barren; for nothing will be impossible for God."

Mary said, "Behold, I am the handmaid of the Lord. May it be done to me according to your word." Then the angel departed from her.

✦ Understanding the Word

The solemnity of the Immaculate Conception has for its Gospel reading the announcement of the angel Gabriel to Mary about the birth of Jesus. Often people focus on Mary's final words to Gabriel as the high point of the passage: "Behold, I am the handmaid of the Lord. May it be done to me according to your word" (Luke 1:38). The actions of Mary that accompany these words are also very important for understanding her response to God's salvation in her life and in the life of the world.

The next thing that Luke writes about following her response is that she "traveled to the hill country" to visit her relative Elizabeth, whom the angel Gabriel had told her was also with child (1:36, 39). Mary will remain with Elizabeth "about three months," a noteworthy time since Gabriel had informed Mary that Elizabeth was six months pregnant (1:36, 56). Elizabeth "was advanced in years" (1:7). Thus, Mary follows her acceptance of God's will in her life with a concerted effort to be of assistance to one in need.

While there her service includes more than practical matters. When Elizabeth praises Mary for believing in the fulfillment of God's word, Mary redirects the praise to God. The Canticle of Mary is focused on God. There are ten declarations in it of what God has done and five descriptions of the characteristics of God (1:46–55). When Mary speaks of herself in this canticle, however, it is always in terms of what God has done for her. God has looked upon her lowliness and done great things for her (1:48a, 49).

Mary's acceptance of God into her life is more than a matter of words. She shows a willingness to help in a practical way and also refocuses a common human tendency to praise human activity toward the reality of God's actions in our world.

The fragment that we hear today from the book of Genesis is the first sad moment in the Bible. We see what happens when we turn from God. When God calls out for them, Adam and Eve go into hiding. In answer to God's question, "Where are you?" the man replies: "I heard you in the garden; but I was afraid, because I was naked, so I hid myself" (Genesis 3:9, 10).

Adam has moved from being the custodian of the garden, entrusted with the care of all that God has made, to a creature skulking around, fearful of being naked before his Creator. Nakedness here is a symbol of being vulnerable, open, obedient before God. But Adam and Eve wanted to be "like gods who know what is good and what is bad" (3:5).

In contrast we have Mary, the handmaid of the Lord, the one who accepts God's intimacy, receiving God's plan into her life and living out God's plan, not her own. Mary is willing to serve as God sees fit. And this willingness to serve extends outward. Her elderly cousin's condition is revealed and Mary goes on the road to be with her until Elizabeth gives birth.

Faith is not a still pond but a river flowing forth in streams of love. Mary's Immaculate Conception did not make her less human but more human, more indebted to God the more she was graced. God graced her appropriately to the divine plan for her. So, too, for each of us.

❖ Consider/Discuss:

- How have I known the grace of God in my life?
- How has this grace flowed forth into actions that benefit those around me?
- How has God's love kept me "free from sin" and more fully alive?

❖ Responding to the Word

Faith leads to action, so we join with the Church in asking God: "Trace in our actions the lines of her love, in our hearts her readiness of faith. Prepare once again a world for your Son" (*Sacramentary*, Alternative Opening Prayer, Solemnity of the Immaculate Conception).

December 13, 2009

THIRD SUNDAY OF ADVENT

Today's Focus: Good Advice, Better News

Only Luke presents us with John giving particular advice to the different groups who came to him. For each group—the crowds, the tax collectors, and the soldiers—John had a specific word for their lives. But for all of them he had the same good news, awakening that part of their soul that had been waiting all their lives for what he was telling them.

FIRST READING
Zephaniah 3: 14–18a

Shout for joy, O daughter Zion!
  Sing joyfully, O Israel!
Be glad and exult with all your heart,
  O daughter Jerusalem!
The LORD has removed the judgment against you,
  he has turned away your enemies;
the King of Israel, the LORD, is in your midst,
  you have no further misfortune to fear.
On that day, it shall be said to Jerusalem:
  Fear not, O Zion, be not discouraged!
The LORD, your God, is in your midst,
  a mighty savior;
he will rejoice over you with gladness,
  and renew you in his love,
he will sing joyfully because of you,
  as one sings at festivals.

PSALM RESPONSE
Isaiah 12:6

Cry out with joy and gladness: for among you is the great and Holy One of Israel.

SECOND READING
Philippians 4: 4–7

Brothers and sisters: Rejoice in the Lord always. I shall say it again: rejoice! Your kindness should be known to all. The Lord is near. Have no anxiety at all, but in everything, by prayer and petition, with thanksgiving, make your requests known to God. Then the peace of God that surpasses all understanding will guard your hearts and minds in Christ Jesus.

GOSPEL
Luke 3:10–18

The crowds asked John the Baptist, "What should we do?" He said to them in reply, "Whoever has two cloaks should share with the person who has none. And whoever has food should do likewise." Even tax collectors came to be baptized and they said to him, "Teacher, what should we do?" He answered them, "Stop collecting more than what is prescribed." Soldiers also asked him, "And what is it that we should do?" He told them, "Do not practice extortion, do not falsely accuse anyone, and be satisfied with your wages."

Now the people were filled with expectation, and all were asking in their hearts whether John might be the Christ. John answered them all, saying, "I am baptizing you with water, but one mightier than I is coming. I am not worthy to loosen the thongs of his sandals. He will baptize you with the Holy Spirit and fire. His winnowing fan is in his hand to clear his threshing floor and to gather the wheat into his barn, but the chaff he will burn with unquenchable fire." Exhorting them in many other ways, he preached good news to the people.

✤ Understanding the Word

What does true repentance look like? This is the topic of the Gospel reading for the Third Sunday of Advent.

Unlike the Gospel of Mark, the Gospels of Matthew and Luke tie repentance for sins to how one lives. Luke is clear: true repentance will show itself in a righteous life (Luke 3:8). Unlike Matthew, Luke takes pains to give examples of what such a life looks like. It involves sharing one's resources rather than trying unjustly to accumulate more. Thus, in Luke's Gospel John the Baptist tells people to share clothes and food with those who are in need (3:11). He advises tax collectors not to cheat people by collecting more than they should (3:13). The soldiers he enjoins not to use their power for extortion and to "be satisfied with your wages" (3:14b); they should not seek to augment their salaries by force.

Significantly, these sayings of John are responses to questions. Only in Luke's Gospel do those who come to be baptized by John ask him specifically what they should do. Different groups do so three times (3:10, 12, 14a). These groups serve as models of seeking for ways in which repentance is made concrete in one's daily activities.

Again, Luke is unique in writing about the great expectations that John engendered in the people (3:15). A sign of this excitement comes right after the Baptist has provided them with concrete advice on how to express a commitment to reform. In this the Baptist provides ministers with an example of how faith energizes people when it reaches them where they live.

The Greek word for repentance is *metanoia*. In the dialogue between John the Baptist and those who come to him to be baptized, Luke portrays repentance as an internal disposition that is revealed in how people use their possessions or desire for increased wealth when there are others who are needy in their midst.

✤ Reflecting on the Word

Years ago I heard Father Joe Champlin, a priest of the diocese of Syracuse, share at a workshop for clergy a wedding homily that offered three words of advice to the couple: Share. Care. Be fair. I wonder now if he got this message from John the Baptist. John gives pretty much this same advice to the people who come to him. He calls the crowds to share their clothing. He tells the tax collectors to care about those whom they were known to overtax. And he urges soldiers not to abuse their power, but to act fairly toward an oppressed people who had little recourse against Roman military might.

These three words of good advice can speak today to our own lives, as individuals and as a nation. They offer a profile of reform, of living in a way that looks beyond oneself to others. Luke's John is very much in line with Luke's call to care for the poor and lowly, the oppressed and the downtrodden.

John knew who he was and who he was not. He preached that "one mightier than I is coming . . . [who] will baptize you with the Holy Spirit and fire" (Luke 3:16). John expected someone who would bring judgment and separate the wheat from the chaff, tossing the worthless into the fire. But the one who came was first of all a "savior," as Luke emphasizes, and as we will hear on Christmas night, Jesus was even better news than John expected. Which is great news for us.

✤ Consider/Discuss:

- What would John tell you to do if you were to ask him?
- Do you see Jesus as a judge with a winnowing fan in his hand to clear the threshing floor of chaff, or as one who came to save us? Are these images irreconcilable?

✤ Responding to the Word

We pray to God today to give us the gift of joy, one of the gifts of the Holy Spirit and of this season, so that we might "rejoice in the Lord always," knowing that "the Lord is near" and will set divine peace as a guard over our hearts and minds (Philippians 4:4, 5).

December 20, 2009

FOURTH SUNDAY OF ADVENT

Today's Focus: God's Unexpected Choices

Picture this scene: Elizabeth, elderly cousin to Mary, once barren, now six months pregnant, speaks only once in the Gospels. On her newly arrived, newly pregnant cousin, Elizabeth pronounces a blessing. As the Holy Spirit sings through Elizabeth, her unborn child leaps for joy at Mary's voice. Elizabeth's blessing is done in all our names.

FIRST
READING
Micah 5:1–4a

Thus says the LORD:
    You, Bethlehem-Ephrathah,
        too small to be among the clans of Judah,
    from you shall come forth for me
        one who is to be ruler in Israel;
    whose origin is from of old,
        from ancient times.
Therefore the Lord will give them up, until the time
    when she who is to give birth has borne,
and the rest of his kindred shall return
    to the children of Israel.
He shall stand firm and shepherd his flock
    by the strength of the LORD,
        in the majestic name of the LORD, his God;
and they shall remain, for now his greatness
    shall reach to the ends of the earth;
    he shall be peace.

PSALM
RESPONSE
Psalm 80:4

Lord, make us turn to you; let us see your face and we shall be saved.

SECOND
READING
Hebrews 10: 5–10

Brothers and sisters: When Christ came into the world, he said:
    "Sacrifice and offering you did not desire,
        but a body you prepared for me;
    in holocausts and sin offerings you took no delight.
    Then I said, 'As is written of me in the scroll,
    behold, I come to do your will, O God.' "

First he says,
    "Sacrifices and offerings, holocausts and sin offerings,
        you neither desired nor delighted in."
    These are offered according to the law. Then he says,
        "Behold, I come to do your will."
    He takes away the first to establish the second.

By this "will," we have been consecrated through the offering of the body of Jesus Christ once for all.

GOSPEL
Luke 1:39–45

Mary set out and traveled to the hill country in haste to a town of Judah, where she entered the house of Zechariah and greeted Elizabeth. When Elizabeth heard Mary's greeting, the infant leaped in her womb, and Elizabeth, filled with the Holy Spirit, cried out in a loud voice and said, "Blessed are you among women, and blessed is the fruit of your womb. And how does this happen to me, that the mother of my Lord should come to me? For at the moment the sound of your greeting reached my ears, the infant in my womb leaped for joy. Blessed are you who believed that what was spoken to you by the Lord would be fulfilled."

❖ Understanding the Word

The concept of the Messiah is rooted in the covenant that God made with King David and his household. Originally the Messiah was a political figure who would restore the rule of the house of David over Israel. Later there evolved a concept of a priestly messiah. In the New Testament the concept is applied to Jesus, who would bring the reign of God to people.

The book of Micah the prophet presents the significance of the Messiah against the backdrop of the overwhelming oppression that the people of Micah's time are experiencing. The Messiah is the one whom the Lord sends from unexpected places to achieve unparalleled results. Micah was an eighth-century B.C. prophet. He lived through the invasion by Assyria of the northern kingdom in 722 B.C. and the consequent deportation of the northern nobles to Assyria and demise of the northern kingdom. Around 710 B.C. the southern kingdom of Judah, to which Micah prophesies, also was invaded by the Assyrians. One can imagine the feeling of *déjà vu* that the people of Judah must have experienced at this time. Would what happened to their northern brothers and sisters happen to them?

Constricting conditions often circumscribe hope. Jerusalem was under siege from the Assyrians. In this situation, Micah calls the city *Bat-gader*, a name that means "fenced-in maiden" (4:14a). He continues speaking of the degradation of the city by saying that the Assyrians "strike on the cheek the ruler of Israel" (4:14b).

It is in this context that Micah prophesies about the coming messiah. This anointed one will come not from the great city of Jerusalem, but from Bethlehem, "too small to be among the clans of Judah" (5:1). In the face of the prevailing weakness of the Jewish leaders in response to the Assyrian threat, the Messiah will come with "the strength of YHWH" (5:3a). The result will be that the people of Judah "will remain" because the Messiah "will be peace" (5:3b, 4).

The Messiah wonderfully upsets conventional expectations in the light of a past that seems to constrict possible outcomes.

My father used to refer to the town of my—and his—birth as a "nickel-and-dime" town. As a child, I was never exactly sure what he meant, but it didn't sound like a compliment. I think it was similar to Micah's words about Bethlehem as "too small to be among the clans of Judah" (5:1). Another description would be a "backwater." Hardly a place deserving of great expectations. Yet, backwater Bethlehem, city of David the shepherd boy, was to be the birthplace of the Messiah—not Jerusalem, center of government and religion, city of David the warrior king.

God's strange choices extend beyond geographical sites to the people on whom God sets eyes. A young betrothed girl up in the north, a barren woman down in the south—these were chosen to play pivotal roles in the story of salvation. The once-barren Elizabeth, soon to bring forth the greatest of all prophets, now proclaims God's most marvelous work and the little one through whom God is working: "Blessed are you among women, and blessed is the fruit of your womb" (Luke 1:42).

Elizabeth cues us to join in the response of the baby in her womb: to allow our hearts and spirits to leap for joy. Again and again God works through those who are open to the Spirit. Blessed are they who place their trust in the Lord who continues to come to give us new life.

❖❖ *Consider/Discuss:*

- Can you think of how God has worked in places and people that you least expected?
- Can you remember how God has worked in your own life in unexpected ways to bring you new life?

❖❖ *Responding to the Word*

After hearing Elizabeth's final words, "Blessed are you who believed that what was spoken to you by the Lord would be fulfilled" (Luke 1:45), we can pray the words of the refrain of today's responsorial psalm: "Lord, make us turn to you; let us see your face and we shall be saved" (Psalm 80:4).

December 25, 2009

THE NATIVITY OF THE LORD
CHRISTMAS MASS AT MIDNIGHT

Today's Focus: Journeying from Gloom to Light

Our Advent journey is over, leaving us on the threshold of the Christmas season. The feasts of this season are themselves a journey into the mystery of our gracious God, who continues to be revealed and given to us in the person of Jesus Christ. Tonight we hear again the story of the first Christmas, a story that includes several journeys.

FIRST READING
Isaiah 9:1–6

The people who walked in darkness
    have seen a great light;
upon those who dwelt in the land of gloom
    a light has shone.
You have brought them abundant joy
    and great rejoicing,
as they rejoice before you as at the harvest,
    as people make merry when dividing spoils.
For the yoke that burdened them,
    the pole on their shoulder,
and the rod of their taskmaster
    you have smashed, as on the day of Midian.
For every boot that tramped in battle,
    every cloak rolled in blood,
    will be burned as fuel for flames.
For a child is born to us, a son is given us;
    upon his shoulder dominion rests.
They name him Wonder-Counselor, God-Hero,
    Father-Forever, Prince of Peace.
His dominion is vast
    and forever peaceful,
from David's throne, and over his kingdom,
    which he confirms and sustains
by judgment and justice,
    both now and forever.
The zeal of the LORD of hosts will do this!

PSALM RESPONSE
Luke 2:11

Today is born our Savior, Christ the Lord.

SECOND READING
Titus 2:11–14

Beloved: The grace of God has appeared, saving all and training us to reject godless ways and worldly desires and to live temperately, justly, and devoutly in this age, as we await the blessed hope, the appearance of the glory of our great God and savior Jesus Christ, who gave himself for us to deliver us from all lawlessness and to cleanse for himself a people as his own, eager to do what is good.

23

GOSPEL
Luke 2:1–14

In those days a decree went out from Caesar Augustus that the whole world should be enrolled. This was the first enrollment, when Quirinius was governor of Syria. So all went to be enrolled, each to his own town. And Joseph too went up from Galilee from the town of Nazareth to Judea, to the city of David that is called Bethlehem, because he was of the house and family of David, to be enrolled with Mary, his betrothed, who was with child. While they were there, the time came for her to have her child, and she gave birth to her firstborn son. She wrapped him in swaddling clothes and laid him in a manger, because there was no room for them in the inn.

Now there were shepherds in that region living in the fields and keeping the night watch over their flock. The angel of the Lord appeared to them and the glory of the Lord shone around them, and they were struck with great fear. The angel said to them, "Do not be afraid; for behold, I proclaim to you good news of great joy that will be for all the people. For today in the city of David a savior has been born for you who is Christ and Lord. And this will be a sign for you: you will find an infant wrapped in swaddling clothes and lying in a manger." And suddenly there was a multitude of the heavenly host with the angel, praising God and saying:

"Glory to God in the highest
and on earth peace to those on whom his favor rests."

❖ Understanding the Word

What an unusual scene for the birth of the Savior of the world! Not surprisingly, we tend to conflate the Matthean and Lukan accounts of the birth of Jesus. In the process we create a portrait of magi with expensive gifts, angelic hosts, and shepherds all around a bucolic scene at night. This composite picture tends to hide the richness of the portrayal that we find in tonight's passage from Luke. Perhaps one way to express this richness is to say that God in Jesus comes to save in the humblest and lowliest of situations.

Only in Luke's account do Joseph and Mary have to leave Nazareth and go on a journey to Bethlehem while Mary is pregnant. This occurs on account of the census reputedly called for by Emperor Caesar Augustus. Rather than being the object of an extensive search by a jealous king, as in Matthew's Gospel, in which King Herod attempts to find the newborn "king of the Jews" (Matthew 2:2), Jesus and his parents are among the masses who are temporarily displaced. Only in Luke's account is Jesus born in a manger "because there was no place for them in the inn" (2:7). In Luke's Gospel there are no wise men who visit Jesus with gifts, but rather humble shepherds who come with testimony.

There is beauty and majesty in the Lukan account, but it occurs precisely in a stark human condition. There is a message and praise conveyed by angels that a savior is born who will bring peace. In the midst of a passage that begins with a reference to an emperor who was honored as a savior for bringing about the "Roman Peace," there is this introduction of the real Savior who brings real peace. This Savior comes, however, not as one of the class of powerful movers of the world, but as one of the simple people who shares in their displacements. A host of angels sings, "Glory to God in the highest / and on earth peace to those on whom his favor rests" (2:14). This glory and peace are manisfested, however, precisely in the divine accompaniment of the poor in their condition.

✤ *Reflecting on the Word*

The Christmas story is a two-part tale with four journeys. First, there is the geographical journey of Joseph and Mary (the second time in a few months for her—and she was pregnant both times) from Galilee to Bethlehem because the emperor's demand for a census required Joseph to register there. Then, the bio-logical journey of the infant from Mary's womb, a place of warmth and comfort, to a world offering no fitting room for his family. At birth, the child was wrapped in strips of cloth to hold his limbs straight, and laid in a feeding trough for animals.

The second part records two other journeys: the angels move from the throne of God to a group of shepherds—laborers held in low esteem—keeping watch by night, delivering to them a joyful message and a song: "Don't be afraid. We bring great news for all people. A savior has been born for you who is Christ/Messiah and Lord/God." Finally, there is the journey across a dark field to the place where the lowliest join the homeless around a newborn in a feeding trough.

Four journeys: across space, into time, bringing joy, eliciting praise. We remember each of these journeys this night and are invited to make our own journey into the mystery of the God who pitched a tent among us in the flesh of a child, and who continues to be born in us now if we open our hearts and minds.

✤ *Consider/Discuss:*

- How can the Incarnation continue to happen in me/us this Christmas, 2009?
- What journey must I make so that Christ can be born in me? From where to where: darkness to light, fear to joy, shedding tears to giv-ing praise and glory?

✤ *Responding to the Word*

We turn to the Father of our Lord Jesus Christ, asking for the gifts of Christmas for ourselves and for our world: joy for all people, peace on earth for all on whom God's favor rests, a new birth in Christ Jesus, and a strengthening of spirit from the food and drink of the Eucharist.

25

December 27, 2009

THE HOLY FAMILY OF JESUS, MARY, AND JOSEPH

Today's Focus: The Tie That Binds

The incarnation of the second person of the Trinity, the Word of God, in the person of Jesus put him in a family, one that did not always understand him, but did provide him a place to grow in wisdom and favor before God. We call them the Holy Family; as such, they comfort and confront us.

FIRST READING
1 Samuel 1: 20–22, 24–28

In those days Hannah conceived, and at the end of her term bore a son whom she called Samuel, since she had asked the LORD for him. The next time her husband Elkanah was going up with the rest of his household to offer the customary sacrifice to the LORD and to fulfill his vows, Hannah did not go, explaining to her husband, "Once the child is weaned, I will take him to appear before the LORD and to remain there forever; I will offer him as a perpetual nazirite."

Once Samuel was weaned, Hannah brought him up with her, along with a three-year-old bull, an ephah of flour, and a skin of wine, and presented him at the temple of the LORD in Shiloh. After the boy's father had sacrificed the young bull, Hannah, his mother, approached Eli and said: "Pardon, my lord! As you live, my lord, I am the woman who stood near you here, praying to the LORD. I prayed for this child, and the LORD granted my request. Now I, in turn, give him to the LORD; as long as he lives, he shall be dedicated to the LORD." Hannah left Samuel there.

PSALM RESPONSE
Psalm 84:5a

Blessed are they who dwell in your house, O Lord.

SECOND READING
1 John 3:1–2, 21–24

Beloved: See what love the Father has bestowed on us that we may be called the children of God. And so we are. The reason the world does not know us is that it did not know him. Beloved, we are God's children now; what we shall be has not yet been revealed. We do know that when it is revealed we shall be like him, for we shall see him as he is.

Beloved, if our hearts do not condemn us, we have confidence in God and receive from him whatever we ask, because we keep his commandments and do what pleases him. And his commandment is this: we should believe in the name of his Son, Jesus Christ, and love one another just as he commanded us. Those who keep his commandments remain in him, and he in them, and the way we know that he remains in us is from the Spirit he gave us.

GOSPEL
Luke 2:41–52

Each year Jesus' parents went to Jerusalem for the feast of Passover, and when he was twelve years old, they went up according to festival custom. After they had completed its days, as they were returning, the boy Jesus remained behind in Jerusalem, but his parents did not know it. Thinking that he was in the caravan, they journeyed for a day and looked for him among their relatives and acquaintances, but not finding him, they returned to Jerusalem to look for him. After three days they found him in the temple, sitting in the midst of the teachers, listening to them and asking them questions, and all who heard him were astounded at his understanding and his answers. When his parents saw him, they were astonished, and his mother said to him, "Son, why have you done this to us? Your father and I have been looking for you with great anxiety." And he said to them, "Why were you looking for me? Did you not know that I must be in my Father's house?" But they did not understand what he said to them. He went down with them and came to Nazareth, and was obedient to them; and his mother kept all these things in her heart. And Jesus advanced in wisdom and age and favor before God and man.

❖ *Understanding the Word*

The story in the Gospel of Luke about the twelve-year-old Jesus and his parents going up to Jerusalem to celebrate the Feast of Passover says much about the perspectives that guide the lives of both Jesus and his mother. Whereas Matthew speaks about the family of Jesus by highlighting Joseph, Luke throws the spotlight on Mary.

First, let us look at the role of Jesus in this passage. He stays behind after the festival and is found in the temple asking the teachers questions (2:43, 46). He is also answering questions put to him with an acuity that astonishes everyone (2:47). When asked why he has done this without telling his parents, he replies with a question that can be translated in two ways: (1) "Did you not know that I must be in my Father's house?" or (2) "Did you not know that I must be about my Father's business?" (2:49b). The words can mean either and in fact they seem to mean both, as the later ministry of the Lukan Jesus will be largely focused on doing God's will in the temple or while journeying to the temple. Already at an early age Jesus focuses on pursuing the particular ministry that God has given him.

As for Mary, she is legitimately worried and puzzled. These emotions are expressed in her words to Jesus after finding him: "Son, why have you done this to us? Your father and I have been looking for you with great anxiety" (2:48). There is much that Mary has experienced that has been perplexing and much that she will experience in the life of her son that will be difficult to grasp in the light of his role as God's Son. But Mary has the disposition to grow in her faith because she is willing to reflect on her experiences of God in her life. Following Jesus' enigmatic answer to her question we hear, "and his mother kept all these things in her heart" (2:51). This is a habit of hers; she does the same thing when she hears what the shepherds say about Jesus after his birth (2:19).

The focus of the child Jesus on his Father's will is balanced by his mother's equally intense focus on seeking this will.

This is the only episode we have about Jesus between the time of his infancy and his baptism in the Jordan as an adult. One might smile at its confirmation that even having the Son of God as an adolescent was no easy thing. But this is more than a story that includes a rare moment of tension within the Holy Family. If he grew in wisdom and grace, I like to think that there were at least several moments when Mary called out the window, "Didn't I tell you not to . . ." Nor is it simply a tale reflecting how the young Jesus sometimes had to navigate conflicting loyalties: obedience to his earthly parents versus the call of his heavenly Father.

Luke reminds us twice in his Gospel that "Jesus advanced in wisdom and age and favor before God and man" (Luke 2:52; see also 2:40). Here he provides us with a story showing Jesus as he grows in wisdom, coming to recognize whose Son he is and what that means: an intense relationship with his Father and all that belongs to and concerns his Father. Here we see him as one "filled with wisdom; and the favor of God was upon him" (2:40).

Perhaps some consolation can be found in realizing that even living in the presence of the Son of God did not remove all anxieties, even for his parents. However, what continued to hold this family together was their mutual desire to do God's will, along with a willingness to ponder, as Mary did time and time again, what exactly all this might mean, trusting in God all the while.

✦ *Consider/Discuss*:

- What does it mean to be a holy family?
- What is your experience of growing in wisdom, favor, grace before God?

✦ *Responding to the Word*

Ask God for the grace to live in peace with all the members of your own family, especially if there are any from whom you feel distant or alienated. Ask God to give all peoples the wisdom to know what it means to "live as the holy family, united in respect and love" (*Sacramentary*, Opening Prayer, Feast of the Holy Family of Jesus, Mary, and Joseph).

January 1, 2010

THE BLESSED VIRGIN MARY, THE MOTHER OF GOD

Today's Focus: Perennially "In"

This solemn feast of Mary is the oldest celebration dedicated to her. Our attention spreads out from the baby to include the only woman usually found in the Nativity scene—though the one in my parish has a woman accompanying the shepherds, carrying what looks like bread in a basket, a nice touch! Mary is set before us this day as model of the Christian life and of the Church.

FIRST READING
Numbers 6: 22–27

The LORD said to Moses: "Speak to Aaron and his sons and tell them: This is how you shall bless the Israelites. Say to them:

The LORD bless you and keep you!
The LORD let his face shine upon you, and be gracious to you!
The LORD look upon you kindly and give you peace!

So shall they invoke my name upon the Israelites, and I will bless them."

PSALM RESPONSE
Psalm 67:2a

May God bless us in his mercy.

SECOND READING
Galatians 4:4–7

Brothers and sisters: When the fullness of time had come, God sent his Son, born of a woman, born under the law, to ransom those under the law, so that we might receive adoption as sons. As proof that you are sons, God sent the Spirit of his Son into our hearts, crying out, "Abba, Father!" So you are no longer a slave but a son, and if a son then also an heir, through God.

GOSPEL
Luke 2:16–21

The shepherds went in haste to Bethlehem and found Mary and Joseph, and the infant lying in the manger. When they saw this, they made known the message that had been told them about this child. All who heard it were amazed by what had been told them by the shepherds. And Mary kept all these things, reflecting on them in her heart. Then the shepherds returned, glorifying and praising God for all they had heard and seen, just as it had been told to them.

When eight days were completed for his circumcision, he was named Jesus, the name given him by the angel before he was conceived in the womb.

The portrait of Mary in the Gospel of Luke shows how God is powerfully present to those on the periphery of the comfortable life provided by society. The shepherds who come to see the newborn Jesus and his family recognize this fact.

In Luke's Gospel Mary is cast as one who is definitely on the border of social acceptance. In contrast to Matthew's Gospel, in which the angel reveals to Joseph how Mary is with child, in Luke's Gospel the angel Gabriel tells Mary how this came to be (Matthew 1:18–22; Luke 1:26–38). One can imagine the precarious position in which Mary is placed, according to Luke. Matthew wrote that Joseph, being just, decided to divorce her quietly. The law allowed for the stoning of a betrothed woman who was found not to be a virgin (Deuteronomy 22:13–21). So it is not only public shame to which Mary would potentially be exposed. Under these conditions it is clear why it would be especially valuable to Mary if the angel told the reason for her pregnancy to Joseph rather than to Mary. But in Luke's Gospel Gabriel relates these things to Mary, who is thus placed in a more awkward position than in Matthew's Gospel. Mary is vulnerable, at risk of not being socially sanctioned or worse.

The Lukan Mary also participates in the plight of the outsider in the birth of Jesus. Only in Luke's Gospel do we read that Mary and Joseph had to journey to Bethlehem while Mary was pregnant. While there she gives birth and must place her son in a manger "because there was on room for them in the inn" (Luke 2:7).

This is where the shepherds find her and her family, and then return to the fields realizing that everything the angels said to them was true (2:20). One of the things that the angels had told them was "on earth peace on those on whom [God's] favor rests" (2:14b). The Lukan perspective of Mary being in a difficult predicament during her pregnancy and labor shows that God's peace is granted to the faithful who are placed in tough situations.

✤✤ Reflecting on the Word

Every New Year's Day the *Washington Post* runs a column declaring what and who are "in" and "out." An interesting item last year was that "pastor" was out and "my person" was in! It reminded me that few things or individuals remain "in" very long. Mary has been one of the few exceptions. From the early days of the church, she has been revered as mother of the Lord and mother of the disciples.

How appropriate to celebrate Mary as Mother of God on January 1, both as a way to begin the New Year and as a way to continue our Christmas celebration. Mary reminds us of what is possible when one says "yes" to God. Her *fiat* ("Let it be") to the angel opened the way for God to enter our world. Through her the Word became flesh, becoming fully human, truly one of us, partaking of our humanity so that we might partake of his divinity.

Over the centuries, Mary has been perennially "in" as a woman of faith, hope, and love. During her life she was "in tune" with all that that God was asking, ever faithful, even though she knew fear, questioned, felt anxiety, and needed to ponder what was happening and what it meant. In our day, with its storms, sorrows, and uncertainties, she can be, as Pope Benedict suggests in his encyclical *Saved in Hope*, our "star of hope," shining with the light of Christ and guiding us along our way. She remains the woman who models love received and returned, loving Christ into life and ministry, loving those entrusted to her care throughout the centuries.

✛ Consider/Discuss:

- How does Mary comfort you most: as woman of faith, hope, or love?
- How does Mary challenge you most: as woman of faith, hope, or love?

✛ *Responding to the Word*

We pray to Mary as mother of all believers to intercede for us, asking her Son to give us in this new year the gift of the faith necessary to face what lies ahead, with a strong hope to know that all will be well, and with the grace to love God and others as she did and continues to do.

January 3, 2010

THE EPIPHANY OF THE LORD

Today's Focus: A Tale for Our Time

The story of the magi is especially meaningful in our day. While our own country is becoming more multicultural and multireligious, the importance of the message of this feast becomes more urgent: God's son Jesus was sent by God to bring all peoples together. This feast of the Epiphany speaks of God's desires that all live in peace as God's children.

FIRST READING
Isaiah 60:1–6

Rise up in splendor, Jerusalem! Your light has come,
   the glory of the Lord shines upon you.
See, darkness covers the earth,
   and thick clouds cover the peoples;
but upon you the LORD shines,
   and over you appears his glory.
Nations shall walk by your light,
   and kings by your shining radiance.
Raise your eyes and look about;
   they all gather and come to you:
your sons come from afar,
   and your daughters in the arms of their nurses.

Then you shall be radiant at what you see,
   your heart shall throb and overflow,
for the riches of the sea shall be emptied out before you,
   the wealth of nations shall be brought to you.
Caravans of camels shall fill you,
   dromedaries from Midian and Ephah;
all from Sheba shall come
   bearing gold and frankincense,
   and proclaiming the praises of the LORD.

PSALM RESPONSE
Psalm 72:11

Lord, every nation on earth will adore you.

SECOND READING
Ephesians 3: 2–3a, 5–6

Brothers and sisters: You have heard of the stewardship of God's grace that was given to me for your benefit, namely, that the mystery was made known to me by revelation. It was not made known to people in other generations as it has now been revealed to his holy apostles and prophets by the Spirit: that the Gentiles are coheirs, members of the same body, and copartners in the promise in Christ Jesus through the gospel.

32

GOSPEL
Matthew 2:
1–12
When Jesus was born in Bethlehem of Judea, in the days of King Herod, behold, magi from the east arrived in Jerusalem, saying, "Where is the newborn king of the Jews? We saw his star at its rising and have come to do him homage." When King Herod heard this, he was greatly troubled, and all Jerusalem with him. Assembling all the chief priests and the scribes of the people, he inquired of them where the Christ was to be born. They said to him, "In Bethlehem of Judea, for thus it has been written through the prophet:

> And you, Bethlehem, land of Judah,
>   are by no means least among the rulers of Judah;
> since from you shall come a ruler,
>   who is to shepherd my people Israel."

Then Herod called the magi secretly and ascertained from them the time of the star's appearance. He sent them to Bethlehem and said, "Go and search diligently for the child. When you have found him, bring me word, that I too may go and do him homage." After their audience with the king they set out. And behold, the star that they had seen at its rising preceded them, until it came and stopped over the place where the child was. They were overjoyed at seeing the star, and on entering the house they saw the child with Mary his mother. They prostrated themselves and did him homage. Then they opened their treasures and offered him gifts of gold, frankincense, and myrrh. And having been warned in a dream not to return to Herod, they departed for their country by another way.

❖ Understanding the Word

The solemnity of the Epiphany celebrates the manifestation of God. The word "epiphany" itself means "to appear" and is often used in reference to the appearance of God. The Church celebrates on this day both the coming of God in Christ and the coming of God in Christ into the lives of Christians.

Last year we looked at the Gospel reading of the arrival of the magi to witness the newborn king (Matthew 2:1–12). Today we reflect on the first reading, which speaks about the effects of God's coming into our own lives. This reading is from a section of the book of Isaiah that scholars call Third Isaiah. Third Isaiah was written when the Jewish people returned from exile in Babylon in the sixth century B.C. Life back home was very difficult, and the prophet writes to give them hope about what God can and will do for them.

Isaiah speaks in poetry, with radical images to counter the spiritual shortsightedness caused by the people's disappointments. These images will provide them with a new perspective that opens their spirits to be able to receive confidently what God's coming means for them. So he appeals to their imaginations to suggest the richness of God for them. It is like light in the midst of darkness (Isaiah 66:1–2). This light will enlighten them regarding how to live. Isaiah says that the people themselves will become this light so that others will use them as examples of how to live (60:3). God comes for the transformation of people, and transformation spreads as more and more see what enlightened living looks like.

Finally, Isaiah writes about God's presence to them in terms resonant with the deepest desires of our hearts: God's coming will create family togetherness and family blessings.

In the light of God's epiphany in Jesus Christ we realize that these blessings are fully realized in the next life. The Isaiah reading informs us, however, of how God is already at work in some ways even now to achieve these ends.

❖ Reflecting on the Word

Matthew's tale is less a story of adventurous seekers than of a luring God, drawing others into the mystery of divinity through the birth of Jesus. A star that guides and wise words that explain are what help lead the magi to their destination. Natural signs and words of revelation are what God works through in our own day to bring us into the presence of Jesus, the Son of God.

The story of the wise men is yet another journey that surrounds the birth of Jesus (see Christmas Midnight for four others). It speaks to all seeking God in today's world. God does not use force to attract others. Angels speak a message of joy for all but give no orders that insist that the shepherds journey through the dark of night to worship. A star appears in the sky but no one forces these astrologers to pack up some gifts and make their way across foreign terrain to kneel and prostrate themselves and do Jesus homage.

At the heart of this story is the message announced in the letter to the Ephesians: God's plan was that everyone be included in the mystery of salvation, that, along with the children of Abraham, "the Gentiles are coheirs, members of the same body, and copartners in the promise in Christ Jesus" (Ephesians 3:6). God wants everyone to share in divine life—*everyone!* Give it your thoughtful consideration.

❖ Consider/Discuss:

- Is the Epiphany message about Jews and Gentiles being co-heirs of the promise in Christ only a message for the early days of the church? How does it speak to the Church in our day?
- What has led you to Christ? How has your own journey been guided by the hand of God?

❖ Responding to the Word

We can pray that the divisions and hatreds that continue to plague our planet will be resolved through the wisdom that is the gift of God. We pray for an increase of wise men and women who are attuned to the signs of God drawing them to join together in worship and live together in peace. The ultimate destination of all people is to arrive in the presence of God.

THE BAPTISM OF THE LORD

Today's Focus: Beloved Children Sent Forth

As this feast of Jesus' baptism brings the Christmas season to a close, we remember this event as another epiphany of the Lord: Jesus stands revealed as beloved Son of the Father as the Holy Spirit descends, and Jesus goes forth led by that Spirit. We, too, are sent forth into Ordinary Time to continue our mission in the world as beloved children of the Father.

FIRST READING
Isaiah 40:1–5, 9–11

Comfort, give comfort to my people,
    says your God.
Speak tenderly to Jerusalem, and proclaim to her
    that her service is at an end,
    her guilt is expiated;
indeed, she has received from the hand of the LORD
    double for all her sins.
        A voice cries out:
In the desert prepare the way of the LORD!
    Make straight in the wasteland a highway for our God!
Every valley shall be filled in,
    every mountain and hill shall be made low;
the rugged land shall be made a plain,
    the rough country, a broad valley.
Then the glory of the LORD shall be revealed,
    and all people shall see it together;
    for the mouth of the LORD has spoken.

Go up onto a high mountain,
    Zion, herald of glad tidings;
cry out at the top of your voice,
    Jerusalem, herald of good news!
Fear not to cry out
    and say to the cities of Judah:
    Here is your God!
Here comes with power
    the Lord GOD,
    who rules by a strong arm;
here is his reward with him,
    his recompense before him.
Like a shepherd he feeds his flock;
    in his arms he gathers the lambs,
carrying them in his bosom,
    and leading the ewes with care.

PSALM RESPONSE
Psalm 104:1

O bless the Lord, my soul.

SECOND READING
Titus 2:11–14; 3:4–7

Beloved: The grace of God has appeared, saving all and training us to reject godless ways and worldly desires and to live temperately, justly, and devoutly in this age, as we await the blessed hope, the appearance of the glory of our great God and savior Jesus Christ, who gave himself for us to deliver us from all lawlessness and to cleanse for himself a people as his own, eager to do what is good.

When the kindness and generous love
    of God our savior appeared,
not because of any righteous deeds we had done
    but because of his mercy,
he saved us through the bath of rebirth
    and renewal by the Holy Spirit,
whom he richly poured out on us
    through Jesus Christ our savior,
so that we might be justified by his grace
    and become heirs in hope of eternal life.

GOSPEL
Luke 3:15–16, 21–22

The people were filled with expectation, and all were asking in their hearts whether John might be the Christ. John answered them all, saying, "I am baptizing you with water, but one mightier than I is coming. I am not worthy to loosen the thongs of his sandals. He will baptize you with the Holy Spirit and fire."

After all the people had been baptized and Jesus also had been baptized and was praying, heaven was opened and the Holy Spirit descended upon him in bodily form like a dove. And a voice came from heaven, "You are my beloved Son; with you I am well pleased."

❖ Understanding the Word

The first reading for the Baptism of the Lord is from the portion of Isaiah called Second Isaiah. It was written shortly before the decisive events in which Cyrus of Persia would defeat the Babylonians and allow the Jewish people in exile in Babylon to return home. Although the first reading speaks of how God is acting through Cyrus, Luke's use of part of this reading shows that he sees God also acting through Jesus in a somewhat analogous way.

The Isaian reading speaks of God putting the divine spirit upon the servant, something that Matthew, Mark, and Luke say happens at Jesus' baptism (Matthew 3:16; Mark 1:10; Luke 3:22). The effect of this Spirit-infusion will be justice for peoples (Isaiah 42:1, 4, 6). This justice is immediately defined, however, in terms of mercy: "To open the eyes of the blind, / to bring out prisoners from confinement, / and from the dungeon, those who live in darkness" (42:7). This is also the way that Luke speaks, in both his Gospel and in his Acts of the Apostles, about the effects of Jesus' baptism. In Acts these effects are summarized neatly. After writing about Jesus' being "anointed with the holy Spirit and power" at baptism, Luke describes this spiritual power being expressed by Jesus "doing good and healing all those oppressed by the devil" (Acts 10:38).

What is instructive is that the ultimate effect of the actualization of this power is a restoration of the relationship with God through forgiveness of sins (Acts 10:43). Thus, the purpose of Jesus' baptism is to bring about justice through mercy. This mercy has concrete effects in our daily lives. Certain healing comes through the divine mercy of Jesus. The final goal of Jesus' baptism and the mercy to us that comes through it is, however, the restoration of the relationship between all human life and God.

❖ Reflecting on the Word

The other night I was looking out the window as the sun was setting and the layers of clouds allowed the sun to create an extraordinary sunset, painting some clouds with a golden hue, while others were orange and red, moving to purple and grey. It was a stunning moment. The baptism of Jesus is one of those brief moments of beauty, occurring in the first three Gospels (and alluded to in the fourth).

Luke's account differs from the others in that the dramatic moment does not occur as Jesus is coming up out of the water but only after his baptism, while he is praying. Luke's Gospel has been called the Gospel of prayer, and from its beginning the adult Jesus is presented as one who prays. At this moment of intimacy, "heaven was opened and the Holy Spirit descended upon him in bodily form like a dove" (Luke 3:21–22). While he was at prayer, the voice spoke to him: "You are my beloved Son; with you I am well pleased" (3:22). From here on we find that Jesus is under the influence of the Holy Spirit, and this Spirit directs him first into the desert to be tested, then into his years of service.

With this solemn celebration of the baptism, we too are sent back into the days called "Ordinary Time," reminded that God has spoken these same words to us at our baptism: You are my son, my daughter. I delight in you. I send you forth to serve as my Son, Jesus, went forth to serve, accompanied by the Holy Spirit.

❖ Consider/Discuss:

- Have you had moments when you experienced yourself as God's beloved child?

- How does your relationship with God flow outward in "Ordinary Time"? Where/who is the Spirit leading you to serve?

❖ Responding to the Word

We pray as Jesus prayed that we might hear the voice of the Father, a voice that speaks of God's love for us. We ask that we might allow that Spirit, God's holy breath that came upon as at our own baptism, to move us out into the world in service to those most in need whom God has set before us.

The readings at the beginning of Ordinary Time for the Lectionary Year C delve into the implications of the gift that has been given to us in Jesus.

The Second Sunday in Ordinary Time presents the miracle at the wedding feast at Cana. This selection from John's Gospel reflects on the burden of a Christian commitment in a society that may be inimical to some Christian perspectives. How God supports us during these times and how we avail ourselves of this support is the focus of this Gospel passage.

We resume hearing from Luke's Gospel on the Third Sunday in Ordinary Time. This day's excerpt explores common conceptions of what will satisfy our deepest needs. In this light, Luke helps listeners to understand how God is the answer to their deepest personal longings.

The liturgical season progresses in the Fourth Sunday in Ordinary Time by addressing the qualities that put people in touch with God's life as it affects them most fundamentally. Luke presents a group that appears to have a strong case to receive God's gifts, only to show why they lack what is necessary to do so. Then Luke refers to two passages from the Old Testament that depict two unlikely people as those whom God blesses. A look at the similarities between these people reveals the qualities that enable them to benefit from the divine life.

Luke continues the development of the theme of beneficial reception of the divine gifts in Jesus in the Gospel selection for the Fifth Sunday in Ordinary Time. In this passage Luke considers both the responsibilities that come with the reception of God's gifts and the memory of God's action in the past that undergirds one's ability to live up to these duties.

Finally, on the Sixth Sunday in Ordinary Time we hear Luke's version of the Beatitudes. Seldom remembered because of the much more popular Matthean version, Luke's Beatitudes energize our commitment to being conduits of the divine gifts to others. These Beatitudes do so by showing how expending oneself for others results in enrichment by God.

January 17, 2010

SECOND SUNDAY IN ORDINARY TIME

Today's Focus: Jesus, Gracious Guest

Jesus goes to a wedding, and at his mother's request somewhat reluctantly changes water into wine. Only in John's Gospel, presented in his Book of Signs (1:19 — 12:50), do we find this event, so we suspect this is more than the act of a gracious guest. Or perhaps that is exactly what it is on the most profound level.

FIRST READING
Isaiah 62:1–5

For Zion's sake I will not be silent,
    for Jerusalem's sake I will not be quiet,
until her vindication shines forth like the dawn
    and her victory like a burning torch.

Nations shall behold your vindication,
    and all the kings your glory;
you shall be called by a new name
    pronounced by the mouth of the LORD.
You shall be a glorious crown in the hand of the LORD,
    a royal diadem held by your God.
No more shall people call you "Forsaken,"
    or your land "Desolate,"
but you shall be called "My Delight,"
    and your land "Espoused."
For the LORD delights in you
    and makes your land his spouse.
As a young man marries a virgin,
    your Builder shall marry you;
and as a bridegroom rejoices in his bride
    so shall your God rejoice in you.

PSALM RESPONSE
Psalm 96:3

Proclaim his marvelous deeds to all the nations.

SECOND READING
1 Corinthians 12: 4–11

Brothers and sisters: There are different kinds of spiritual gifts but the same Spirit; there are different forms of service but the same Lord; there are different workings but the same God who produces all of them in everyone. To each individual the manifestation of the Spirit is given for some benefit. To one is given through the Spirit the expression of wisdom; to another, the expression of knowledge according to the same Spirit; to another, faith by the same Spirit; to another, gifts of healing by the one Spirit; to another, mighty deeds; to another, prophecy; to another, discernment of spirits; to another, varieties of tongues; to another, interpretation of tongues. But one and the same Spirit produces all of these, distributing them individually to each person as he wishes.

GOSPEL
John 2:1–11

There was a wedding at Cana in Galilee, and the mother of Jesus was there. Jesus and his disciples were also invited to the wedding. When the wine ran short, the mother of Jesus said to him, "They have no wine." And Jesus said to her, "Woman, how does your concern affect me? My hour has not yet come." His mother said to the servers, "Do whatever he tells you." Now there were six stone water jars there for Jewish ceremonial washings, each holding twenty to thirty gallons. Jesus told them, "Fill the jars with water." So they filled them to the brim. Then he told them, "Draw some out now and take it to the headwaiter." So they took it. And when the headwaiter tasted the water that had become wine, without knowing where it came from—although the servers who had drawn the water knew—, the headwaiter called the bridegroom and said to him, "Everyone serves good wine first, and then when people have drunk freely, an inferior one; but you have kept the good wine until now." Jesus did this as the beginning of his signs at Cana in Galilee and so revealed his glory, and his disciples began to believe in him.

❖ Understanding the Word

The Gospel reading today recounts the first miracle of Jesus in the Gospel of John. In this Gospel the miracles are called "signs" because they witness to who Jesus is. This first miracle changes water into wine at the wedding feast at Cana. It portrays Jesus as the ample provision for the spirits of his disciples no matter in what situation they find themselves.

The Johannine Christians appear to have been cast out of synagogue fellowship (John 9:34; 12:42; 16:2). We should not minimize the psychological effects of this expulsion because humans are social creatures through and through. Ostracism cuts to the very heart of our social needs.

The first sign of Jesus addresses this most basic psychological need for the joy that comes through human companionship. When wine has run out at the wedding, Jesus changes water into wine (John 2:3–10). The rest, refreshment, and celebration may continue. If the commitment of the disciples to Jesus separates them from their larger society, they need not worry. Jesus gives them the wine that is often symbolic of joy both in the Old Testament and in other ancient Mediterranean writings.

At the same time, Jesus provides his disciples a new perspective on the social sufferings they experience, a perspective that also sustains them in troubling times. The response of Jesus to his mother when she notifies him, "They have no wine," is "Woman, how does your concern affect me? My hour has not yet come" (2:4). Jesus' "hour" is a reference to the time of his death. So while Jesus does change the water into wine, thus prolonging the joy of the wedding feast, he seems to be strangely unconcerned with the matter because of his focus on his hour. This puts into perspective the concern for present sufferings and the joy that God provides in the midst of them. There is something even more joyful to which all suffering leads.

40

In such ways the miracle at Cana signifies the joy that God provides in the present and in the future as a means to sustain the faithful in their sufferings.

✦ Reflecting on the Word

The wine runs out. Party's over! A disaster at a wedding. An embarrassment for the hosts and a disgrace for the married couple. Mary notices, goes to her son, and says ever so quietly, "They have no wine" (John 2:3). This is one of only two recorded exchanges in the Gospels between Jesus and Mary (the other occurs in Luke 2:41–52). Jesus' filial response here is not exactly enthusiastic: "Woman, how does your concern affect me? My hour has not yet come" (2:4). Nevertheless, the result is six water jars, each holding twenty to thirty gallons of water, turned into what the headwaiter declares to be the really good stuff.

The first half of John's Gospel is called the Book of Signs, so we should look deeper than Jesus coming through at the last minute to keep the party going. True, Jesus seemed to like parties and didn't draw the line regarding with whom he would eat and drink (another sign!). So what are we to take from this event?

First, Jesus is more than a wedding guest in John's Gospel; he is the bridegroom, sent by God, come to woo and wed a new bride, a new Israel, joining Jews and Gentiles into one body. As a harbinger of this, the poet Richard Crashaw says, "The conscious water saw its God and blushed."

The nuptials were eventually held at "the hour" Jesus referred to here, when he was lifted up on the cross, drawing all things to himself. So, the joy of that early wedding at Cana was merely a shadow of the joy awaiting us in the kingdom, one that we anticipate even now whenever we lift the wedding cup of the Eucharist to our lips.

✦ Consider/Discuss:

- Consider having a glass of "good wine." Savor it. What effect does it have on you? How does this experience relate to the joy of the kingdom of God?
- Do you ever relate to God or Jesus as the bridegroom?

✦ Responding to the Word

Pray over the words of the prophet Isaiah, speaking in God's name, in today's first reading: "As a young man marries a virgin, / your Builder shall marry you; and as a bridegroom rejoices in his bride / so shall your God rejoice in you" (Isaiah 62:5).

January 24, 2010

THIRD SUNDAY IN ORDINARY TIME

Today's Focus: God's Word, a Lamp for Our Feet

Both today's Gospel and the reading from Nehemiah remind us that the word of God found in the Torah, the prophets, and the writings of the Old Testament has been an ongoing source of conversion, wisdom, encouragement, and self-understanding for Israel. Jesus, too, came to understand his mission through the words of Isaiah. This same word speaks to us in our day.

FIRST READING
Nehemiah 8: 2–4a, 5–6, 8–10

Ezra the priest brought the law before the assembly, which consisted of men, women, and those children old enough to understand. Standing at one end of the open place that was before the Water Gate, he read out of the book from daybreak till midday, in the presence of the men, the women, and those children old enough to understand; and all the people listened attentively to the book of the law. Ezra the scribe stood on a wooden platform that had been made for the occasion. He opened the scroll so that all the people might see it—for he was standing higher up than any of the people—; and, as he opened it, all the people rose. Ezra blessed the Lord, the great God, and all the people, their hands raised high, answered, "Amen, amen!" Then they bowed down and prostrated themselves before the Lord, their faces to the ground. Ezra read plainly from the book of the law of God, interpreting it so that all could understand what was read. Then Nehemiah, that is, His Excellency, and Ezra the priest-scribe and the Levites who were instructing the people said to all the people: "Today is holy to the Lord your God. Do not be sad, and do not weep"—for all the people were weeping as they heard the words of the law. He said further: "Go, eat rich foods and drink sweet drinks, and allot portions to those who had nothing prepared; for today is holy to our Lord. Do not be saddened this day, for rejoicing in the Lord must be your strength!"

PSALM RESPONSE
John 6:63c

Your words, Lord, are Spirit and life.

In the shorter form of the reading, the passages in brackets are omitted.

SECOND READING
1 Corinthians 12:12–30 or 12:12–14, 27

Brothers and sisters: As a body is one though it has many parts, and all the parts of the body, though many, are one body, so also Christ. For in one Spirit we were all baptized into one body, whether Jews or Greeks, slaves or free persons, and we were all given to drink of one Spirit.

Now the body is not a single part, but many. [If a foot should say, "Because I am not a hand I do not belong to the body," it does not for this reason belong any less to the body. Or if an ear should say, "Because I am not an eye I do not belong to the body," it does not for this reason belong any less to the body. If the whole body were an eye, where would the hearing be? If the whole body were hearing, where would the sense of smell be? But as it is, God placed the parts, each one of them, in the body as he intended. If they were all one part, where would the body be? But as it is, there are many parts, yet one body. The eye cannot say to the hand, "I do not need you," nor again the head to the feet, "I do not need you." Indeed, the parts of the body that seem to be weaker are all the more necessary, and those parts of the body that we consider less honorable we surround with greater honor, and our less presentable parts are treated with greater propriety, whereas our more presentable parts do not need this. But God has so constructed the body as to give greater honor to a part that is without it, so that there may be no division in the body, but that the parts may have the same concern for one another. If one part suffers, all the parts suffer with it; if one part is honored, all the parts share its joy.]

Now you are Christ's body, and individually parts of it. [Some people God has designated in the church to be, first, apostles; second, prophets; third, teachers; then, mighty deeds; then gifts of healing, assistance, administration, and varieties of tongues. Are all apostles? Are all prophets? Are all teachers? Do all work mighty deeds? Do all have gifts of healing? Do all speak in tongues? Do all interpret?]

GOSPEL
Luke 1:1–4; 4:14–21

Since many have undertaken to compile a narrative of the events that have been fulfilled among us, just as those who were eyewitnesses from the beginning and ministers of the word have handed them down to us, I too have decided, after investigating everything accurately anew, to write it down in an orderly sequence for you, most excellent Theophilus, so that you may realize the certainty of the teachings you have received.

Jesus returned to Galilee in the power of the Spirit, and news of him spread throughout the whole region. He taught in their synagogues and was praised by all.

He came to Nazareth, where he had grown up, and went according to his custom into the synagogue on the sabbath day. He stood up to read and was handed a scroll of the prophet Isaiah. He unrolled the scroll and found the passage where it was written:

43

> The Spirit of the Lord is upon me,
>   because he has anointed me
>   to bring glad tidings to the poor.
> He has sent me to proclaim liberty to captives
>   and recovery of sight to the blind,
>   to let the oppressed go free,
>   and to proclaim a year acceptable to the Lord.

Rolling up the scroll, he handed it back to the attendant and sat down, and the eyes of all in the synagogue looked intently at him. He said to them, "Today this Scripture passage is fulfilled in your hearing."

❖ Understanding the Word

The mission of Jesus in Luke's Gospel is to provide the peace that the suffering need and that only God can give. The Roman Emperor Augustus had initiated a period of time that was hailed as the *Pax Romana* or "Roman peace." Augustus was not slow to advertise his accomplishments. He took upon himself the titles "Son of God," "God," "Redeemer," "Lord," and "Savior of the World," among others. Augustus also took care to promote the peace he had brought in monuments. Perhaps the most famous is the Altar of Augustan Peace, erected in Rome in 9 B.C. Four major scenes depicted on the front and rear of the altar represent religion, war, victory, and the peace to which Augustus has led the empire.

Despite the relative infrequency of wars, the Augustan peace did not deliver the needy from many of their needs nor did it fulfill the deepest yearnings of people. According to Luke, God comes in Jesus to address these primal needs and desires. The angels who announce Jesus' birth to the shepherds sing, "Glory to God in the highest / and on earth peace to those on whom his favor rests" (Luke 2:14). This peace appears to draw upon the Hebrew concept of *shalom*, which is not simply the absence of strife but also includes a fullness of life.

Today's Gospel presents the first words the Lukan Jesus speaks at the beginning of his ministry. Unlike the Gospels of Matthew and Mark, this message is not expressed in terms of the coming of the reign of God (Matthew 4:17; Mark 1:15). Rather, Luke adopts words from the prophet Isaiah "to proclaim a year acceptable to the Lord" (Luke 4:18–19). In other words, the time that is truly significant is not the epoch initiated by Augustus Caesar but that initiated by God in Jesus. The images in Jesus' words express the liberty and joy that is God's ultimate gift.

There are always many proclamations about the goods that come to us. Only one good from one Source, however, fulfills our most basic and important needs.

✤ Reflecting on the Word

The book of Isaiah has been called the fifth Gospel, so often do the Gospel writers use it for proclaiming Jesus as Christ, the long-awaited Messiah and Son of God. In today's Gospel reading, Jesus begins to move through his home territory of Galilee "in the power of the Spirit" (Luke 4:14), the same Spirit that descended on him after his baptism. He then goes to his hometown of Nazareth and to the synagogue on the Sabbath.

A hush must have fallen on the room as he walked to the place of reading and searched the scroll to find this passage. They had been hearing about his time in Galilee and how all had praised his teaching. What would he say to them? He chose Isaiah's words (61:1–2a) about one anointed by the Spirit who would preach good news to the poor, bring liberty to captives, and, at the heart of these lines, exercise a ministry of compassion, a reference to another citation from Isaiah (see 42:6b).

This three-part mission continues to be the work of the Church: preaching the Gospel, working for social justice, and reaching out to all peoples in compassion. At the beginning of his ministry, Jesus announced that this work was being fulfilled in the hearing of his listeners by what he was doing. The Spirit works to do the same today through us.

✤ Consider/Discuss:

- How do you live out this three-part mission in your life: proclaiming Jesus by word, deed, and a life signaling God's compassion for all?
- Does the word of God nourish your prayer, your meditation, your time with God?

✤ Responding to the Word

When Ezra read from the book of the law of God, explaining it so the people could understand, they wept, but he said to them: "Go, eat rich foods and drink sweet drinks, and allot portions to those who had nothing prepared; for today is holy to our LORD. Do not be saddened this day, for rejoicing in the LORD must be your strength!" (Nehemiah 8:10). Ask God to let the divine word bring joy to your heart.

January 31, 2010

FOURTH SUNDAY IN ORDINARY TIME

Today's Focus: A God Not to Be Hemmed In

Today we hear God telling Jeremiah that he is being sent forth as a prophet to the nations and that his own people will fight against him but not prevail. Jesus' own townspeople try to kill him when he challenges their resistance to the notion that God reaches out beyond Israel. In both cases, people are enraged enough to kill the prophet who challenges their limited understanding. But the prophetic word prevails.

FIRST READING
Jeremiah 1:4–5, 17–19

The word of the LORD came to me, saying:
Before I formed you in the womb I knew you,
 before you were born I dedicated you,
 a prophet to the nations I appointed you.

But do you gird your loins;
 stand up and tell them
 all that I command you.
Be not crushed on their account,
 as though I would leave you crushed before them;
for it is I this day
 who have made you a fortified city,
a pillar of iron, a wall of brass,
 against the whole land:
against Judah's kings and princes,
 against its priests and people.
They will fight against you but not prevail over you,
 for I am with you to deliver you, says the LORD.

PSALM RESPONSE
Psalm 71:15ab

I will sing of your salvation.

SECOND READING
1 Corinthians 12:31 – 13:13

Brothers and sisters: [Strive eagerly for the greatest spiritual gifts. But I shall show you a still more excellent way.

If I speak in human and angelic tongues, but do not have love, I am a resounding gong or a clashing cymbal. And if I have the gift of prophecy, and comprehend all mysteries and all knowledge; if I have all faith so as to move mountains, but do not have love, I am nothing. If I give away everything I own, and if I hand my body over so that I may boast, but do not have love, I gain nothing.]

Love is patient, love is kind. It is not jealous, it is not pompous, it is not inflated, it is not rude, it does not seek its own interests, it is not quick-tempered, it does not brood over injury, it does not rejoice over wrongdoing but rejoices with the truth. It bears all things, believes all things, hopes all things, endures all things.

Love never fails. If there are prophecies, they will be brought to nothing; if tongues, they will cease; if knowledge, it will be brought to nothing. For we know partially and we prophesy partially, but when the perfect comes, the partial will pass away. When I was a child, I used to talk as a child, think as a child, reason as a child; when I became a man, I put aside childish things. At present we see indistinctly, as in a mirror, but then face to face. At present I know partially; then I shall know fully, as I am fully known. So faith, hope, love remain, these three; but the greatest of these is love.

GOSPEL
Luke 4:21–30

Jesus began speaking in the synagogue, saying: "Today this Scripture passage is fulfilled in your hearing." And all spoke highly of him and were amazed at the gracious words that came from his mouth. They also asked, "Isn't this the son of Joseph?" He said to them, "Surely you will quote me this proverb, 'Physician, cure yourself,' and say, 'Do here in your native place the things that we heard were done in Capernaum.'" And he said, "Amen, I say to you, no prophet is accepted in his own native place. Indeed, I tell you, there were many widows in Israel in the days of Elijah when the sky was closed for three and a half years and a severe famine spread over the entire land. It was to none of these that Elijah was sent, but only to a widow in Zarephath in the land of Sidon. Again, there were many lepers in Israel during the time of Elisha the prophet; yet not one of them was cleansed, but only Naaman the Syrian."

When the people in the synagogue heard this, they were all filled with fury. They rose up, drove him out of the town, and led him to the brow of the hill on which their town had been built, to hurl him down headlong. But Jesus passed through the midst of them and went away.

✦ Understanding the Word

In last Sunday's Gospel Jesus proclaimed the good news of relief and joy to all who are suffering. In today's Gospel Jesus explains how to be receptive to this gift.

Jesus has just read from the prophet Isaiah in the synagogue in his hometown of Nazareth. He anticipates that the people there will ask him to do good there, as he did in Capernaum, that they will claim the privilege of the hometown (Luke 4:23). But, Jesus says, the local boy is accepted as one of them only as long as his message conforms to local views. The residents of Nazareth feel that Jesus should first do good to the residents of his own native village. Jesus responds, however, that generosity of spirit is what shows the real closeness that enables a special relationship with God and not the proximity of having grown up together.

47

This is the reason that Jesus refers to two passages from the Old Testament. In each passage a foreigner showed a magnanimity that resonates with the divine gifts. These foreigners were the ones to whom God shows mercy and not Israelites. Thus, Elijah was sent to a Gentile widow when there was a famine for three and a half years (4:25–26). In this story in First Kings the woman accedes to Elijah's request for water and bread even though she and her son have only enough for a small meal left before they are without food altogether (1 Kings 17:10–15). Similarly, Jesus says that only the foreign leper Naaman was cured by Elisha the prophet (Luke 4:27). Naaman shows a generous response to God's healing of him (2 Kings 5:5, 15, 23–24).

The reaction of his own people to these words of Jesus is extreme. They take him up to a precipice and try to hurl him over (Luke 4:29). The distinction that they think is due them is something that every group zealously guards. But Jesus grounds distinction in the large-heartedness and open-handedness that freely shares one's gifts. These qualities make people receptive to God's gifts in their own lives.

❖ Reflecting on the Word

Prophets tend not to be very popular. They get thrown in jail, ridiculed, beaten up, or killed. The leaders of Jerusalem once had Jeremiah thrown in a cistern, where he would have died if someone had not interceded for him with the king. Today we hear how the people of Nazareth would have killed Jesus if he had not given them the slip.

In both cases, people did not want a message that God was sending them through the prophets. Jeremiah had to tell the leaders that their time had run out because of their infidelity to the covenant. God was leaving them to their own devices, allowing Jerusalem to be destroyed by the Babylonians. Jesus confronts his own townspeople by admonishing them that they should be like that woman whom Elijah helped and that leper Elisha sent to wash in the Jordan. Both of these Gentiles had faith they should imitate. But the villagers only wanted a God who would wreak vengeance on the Gentiles, a God who only worked wonders for them and who was confined within the boundaries of Israel.

Sometimes we may want to keep God in a little box of our own making, limiting God to the boundaries of the church building or maybe even just the tabernacle. That way we go and visit God when we have time or need something, but we hope that God will not bother us too much with any burdensome demands. The God of Israel was never satisfied with confinement, even in something the size of the temple. And Jesus would not allow himself to be constricted in his own day concerning whom he associated or ate with or even touched. Tight quarters wouldn't do, not then but especially once he was raised from the tomb!

❖ Consider/Discuss:

- Has anything ever happened to challenge your idea or image of God?
- Have you ever met a prophet who upset your world?

❖ Responding to the Word

We pray that we will hear when God sends a challenging word to us, calling us to expand our boundaries and allow God to work in new and surprising ways. Lord, let us be open to your Spirit who moves as the Spirit wills.

February 7, 2010

FIFTH SUNDAY IN ORDINARY TIME

Today's Focus: Encountering the Holiness of God

Rarely do all three readings have a common thread. Today we can find one: our unworthiness before the holiness of God. Isaiah, Paul, and Peter all had an experience of what it means to be in the presence of the living God: All bow down in the presence of divinity and then all are sent forth to do God's work.

FIRST READING
Isaiah 6:1–2a, 3–8

In the year King Uzziah died, I saw the Lord seated on a high and lofty throne, with the train of his garment filling the temple. Seraphim were stationed above.

They cried one to the other, "Holy, holy, holy is the LORD of hosts! All the earth is filled with his glory!" At the sound of that cry, the frame of the door shook and the house was filled with smoke.

Then I said, "Woe is me, I am doomed! For I am a man of unclean lips, living among a people of unclean lips; yet my eyes have seen the King, the LORD of hosts!" Then one of the seraphim flew to me, holding an ember that he had taken with tongs from the altar.

He touched my mouth with it, and said, "See, now that this has touched your lips, your wickedness is removed, your sin purged."

Then I heard the voice of the Lord saying, "Whom shall I send? Who will go for us?" "Here I am," I said; "send me!"

PSALM RESPONSE
Psalm 138:1c

In the sight of the angels I will sing your praises, Lord.

For a shorter reading, omit the passages in brackets.

SECOND READING
1 Corinthians 15:1–11 or 15:3–8, 11

[I am reminding you,] brothers and sisters,[of the gospel I preached to you, which you indeed received and in which you also stand. Through it you are also being saved, if you hold fast to the word I preached to you, unless you believed in vain. For] I handed on to you as of first importance what I also received: that Christ died for our sins in accordance with the Scriptures; that he was buried; that he was raised on the third day in accordance with the Scriptures; that he appeared to Cephas, then to the Twelve. After that, he appeared to more than five hundred brothers at once, most of whom are still living, though some have fallen asleep. After that he appeared to James, then to all the apostles. Last of all, as to one born abnormally, he appeared to me. [For I am the least of the apostles, not fit to be called an apostle, because I persecuted the church of God. But by the grace of God I am what I am, and his grace to me has not been ineffective. Indeed, I have toiled harder than all of them; not I, however, but the grace of God that is with me.] Therefore, whether it be I or they, so we preach and so you believed.

GOSPEL
Luke 5:1–11

While the crowd was pressing in on Jesus and [text obscured] of God, he was standing by the Lake of Gennesa[text obscured] boats there alongside the lake; the fishermen had [text obscured] and were washing their nets. Getting into one of the boats, [text obscured] belonging to Simon, he asked him to put out a short distance fr[om] the shore. Then he sat down and taught the crowds from the boat. After he had finished speaking, he said to Simon, "Put out into deep water and lower your nets for a catch." Simon said in reply, "Master, we have worked hard all night and have caught nothing, but at your command I will lower the nets." When they had done this, they caught a great number of fish and their nets were tearing. They signaled to their partners in the other boat to come to help them. They came and filled both boats so that the boats were in danger of sinking. When Simon Peter saw this, he fell at the knees of Jesus and said, "Depart from me, Lord, for I am a sinful man." For astonishment at the catch of fish they had made seized him and all those with him, and likewise James and John, the sons of Zebedee, who were partners of Simon. Jesus said to Simon, "Do not be afraid; from now on you will be catching men." When they brought their boats to the shore, they left everything and followed him.

❖❖ Understanding the Word

The account of Jesus' calling of the first apostles completes the circle of divine gift-human gift-divine gift in chapters 4 and 5 of Luke's Gospel. Last Sunday we heard that God brings through Jesus relief and joy for all who are oppressed in any way. Those who are receptive to these gifts are those who are themselves generous in sharing their own gifts with others (Luke 4:18–30).

Now Jesus calls the first apostles—Simon, John, and James—to share in his ministry (5:1–11). The call comes at a low point in the lives of these soon-to-be apostles. They had been fishing all night and had caught nothing (5:5). According to Simon this fruitless work had been difficult. Despite tiredness and disappointment, Simon readily accedes to Jesus' request to take him a little way from shore so that Jesus can teach people from Simon's boat (5:3). As if all this were not enough, Jesus now asks Simon to go back out into deep water and cast his nets again (5:4). This action would have seemed to most both futile and annoying, so soon revisiting the scene of their ineffective labors—and after they had been washing their nets (5:2).

When Simon catches so many fish that he has to request his "partners in the other boat" to help him, he asks Jesus to leave him because he is a sinner (5:7–8). What Simon is saying is that he is not worthy of this gift. Jesus responds, however, that Simon's unworthiness does not require him to be separated from Jesus. A gift is not for possessing but for sharing. The gift does not stop at Simon, who therefore need not worry about his merit. Simon is to be a mediator of gifts. Thus, Jesus tells Simon, "Do not be afraid; from now on you will be catching men" (5:11). This reference is to the teaching Jesus had just been providing the crowds while in Simon's boat (5:3).

james received prepares them to be bearers of the
...thers. They are able to leave everything and follow
... experienced God's sustaining and generous gift during
...pointment, frustration, and need (5:11).

... the Word

...any people seem to have moved from fearing God to becoming
ve..., ...with God. After all, God is love and Jesus is our brother and the Holy
Spirit ... ...t dove that not only came upon Jesus at his baptism but upon us at
ours. So don't worry—be happy.

I am not calling for a return to living in abject fear before a wrathful God or
stoking up the old torturous hell peopled by souls condemned by scrupulosity.
But there must be some truth to the experience that Isaiah, Paul, and Peter witness to today: our unworthiness before God. The reaction of Isaiah ("Woe is me. I
am doomed!" [Isaiah 6:3]) is most understandable, what with the cry of seraphim
shaking the door of the great temple of Solomon and smoke billowing around the
Lord up there on a high throne. Who wouldn't shudder? Paul's experience on the
road to Damascus, briefly related today, certainly must have sent a ripple of fear
and trembling through him.

But Peter's experience seems more puzzling. This fellow Galilean comes along
and tells experienced fishermen where to catch fish after they had failed to do so
all night. What evokes Peter's "Depart from me, Lord, for I am a sinful man" (Luke
5:8)? This must be fear talking because Jesus replies, "Do not be afraid" (5:10).

Have we domesticated God? Have we turned Jesus simply into another
"buddy"? Have we lost sight of the fact that this is the living God: Creator,
Redeemer, and Sanctifier? Might a little awe and trembling be in order on occasion? After all, at every Mass we say right before receiving Communion, "Lord, I
am not worthy to receive you, but only say the word and I shall be healed."

❖ Consider/Discuss:

- Was it their attitude of awe and recognition of unworthiness that
allowed God to send forth all three of these men to do great things?

- Have you noticed how often in the Gospel someone—usually an
angel or Jesus—says, "Do not be afraid"? Does that speak to us
today? Should it?

❖ Responding to the Word

We might pray the line from today's Mass that serves as an introductory anti-
phon: "Come, let us worship the Lord. Let us bow down in the presence of our
maker, for he is the Lord our God" (Psalm 94:6–7).

February 14, 2010

SIXTH SUNDAY IN ORDINARY TIME

Today's Focus: A Very Strange Valentine's Message

On this Valentine's Day God's word confronts us with some unnerving "either/or" choices: either trusting in human beings or trusting in the Lord, being either poor or rich, hungry or full, weeping or laughing, hated or spoken well of. "Do we have to choose?" you might ask. Short answer: Yes.

FIRST READING
Jeremiah 17:5–8

Thus says the LORD:
>Cursed is the one who trusts in human beings,
>>who seeks his strength in flesh,
>>whose heart turns away from the LORD.
>He is like a barren bush in the desert
>>that enjoys no change of season,
>but stands in a lava waste,
>>a salt and empty earth.
>Blessed is the one who trusts in the LORD,
>>whose hope is the LORD.
>He is like a tree planted beside the waters
>>that stretches out its roots to the stream:
>it fears not the heat when it comes;
>>its leaves stay green;
>in the year of drought it shows no distress,
>>but still bears fruit.

PSALM RESPONSE
Psalm 40:5a

Blessed are they who hope in the Lord.

SECOND READING
1 Corinthians 15: 12, 16–20

Brothers and sisters: If Christ is preached as raised from the dead, how can some among you say there is no resurrection of the dead? If the dead are not raised, neither has Christ been raised, and if Christ has not been raised, your faith is vain; you are still in your sins. Then those who have fallen asleep in Christ have perished. If for this life only we have hoped in Christ, we are the most pitiable people of all.

But now Christ has been raised from the dead, the firstfruits of those who have fallen asleep.

GOSPEL
Luke 6:17,
20–26

Jesus came down with the Twelve and stood on a stretch of level ground with a great crowd of his disciples and a large number of the people from all Judea and Jerusalem and the coastal region of Tyre and Sidon.

And raising his eyes toward his disciples he said:

"Blessed are you who are poor,
   for the kingdom of God is yours.
Blessed are you who are now hungry,
   for you will be satisfied.
Blessed are you who are now weeping,
   for you will laugh.
Blessed are you when people hate you,
   and when they exclude and insult you,
and denounce your name as evil
on account of the Son of Man.

Rejoice and leap for joy on that day! Behold, your reward will be great in heaven. For their ancestors treated the prophets in the same way.

But woe to you who are rich,
   for you have received your consolation.
Woe to you who are filled now,
   for you will be hungry.
Woe to you who laugh now,
   for you will grieve and weep.
Woe to you when all speak well of you,
   for their ancestors treated the false prophets in this way."

❖❖ *Understanding the Word*

We are more accustomed to Matthew's version of the Beatitudes. Luke's version, however, has its own beauty and significance in relation to the context in which it is placed.

Matthew's Beatitudes may initially seem richer and more spiritually significant. There are nine Matthean Beatitudes compared to only four Lukan ones (Matthew 5:3–11; Luke 6:20–23). Moreover, two of the Beatitudes that Matthew and Luke share seem decidedly richer in their Matthean version. While Luke talks about the poor and the hungry being blessed, Matthew qualifies these groups as "the poor in spirit" and those "who hunger and thirst for righteousness" (Mattew 5:3, 6; Luke 6:20–21).

Luke's version of the Beatitudes encourages the disciples to continue to be generous stewards of the divine gifts in the face of their own present material and emotional needs. Thus, while the Matthean Beatitudes are addressed to disciples and crowds alike, Luke's are directed solely to the disciples, responding to their present situation. So Luke has no Beatitudes about the meek and the peacemakers because the Lukan disciples are not presently exercising that quality and function. Luke speaks of the poor and the hungry, those who are sorrowful and have been insulted, excluded, and denounced because of Jesus. All these experiences are what has just happened to them in Luke's Gospel. The disciples have been hungry and eaten grain that they picked on the Sabbath (6:1). This has incurred the displeasure of the Pharisees (6:2). They have also been criticized by the Pharisees for their dietary practices in general (5:33). Finally, they have accepted the risk of poverty in order to follow Jesus: whereas in Matthew and Mark's Gospels the first disciples leave their father and their nets to follow Jesus, Luke writes that they left everything (Luke 5:11).

The Beatitudes inform the disciples that divine bounty comes in what looks like human depletion. Their own self-gift and the needy state it places them in are the elements of their commitment through which the Godly gift comes to others.

✣ Reflecting on the Word

What a set of readings for Valentine's Day! Cursed are those who trust in human beings! Woe to you who laugh now! Woe when all speak well of you! Blessed are you who are poor, hungry, weeping, hated, excluded, and insulted. This is the word of the Lord? This is the God who is love?

To begin with, our God is a passionate God, passionately in love with us. "I am a jealous God" was what God said to Moses. God wants to come first—that is the bottom line here. Not that we can't love others, but that only God is God who is worthy of all our love.

Jesus came to create a new family. Remember, his own family didn't understand him; they even thought he was crazy and came to bring him home. Jesus came to form a family of those who do the will of God. He appointed apostles not just to preach and heal but to be with him.

Luke's sermon on the plain (6:20–49) outlines what life in the kingdom is like now. If you live in the kingdom, you stand with the poor, the hungry, the grieving, and most of all, with those who are hated and excluded and denounced on account of the Son of Man (6:20–22).

✣ Consider/Discuss:

- Why would a person be cursed for trusting in other human beings? Is that always in opposition to trusting in God?
- Would you find your name under the woe listing or the blessed listing? With Lent approaching, how might these words of Jesus call you to conversion?

✣ Responding to the Word

Ask God to give you a heart that puts its trust in the Lord, that is willing to take action to show solidarity with the poor, the homeless, the oppressed, the grieving. Ask Jesus to reveal himself as the bridegroom, as love incarnate, as the compassion of God, and to bring you into this relationship of love.

Let us look at the movement of the Lenten readings. The way that they progress makes powerful statements about temptation, prayer, the power of the Spirit, suffering, reconciliation, interior dispositions, harmful or healthy ways of treating others, signs of resurrection, and Christian service.

The Gospel on the first Sunday of Lent shows us how the power of the Spirit in our lives and ministries enables us to resist the temptations that we all face. The next Sunday, Luke's account of the Transfiguration provides for us another dimension of prayer: how it may open our lives to a perspective-enriching experience of God. By contrast, perspectives shared in human society are often wrong. Luke's Gospel reading for the Third Sunday of Lent in Year C takes on one such conception that has had amazing staying power throughout many cultures, and replaces it with a view that provides energy for moral growth. On the same Sunday in Year A we have an example from the book of Exodus of a common (but incorrect) notion about suffering, and a corrected perspective that shows how to respond to suffering in a way that strengthens one's relationship with God.

The next few Sundays reflect on what it is to be a new creation in Christ and what kind of responsibilities this gift entails. The rich description of this gift in Second Corinthians on the Fourth Sunday of Lent in Year C inspires us to respond generously to it. The first reading for the Fourth Sunday of Lent in Year A shows us how renewed life has its roots in our interior dispositions, while the Gospel for the Fifth Sunday of Lent in Year C moves outward to show us how to live in ways that heal others and do not afflict them.

Finally, the three readings for the Fifth Sunday of Lent in Year A and the three readings for Palm Sunday of the Lord's Passion guide us, respectively, toward seeing signs of resurrection in our daily life and proceeding toward this new life through commitment to service. The reading from Ezekiel on the Fifth Sunday of Lent, Year A, helps us to see new life arising out of repentance, while the reading from the Letter to the Romans shows that the righteousness that arises out of repentance leads to actual resurrection. This occurs because righteousness comes from the Spirit that raised Jesus dwelling in us. The Gospel for that same Sunday depicting the raising of Lazarus encourages us to see, in our experiences of the restoration of life, signs of the resurrection that is God's promise. The three readings for Palm Sunday of the Lord's Passion clarify various dimensions of Christian service that lead to resurrection and portray the ultimate example of such service.

February 21, 2010

FIRST SUNDAY OF LENT

Today's Focus: Springtime in the Desert

In one of the prefaces for Lent, the presider prays in the name of the community: "Each year you give us this joyful season when we prepare to celebrate the paschal mystery with mind and heart renewed" (Sacramentary, Preface for Lent I). Lent, which means spring, becomes joyful when we turn our hearts and minds toward God.

FIRST READING
Deuteronomy 26: 4–10

Moses spoke to the people, saying: "The priest shall receive the basket from you and shall set it in front of the altar of the LORD, your God. Then you shall declare before the LORD, your God, 'My father was a wandering Aramean who went down to Egypt with a small household and lived there as an alien. But there he became a nation great, strong, and numerous. When the Egyptians mal-treated and oppressed us, imposing hard labor upon us, we cried to the LORD, the God of our fathers, and he heard our cry and saw our affliction, our toil, and our oppression. He brought us out of Egypt with his strong hand and outstretched arm, with terrifying power, with signs and wonders; and bringing us into this country, he gave us this land flowing with milk and honey. Therefore, I have now brought you the firstfruits of the products of the soil which you, O LORD, have given me.' And having set them before the Lord, your God, you shall bow down in his presence."

PSALM RESPONSE
Psalm 91:15b

Be with me, Lord, when I am in trouble.

SECOND READING
Romans 10: 8–13

Brothers and sisters: What does Scripture say?

The word is near you,
in your mouth and in your heart

—that is, the word of faith that we preach—, for, if you confess with your mouth that Jesus is Lord and believe in your heart that God raised him from the dead, you will be saved. For one believes with the heart and so is justified, and one confesses with the mouth and so is saved. For the Scripture says,

No one who believes in him will be put to shame.

For there is no distinction between Jew and Greek; the same Lord is Lord of all, enriching all who call upon him. For "everyone who calls on the name of the Lord will be saved."

GOSPEL
Luke 4:1–13

Filled with the Holy Spirit, Jesus returned from the Jordan and was led by the Spirit into the desert for forty days, to be tempted by the devil. He ate nothing during those days, and when they were over he was hungry. The devil said to him, "If you are the Son of God, command this stone to become bread." Jesus answered him, "It is written,

One does not live on bread alone."

Then he took him up and showed him all the kingdoms of the world in a single instant. The devil said to him, "I shall give to you all this power and glory; for it has been handed over to me, and I may give it to whomever I wish. All this will be yours, if you worship me." Jesus said to him in reply, "It is written:

You shall worship the Lord, your God,
and him alone shall you serve."

Then he led him to Jerusalem, made him stand on the parapet of the temple, and said to him, "If you are the Son of God, throw yourself down from here, for it is written:

He will command his angels concerning you, to guard you,
and:
With their hands they will support you,
lest you dash your foot against a stone."
Jesus said to him in reply, "It also says,
You shall not put the Lord, your God, to the test."

When the devil had finished every temptation, he departed from him for a time.

❖ Understanding the Word

The Gospel reading today shows how the very obstacles to ministry can be a source of strength if they are met correctly.

After Jesus' baptism he is led by the Spirit into the desert, where he fasts for forty days. This is his identification with the experience of the Israelites in the wilderness for forty years following the Exodus. For the generations of both Moses and Jesus the wilderness experience is a time of testing. God tests the wilderness generation (Exodus 16:4), and the devil tempts Jesus (Luke 4:1–13). While the Israelites repeatedly failed their tests, however, Jesus successfully resists the three temptations.

The challenges confronted by Jesus represent three temptations that are common to all people, temptations that turn us away from others and into ourselves. The inducement to turn a stone into bread tests our trust in God to sustain our life at difficult times. The enticement to worship the devil in return for all the kingdoms of the world speaks to the pull that riches and power exert over our hearts. Finally, the temptation to jump from the parapet of the temple represents the tug that self-glorification exerts in our lives.

In Luke's version of this story, which is the Gospel for today, after successfully resisting the temptations Jesus moves to his ministry "in the power of the Spirit" (4:14). It was the Spirit who led Jesus into the desert where the temptations began (4:1-2). Luke is saying that by resisting the attempts (1) to think and act as if we sustain our own lives, (2) to make wealth and power our goals, and (3) to exult in our own glorification, we live in "the power of the Spirit" from which effective ministry develops and through which it progresses.

Only Luke writes that after his baptism Jesus was praying when the Spirit first descended upon him and then led him into the desert (3:21–22; 4:1). In doing so, Luke is suggesting that in order for Christians to stand firm against temptations they need to remain rooted in prayer.

❖ Reflecting on the Word

Food, Fortune, Fame—they sound like categories from the quiz show *Jeopardy*. "Feed yourself, you're starving," Satan said to Jesus, showing up at high noon, I imagine, when the sun was most brutal. After more than a month of daytime heat and nighttime cold, no food, and no one else in sight, Jesus could not have had much energy. But it wasn't strength for a physical fight that was needed; it was strength of the Spirit. And Jesus was not lacking that. The Spirit had come upon him at his baptism and had driven him into the wilderness. That Spirit does not abandon him now.

First temptation: Use your power to feed yourself. Jesus' answer: God's word is my food. Second temptation: Bend the knee to me in exchange for all the kingdoms of the world. Jesus' answer: Only God deserves worship; the only kingdom worth having is God's. Third temptation: Check to see if God is with you by throwing yourself off the temple. Jesus' answer: You don't test God; you trust God.

Just as Israel was tempted in the desert not to place their trust in the God who delivered them from Egypt, so Jesus is tempted. But Jesus is the new Israel, the ideal Israel, the beloved Son. He professes faith in the God of Israel, his beloved Father.

That same Spirit who was with Jesus in his time of testing is with us today. The issue is not all that different: Where do we place our trust? Whose voice do we obey?

✢ Consider/Discuss:

- What temptations do you face in life that draw you away from God?
- In whom or what do you put your trust?

✢ Responding to the Word

The ancient creed of Israel recognized God working in their history "with his strong hand and outstretched arm" (Deuteronomy 26:8), bringing them from a land of slavery to a place "flowing with milk and honey" (26:9). Slowly say the Nicene Creed or the Apostles' Creed. Allow the words to bring you more deeply into the mystery of God.

February 28, 2010

SECOND SUNDAY OF LENT

Today's Focus: A Glimpse of Glory

Lent reminds us that our final destination is glory, our "citizenship is in heaven" (Philippians 3:20). The Transfiguration was a moment when Jesus' disciples caught a glimpse of him in glory. Moments of glory do not last long, but they continue to occur. This is more likely to happen when we "listen to him" (Luke 9:35).

FIRST READING
Genesis 15: 5–12, 17–18

The Lord God took Abram outside and said, "Look up at the sky and count the stars, if you can. Just so," he added, "shall your descendants be." Abram put his faith in the LORD, who credited it to him as an act of righteousness.

He then said to him, "I am the LORD who brought you from Ur of the Chaldeans to give you this land as a possession." "O Lord GOD," he asked, "how am I to know that I shall possess it?" He answered him, "Bring me a three-year-old heifer, a three-year-old she-goat, a three-year-old ram, a turtledove, and a young pigeon." Abram brought him all these, split them in two, and placed each half opposite the other; but the birds he did not cut up. Birds of prey swooped down on the carcasses, but Abram stayed with them. As the sun was about to set, a trance fell upon Abram, and a deep, terrifying darkness enveloped him.

When the sun had set and it was dark, there appeared a smoking fire pot and a flaming torch, which passed between those pieces. It was on that occasion that the LORD made a covenant with Abram, saying: "To your descendants I give this land, from the Wadi of Egypt to the Great River, the Euphrates."

PSALM RESPONSE
Psalm 27:1a

The Lord is my light and my salvation.

In the shorter form of the reading, the passage in brackets is omitted.

SECOND READING
Philippians 3: 17 — 4:1 or 3:20 — 4:1

[Join with others in being imitators of me, brothers and sisters, and observe those who thus conduct themselves according to the model you have in us. For many, as I have often told you and now tell you even in tears, conduct themselves as enemies of the cross of Christ. Their end is destruction. Their God is their stomach; their glory is in their "shame." Their minds are occupied with earthly things. But] our citizenship is in heaven, and from it we also await a savior, the Lord Jesus Christ. He will change our lowly body to conform with his glorified body by the power that enables him also to bring all things into subjection to himself.

Therefore, my brothers and sisters, whom I love and long for, my joy and crown, in this way stand firm in the Lord.

GOSPEL
Luke 9:28b–36

Jesus took Peter, John, and James and went up the mountain to pray. While he was praying his face changed in appearance and his clothing became dazzling white. And behold, two men were conversing with him, Moses and Elijah, who appeared in glory and spoke of his exodus that he was going to accomplish in Jerusalem. Peter and his companions had been overcome by sleep, but becoming fully awake, they saw his glory and the two men standing with him. As they were about to part from him, Peter said to Jesus, "Master, it is good that we are here; let us make three tents, one for you, one for Moses, and one for Elijah." But he did not know what he was saying. While he was still speaking, a cloud came and cast a shadow over them, and they became frightened when they entered the cloud. Then from the cloud came a voice that said, "This is my chosen Son; listen to him." After the voice had spoken, Jesus was found alone. They fell silent and did not at that time tell anyone what they had seen.

❖ Understanding the Word

The Lukan story of the Transfiguration signals Jesus' recognition of the sustaining and empowering function of vision for his disciples. He had just told them in no uncertain terms the extent to which they must be willing to follow him in discipleship: "If anyone wishes to come after me, he must deny himself and take up his cross daily and follow me. For whoever wishes to save his life will lose it, but whoever loses his life for my sake will save it" (Luke 9:23–24).

Now Jesus takes the leaders of the disciples with him up a mountain and provides them with both the experience of the glory that awaits the faithful disciple and the perspective to sustain and empower them on the way. First, while praying on the mountain Jesus' face becomes changed and his clothes become "dazzling white" (9:29). Second, while Matthew and Mark also write that Moses and Elijah appeared, only Luke writes that they appeared "in glory" (9:31). There were traditions of Moses and Elijah having ascended into the heavens. Thus, these two figures give the disciples an experience of what the end of the sometimes difficult journey is like. Third, only Luke also stresses that not only does a cloud overshadow them when the divine voice comes, but also that Peter, James, and John enter the cloud (9:34). The cloud is a symbol of God's presence, as it was during the Exodus and wilderness wanderings. They are taken into the divine presence when they hear the voice confirming Jesus.

Jesus also gives them perspective to help them be faithful on the way. Only Luke says that Moses and Elijah talk about Jesus' "exodus that he was going to accomplish in Jerusalem" (9:30–31). So the leaders of the apostles receive the perspective that life is a journey with hardships, like the Exodus, but for the stalwart disciple life will result in a glorious conclusion.

Thus, Luke encourages us to take time apart to be open to the experience of God and the godly perspective that energizes our commitments. Given the importance of prayer for Luke, it hardly seems accidental that these come while Jesus is at prayer.

Every so often life gives you a glimpse of glory: a moment of beauty in a sunset, of goodness in a person, of truth in words spoken, of peace and well-being. Sometimes it comes suddenly; other times it's been there all along but you haven't been paying much attention. But it is real and you know it is a glimpse of glory.

This is what happened to Peter, James, and John. Jesus often went off to pray during their time with him, traveling through towns and villages. Luke makes a special point of telling us this more than once. At these times he would experience the presence of his Father. Now, while he is praying with his friends, the Father again draws near, not just to Jesus this time but to his disciples, too.

But first there are Moses and Elijah, also in a state of glory, speaking to Jesus about his coming death, his "exodus," his passing over into glory. And Jesus will go on to speak to his disciples about his coming death, which they will not want to hear. But for now they are given a glimpse of glory, of what is at the end of the road.

Every so often we need a reminder of what we are destined for, that our citizenship is in heaven. We need to be reminded of the promise that our Savior will come and "change our lowly body to conform with his glorified body" (Philippians 3:21). For the present, we need to heed the Father's words: "This is my chosen Son; listen to him" (Luke 9:35).

❖ *Consider/Discuss*:

- Do you think of yourself as destined for glory? Let your imagination consider what it will be like.
- Have you had your own glimpse of glory, a taste of the transcendent, any time recently?

❖ *Responding to the Word*

While we pray that one day we will see the Lord in his glory, we can also ask, even now, that we may receive a glimpse of that glory as we walk by faith. We pray that we may live in awareness of the presence of God.

March 7, 2010

THIRD SUNDAY OF LENT, YEAR C

Today's Focus: It's Time to Turn—Now

Lent is a time for conversion, for turning toward God and away from anything that separates us from God. Today we hear the story of Moses turning toward a burning bush and finding the living and saving God. Jesus turns us toward a fig tree.

For pastoral reasons, the readings given for Year A may be used in place of these readings. See page 68.

FIRST READING
Exodus 3:1–8a, 13–15

Moses was tending the flock of his father-in-law Jethro, the priest of Midian. Leading the flock across the desert, he came to Horeb, the mountain of God. There an angel of the LORD appeared to Moses in fire flaming out of a bush. As he looked on, he was surprised to see that the bush, though on fire, was not consumed. So Moses decided, "I must go over to look at this remarkable sight, and see why the bush is not burned."

When the LORD saw him coming over to look at it more closely, God called out to him from the bush, "Moses! Moses!" He answered, "Here I am." God said, "Come no nearer! Remove the sandals from your feet, for the place where you stand is holy ground. I am the God of your fathers," he continued, "the God of Abraham, the God of Isaac, the God of Jacob." Moses hid his face, for he was afraid to look at God. But the LORD said, "I have witnessed the affliction of my people in Egypt and have heard their cry of complaint against their slave drivers, so I know well what they are suffering. Therefore I have come down to rescue them from the hands of the Egyptians and lead them out of that land into a good and spacious land, a land flowing with milk and honey."

Moses said to God, "But when I go to the Israelites and say to them, 'The God of your fathers has sent me to you,' if they ask me, 'What is his name?' what am I to tell them?" God replied, "I am who am." Then he added, "This is what you shall tell the Israelites: I AM sent me to you."

God spoke further to Moses, "Thus shall you say to the Israelites: The LORD, the God of your fathers, the God of Abraham, the God of Isaac, the God of Jacob, has sent me to you.

"This is my name forever; thus am I to be remembered through all generations."

PSALM RESPONSE
Psalm 103:8a

The Lord is kind and merciful.

SECOND
READING
1 Corinthians 10:
1–6, 10–12 I do not want you to be unaware, brothers and sisters, that our ancestors were all under the cloud and all passed through the sea, and all of them were baptized into Moses in the cloud and in the sea. All ate the same spiritual food, and all drank the same spiritual drink, for they drank from a spiritual rock that followed them, and the rock was the Christ. Yet God was not pleased with most of them, for they were struck down in the desert.

These things happened as examples for us, so that we might not desire evil things, as they did. Do not grumble as some of them did, and suffered death by the destroyer. These things happened to them as an example, and they have been written down as a warning to us, upon whom the end of the ages has come. Therefore, whoever thinks he is standing secure should take care not to fall.

GOSPEL
Luke 13:1–9

Some people told Jesus about the Galileans whose blood Pilate had mingled with the blood of their sacrifices. Jesus said to them in reply, "Do you think that because these Galileans suffered in this way they were greater sinners than all other Galileans? By no means! But I tell you, if you do not repent, you will all perish as they did! Or those eighteen people who were killed when the tower at Siloam fell on them—do you think they were more guilty than everyone else who lived in Jerusalem? By no means! But I tell you, if you do not repent, you will all perish as they did!"

And he told them this parable: "There once was a person who had a fig tree planted in his orchard, and when he came in search of fruit on it but found none, he said to the gardener, 'For three years now I have come in search of fruit on this fig tree but have found none. So cut it down. Why should it exhaust the soil?' He said to him in reply, 'Sir, leave it for this year also, and I shall cultivate the ground around it and fertilize it; it may bear fruit in the future. If not you can cut it down.'"

❖❖ Understanding the Word

Most of us might think that we do quite well at living the way we should in comparison to how all people live their lives. It is, decision scientists tell us, a self-affirming bias that people have and one that has been demonstrated in tests. In today's Gospel passage, Jesus counters this bias in order to motivate in us a higher degree of commitment to moral growth.

What occasions this teaching of Jesus is the report that Pilate had slaughtered some Galileans. The way this news is conveyed is especially gruesome: it is said that the Roman leader had mingled their blood "with the blood of their sacrifices" (Luke 13:1). Immediately Jesus discerns an attitude that lurks behind these words. He senses a common defense mechanism that people use to deal with the horrors of the world: those who experience them must in some way have brought them upon themselves. Thus it was, and still is, a common attitude to attribute suffering to the sinfulness of the afflicted person. In some cases this is almost a knee-jerk reaction that must be countered. This attitude gives us a sense of control over our lives. We feel that if we live well we can stay clear of the problems in life.

Jesus stands this idea on its head. He says that people who experience tragedies are not worse sinners than anyone else (13:2, 4). Rather all need to repent or they will perish as did those who experienced disasters (13:3, 5). This perishing refers to the apocalyptic destruction at the end of time that Jesus had been talking about in portions of chapter 12. The idea is that everyone is in need of repentance. This perspective subverts the bias that we are living well and inspires us to further growth.

❖ Reflecting on the Word

"MYOB," we would say to each other when I was growing up. "MYOB"—"Mind your own business." It was one of those sayings planted at an early age. Don't be nosy. Look to your own affairs and not to the concerns of others.

Jesus seems to be saying something similar in the first part of the Gospel today. People are telling him about these terrible tragedies that have been happening—Pilate's brutal treatment of some Galileans and a tower that had fallen and killed a crowd. Their world view came from such revered books as Deuteronomy, which said that the good prosper and the wicked are punished. So if something awful happens, the victims must have done something to deserve it.

Jesus takes a different approach. He tells the people that they should look to their own lives and see what is going on there. What kind of fruit are their lives bearing? The point of the parable seems to be that time is running out. The hour of grace (*kairos*) is now. Don't assume there's a lot of time (*chronos*) left. And Paul underlines this when he writes that "whoever thinks he is standing secure should take care not to fall" (1 Corinthians 10:12).

God continues to speak to us through Jesus in the Gospel, calling us to draw closer, to turn our lives more fully toward God so God can enter. The call to repentance was the basic message that Jesus preached. This message has not changed. Many have heard it; not all have responded.

❖ Consider/Discuss:

- Do we distract ourselves from attending to what needs to be done in our lives by focusing on the situation of others?
- How is God asking us, individually and communally, to bear fruit in our lives?

❖ Responding to the Word

We pray that we may hear God's call in our own lives, and that we might take advantage of this holy season to reflect on how God is calling us to change and live in the grace of God more fully.

March 7, 2010

THIRD SUNDAY OF LENT, YEAR A

Today's Focus: Water, the First Gift

The Gospels that we hear for the next three weeks were chosen because of their special importance for those undergoing Christian initiation at the Easter Vigil. Today's Gospel presents Jesus as one who offers living water, water that will well up within us as a source of eternal life.

FIRST READING
Exodus 17: 3–7

In those days, in their thirst for water, the people grumbled against Moses, saying, "Why did you ever make us leave Egypt? Was it just to have us die here of thirst with our children and our livestock?" So Moses cried out to the LORD, "What shall I do with this people? A little more and they will stone me!" The LORD answered Moses, "Go over there in front of the people, along with some of the elders of Israel, holding in your hand, as you go, the staff with which you struck the river. I will be standing there in front of you on the rock in Horeb. Strike the rock, and the water will flow from it for the people to drink." This Moses did, in the presence of the elders of Israel. The place was called Massah and Meribah, because the Israelites quarreled there and tested the LORD, saying, "Is the LORD in our midst or not?"

PSALM RESPONSE
Psalm 95:8

If today you hear his voice, harden not your hearts.

SECOND READING
Romans 5: 1–2, 5–8

Brothers and sisters: Since we have been justified by faith, we have peace with God through our Lord Jesus Christ, through whom we have gained access by faith to this grace in which we stand, and we boast in hope of the glory of God.

And hope does not disappoint, because the love of God has been poured out into our hearts through the Holy Spirit who has been given to us. For Christ, while we were still helpless, died at the appointed time for the ungodly. Indeed, only with difficulty does one die for a just person, though perhaps for a good person one might even find courage to die. But God proves his love for us in that while we were still sinners Christ died for us.

GOSPEL
John 4:5–42 or
4:5–15, 19b–26,
39a, 40–42

Jesus came to a town of Samaria called Sychar, near the plot of land that Jacob had given to his son Joseph. Jacob's well was there. Jesus, tired from his journey, sat down there at the well. It was about noon.

A woman of Samaria came to draw water. Jesus said to her, "Give me a drink." His disciples had gone into the town to buy food. The Samaritan woman said to him, "How can you, a Jew, ask me, a Samaritan woman, for a drink?"—For Jews use nothing in common with Samaritans.—Jesus answered and said to her, "If you knew the gift of God and who is saying to you, 'Give me a drink,' you would have asked him and he would have given you living water." The woman said to him, "Sir, you do not even have a bucket and the cistern is deep; where then can you get this living water? Are you greater than our father Jacob, who gave us this cistern and drank from it himself with his children and his flocks?" Jesus answered and said to her, "Everyone who drinks this water will be thirsty again; but whoever drinks the water I shall give will never thirst; the water I shall give will become in him a spring of water welling up to eternal life." The woman said to him, "Sir, give me this water, so that I may not be thirsty or have to keep coming here to draw water."

[Jesus said to her, "Go call your husband and come back." The woman answered and said to him, "I do not have a husband." Jesus answered her, "You are right in saying, 'I do not have a husband.' For you have had five husbands, and the one you have now is not your husband. What you have said is true." The woman said to him, "Sir,] I can see that you are a prophet. Our ancestors worshiped on this mountain; but you people say that the place to worship is in Jerusalem." Jesus said to her, "Believe me, woman, the hour is coming when you will worship the Father neither on this mountain nor in Jerusalem. You people worship what you do not understand; we worship what we understand, because salvation is from the Jews. But the hour is coming, and is now here, when true worshipers will worship the Father in Spirit and truth; and indeed the Father seeks such people to worship him. God is Spirit, and those who worship him must worship in Spirit and truth."

The woman said to him, "I know that the Messiah is coming, the one called the Christ; when he comes, he will tell us everything." Jesus said to her, "I am he, the one speaking with you."

[At that moment his disciples returned, and were amazed that he was talking with a woman, but still no one said, "What are you looking for?" or "Why are you talking with her?" The woman left her water jar and went into the town and said to the people, "Come see a man who told me everything I have done. Could he possibly be the Christ?" They went out of the town and came to him. Meanwhile, the disciples urged him, "Rabbi, eat." But he said to them, "I have food to eat of which you do not know." So the disciples said to one another, "Could someone have brought him something to eat?" Jesus said to them, "My food is to do the will of the one who sent me and to finish his work. Do you not say, 'In four months the harvest will be here'? I tell you, look up and see the fields ripe for the harvest. The reaper is already receiving payment and gathering crops for eternal life, so that the sower and reaper can rejoice together. For here the saying is verified that 'One sows and another reaps.' I sent you to reap what you have not worked for; others have done the work, and you are sharing the fruits of their work."]

Many of the Samaritans of that town began to believe in him [because of the word of the woman who testified, "He told me everything I have done."] When the Samaritans came to him, they invited him to stay with them; and he stayed there two days. Many more began to believe in him because of his word, and they said to the woman, "We no longer believe because of your word; for we have heard for ourselves, and we know that this is truly the savior of the world."

✢ Understanding the Word

In today's first reading we find that when people encounter difficult times they tend to test God rather than use the opportunity to express their faith. The people are upset with Moses because they have found no water at the place where they have encamped after their journey by day in the desert (Exodus 17:1–2a).

Moses interprets this reaction by the people as a testing of God (17:2b). This phrase is significant because it had just been used by God in the previous chapter of the book of Exodus. God had promised to rain down manna from the heavens to sustain the people. God had told them to gather the manna on only six days, collecting enough on the sixth day to sustain them on the seventh. Thus God would test the people to see whether or not they would listen (16:4–5). Would the wilderness generation trust in God's sustaining presence in difficult times? They failed the test in Exodus 16 by going out on the seventh day to gather manna. They were, after all, in the desert, where food is scarce.

They also fail the test in today's passage. Moses' reaction shows that the people have not understood the function of difficult times in the development of their relationship with God. By not trusting in God's provision they have put God to the test. They should have trusted and thus passed the test of their belief in God's providence.

70

This passage from Exodus reconfigures the way that we look upon trying situations. People commonly try God in these times by questioning the divine saving presence. These times are, however, opportunities to express our trust in God.

✤ Reflecting on the Word

From the beginning, God worked with water. Chapter one of Genesis shows God separating water from the sky and the earth. In chapter two, God causes a stream to rise from the earth to water all the surface of the dry land so that a garden can spring up. And from the dust—with a little water—God makes the first human creature and then breathes life into him.

When Moses led Israel out into the desert and the people began to grumble because they found themselves without water, God sent Moses over to strike a rock. Out came cool clear water.

Jesus hung around water quite a bit, too, calling his first disciples from the fishing boats up in Galilee. Not only did he calm the water, he even walked on it. But of all the occasions that connect Jesus with water, none is more pregnant with meaning than the time he spent with a Samaritan woman at a well. She had come to slake her thirst, to get water for cooking and washing. What she found was the one who could give her water of a different kind.

"Everyone who drinks this water will be thirsty again; but whoever drinks the water I shall give will never thirst; the water I shall give will become in [them] a spring of water welling up to eternal life" (John 4:14).

We were baptized with water and the Holy Spirit. On that day the Holy Spirit was poured into our hearts.

✤ Consider/Discuss:

- What would life be like without water? How many ways do we depend on water?
- What does it mean to drink the water that Jesus gives? How does it take away our thirst?

✤ Responding to the Word

We pray that the Father may give us a thirst both for Jesus and for the eternal life he brings. Jesus, the living water, will preserve our spirits from becoming dry and our hearts from become hardened. We pray the Holy Spirit to lead us to the wellspring of salvation.

March 14, 2010

FOURTH SUNDAY OF LENT, YEAR C

Today's Focus: What Does a New Creation Look Like?

The movement of Lent is a journey to Easter, when we will renew our baptismal promises and pledge once more to live a life that renounces the power and attraction of evil and commit ourselves more fully to living life in union with the Trinity. Today's readings offer us some images of what it means to be a new creation.

For pastoral reasons, the readings given for Year A may be used in place of these readings. See page 76.

FIRST READING
Joshua 5:9a, 10–12

The LORD said to Joshua, "Today I have removed the reproach of Egypt from you."

While the Israelites were encamped at Gilgal on the plains of Jericho, they celebrated the Passover on the evening of the fourteenth of the month. On the day after the Passover, they ate of the produce of the land in the form of unleavened cakes and parched grain. On that same day after the Passover, on which they ate of the produce of the land, the manna ceased. No longer was there manna for the Israelites, who that year ate of the yield of the land of Canaan.

PSALM RESPONSE
Psalm 34:9a

Taste and see the goodness of the Lord.

SECOND READING
2 Corinthians 5: 17–21

Brothers and sisters: Whoever is in Christ is a new creation: the old things have passed away; behold, new things have come. And all this is from God, who has reconciled us to himself through Christ and given us the ministry of reconciliation, namely, God was reconciling the world to himself in Christ, not counting their trespasses against them and entrusting to us the message of reconciliation. So we are ambassadors for Christ, as if God were appealing through us. We implore you on behalf of Christ, be reconciled to God. For our sake he made him to be sin who did not know sin, so that we might become the righteousness of God in him.

GOSPEL
Luke 15:1–3,
11–32

Tax collectors and sinners were all drawing near to listen to Jesus, but the Pharisees and scribes began to complain, saying, "This man welcomes sinners and eats with them." So to them Jesus addressed this parable: "A man had two sons, and the younger son said to his father, 'Father give me the share of your estate that should come to me.' So the father divided the property between them. After a few days, the younger son collected all his belongings and set off to a distant country where he squandered his inheritance on a life of dissipation. When he had freely spent everything, a severe famine struck that country, and he found himself in dire need. So he hired himself out to one of the local citizens who sent him to his farm to tend the swine. And he longed to eat his fill of the pods on which the swine fed, but nobody gave him any. Coming to his senses he thought, 'How many of my father's hired workers have more than enough food to eat, but here am I, dying from hunger. I shall get up and go to my father and I shall say to him, "Father, I have sinned against heaven and against you. I no longer deserve to be called your son; treat me as you would treat one of your hired workers."' So he got up and went back to his father. While he was still a long way off, his father caught sight of him, and was filled with compassion. He ran to his son, embraced him and kissed him. His son said to him, 'Father, I have sinned against heaven and against you; I no longer deserve to be called your son.' But his father ordered his servants, 'Quickly bring the finest robe and put it on him; put a ring on his finger and sandals on his feet. Take the fattened calf and slaughter it. Then let us celebrate with a feast, because this son of mine was dead, and has come to life again; he was lost, and has been found.' Then the celebration began. Now the older son had been out in the field and, on his way back, as he neared the house, he heard the sound of music and dancing. He called one of the servants and asked what this might mean. The servant said to him, 'Your brother has returned and your father has slaughtered the fattened calf because he has him back safe and sound.' He became angry, and when he refused to enter the house, his father came out and pleaded with him. He said to his father in reply, 'Look, all these years I served you and not once did I disobey your orders; yet you never gave me even a young goat to feast on with my friends. But when your son returns who swallowed up your property with prostitutes, for him you slaughter the fattened calf.' He said to him, 'My son, you are here with me always; everything I have is yours. But now we must celebrate and rejoice, because your brother was dead and has come to life again; he was lost and has been found.'"

In today's second reading Paul explains what it is to be a new creation in Christ, how that has occurred, and how it continues.

We are reconciled to God in Christ (2 Corinthians 5:18). Reconciliation means that God did not make our sins an obstacle to reunification (5:19). God's intent to reconcile humanity is so great that this mission has been extended through the ministry of Paul and his coworkers (5:18). So much does God wish to be united with us that God "appeals" to us through Paul, who mirrors this divine desire by "imploring" people to act in ways that make this reconciliation possible (5:20).

When such reconciliation occurs, we become a new creation. In other words, new life is given through a new association. Because this association is with God, this new life is God's life. This is why Paul says that those who are reconciled "become the righteousness of God" in Christ (5:21). The new creation, then, is a change from the type of life that a person has led, a shift from alienation from God to union with God.

The union occurs through our becoming "the righteousness of God." The word *dikaiosune*, which our Bible translates as "righteousness," also means "justice." This characteristic was considered in both the Jewish and Greek cultures to be the key virtue. Paul claims that the new creation makes people not only have this essence of humanity in them, but also to be reconfigured into "the righteousness of God."

This perspective energizes us for the task of remaining reconciled to God by adhering to the message. Paul implores the Corinthians to "be reconciled to God" (5:20b). The gift of being a new creation is one that must be accepted continually through personal effort to be open to God's gift.

❖ *Reflecting on the Word*

When Israel packed its few bags and went rushing out of Egypt, God's chosen people began a journey into being a new creation, from being a nation of slaves to being a nation of free men and women, a people under the heel of Egypt to one joined to God by the covenant, a community that ate manna (which literally means "What is it?") to one that ate the produce of the promised land. This journey took forty years and it wasn't easy.

When the prodigal son finally "came to his senses" and realized he would be better off back home as a hired worker than stealing slop from the pigs, he began a journey from being lost to being found, from being dead to being alive. This journey did not take forty years, but how do you measure in clock time a journey that transforms the heart? This journey wasn't easy either.

The path to being a new creation can take forty years, forty days, forty minutes, or forty seconds. Sometime it involves an outer journey; it is always an inner one. It is difficult—dying to self always is. What matters is that we make it. Because the end result is the radiance of a people, or a son or daughter, who has finally arrived where they belong, at a party where the Father has an arm around them and the older brother who brought this about through his saving death is standing at the Father's side, with the Spirit hovering above them all.

- Where have you come from this Lent and where do you see yourself arriving?
- What does it mean in your life to see yourself as being a new creation in Christ?

❖ *Responding to the Word*

We pray that whatever form our journey takes, we will persevere in becoming, individually and communally, a new creation. We ask the Father to send forth the Holy Spirit upon us so that we will be recreated as this same Spirit continues to renew the face of the earth.

March 14, 2010

FOURTH SUNDAY OF LENT, YEAR A

Today's Focus: Blindness

Having sight does not preclude blindness. Sometimes we choose to be blind to what is right in front of us. Today's scriptures give us the blind and the sighted. But it is not just a matter of looking through one's eyes. Seeing with faith demands the touch of God.

FIRST READING
1 Samuel 16: 1b, 6–7, 10–13a

The LORD said to Samuel: "Fill your horn with oil, and be on your way. I am sending you to Jesse of Bethlehem, for I have chosen my king from among his sons."

As Jesse and his sons came to the sacrifice, Samuel looked at Eliab and thought, "Surely the Lord's anointed is here before him." But the LORD said to Samuel: "Do not judge from his appearance or from his lofty stature, because I have rejected him. Not as man sees does God see, because man sees the appearance but the LORD looks into the heart." In the same way Jesse presented seven sons before Samuel, but Samuel said to Jesse, "The LORD has not chosen any one of these." Then Samuel asked Jesse, "Are these all the sons you have?" Jesse replied, "There is still the youngest, who is tending the sheep." Samuel said to Jesse, "Send for him; we will not begin the sacrificial banquet until he arrives here." Jesse sent and had the young man brought to them. He was ruddy, a youth handsome to behold and making a splendid appearance. The LORD said, "There—anoint him, for this is the one!" Then Samuel, with the horn of oil in hand, anointed David in the presence of his brothers; and from that day on, the spirit of the LORD rushed upon David.

PSALM RESPONSE
Psalm 23:1

The Lord is my shepherd; there is nothing I shall want.

SECOND READING
Ephesians 5: 8–14

Brothers and sisters: You were once darkness, but now you are light in the Lord. Live as children of light, for light produces every kind of goodness and righteousness and truth. Try to learn what is pleasing to the Lord. Take no part in the fruitless works of darkness; rather expose them, for it is shameful even to mention the things done by them in secret; but everything exposed by the light becomes visible, for everything that becomes visible is light. Therefore, it says:
"Awake, O sleeper,
and arise from the dead,
and Christ will give you light."

GOSPEL
John 9:1–41 or
9:1, 6–9, 13–17,
34–38

As Jesus passed by he saw a man blind from birth. [His disciples asked him, "Rabbi, who sinned, this man or his parents, that he was born blind?" Jesus answered, "Neither he nor his parents sinned; it is so that the works of God might be made visible through him. We have to do the works of the one who sent me while it is day. Night is coming when no one can work. While I am in the world, I am the light of the world." When he had said this,] he spat on the ground and made clay with the saliva, and smeared the clay on his eyes, and said to him, "Go wash in the Pool of Siloam"—which means Sent—. So he went and washed, and came back able to see.

His neighbors and those who had seen him earlier as a beggar said, "Isn't this the one who used to sit and beg?" Some said, "It is, " but others said, "No, he just looks like him." He said, "I am." [So they said to him, "How were your eyes opened?" He replied, "The man called Jesus made clay and anointed my eyes and told me, 'Go to Siloam and wash.' So I went there and washed and was able to see." And they said to him, "Where is he?" He said, "I don't know."]

They brought the one who was once blind to the Pharisees. Now Jesus had made clay and opened his eyes on a sabbath. So then the Pharisees also asked him how he was able to see. He said to them, "He put clay on my eyes, and I washed, and now I can see." So some of the Pharisees said, "This man is not from God, because he does not keep the sabbath." But others said, "How can a sinful man do such signs?" And there was a division among them. So they said to the blind man again, "What do you have to say about him, since he opened your eyes?" He said, "He is a prophet."

[Now the Jews did not believe that he had been blind and gained his sight until they summoned the parents of the one who had gained his sight. They asked them, "Is this your son, who you say was born blind? How does he now see?" His parents answered and said, "We know that this is our son and that he was born blind. We do not know how he sees now, nor do we know who opened his eyes. Ask him, he is of age; he can speak for himself." His parents said this because they were afraid of the Jews, for the Jews had already agreed that if anyone acknowledged him as the Christ, he would be expelled from the synagogue. For this reason his parents said, "He is of age; question him."

So a second time they called the man who had been blind and said to him, "Give God the praise! We know that this man is a sinner." He replied, "If he is a sinner, I do not know. One thing I do know is that I was blind and now I see." So they said to him, "What did he do to you? How did he open your eyes?" He answered them, "I told you already and you did not listen. Why do you want to hear it again? Do you want to become his disciples, too?" They ridiculed him and said, "You are that man's disciple; we are disciples of Moses! We know that God spoke to Moses, but we do not know where this one is from." The man answered and said to them, "This is what is so amazing, that you do not know where he is from, yet he opened my eyes. We know that God does not listen to sinners, but if one is devout and does his will, he listens to him. It is unheard of that anyone ever opened the eyes of a person born blind. If this man were not from God, he would not be able to do anything."] They answered and said to him, "You were born totally in sin, and are you trying to teach us?" Then they threw him out.

When Jesus heard that they had thrown him out, he found him and said, "Do you believe in the Son of Man?" He answered and said, "Who is he, sir, that I may believe in him?" Jesus said to him, "You have seen him, the one speaking with you is he." He said, "I do believe, Lord," and he worshiped him. [Then Jesus said, "I came into this world for judgment, so that those who do not see might see, and those who do see might become blind."

Some of the Pharisees who were with him heard this and said to him, "Surely we are not also blind, are we?" Jesus said to them, "If you were blind, you would have no sin; but now you are saying, 'We see,' so your sin remains."]

✜ *Understanding the Word*

The first reading is about the anointing of David as king over Israel. The passage is part of a larger biblical tradition of God judging people in ways that are very different from the ways that people judge each other.

The Lord calls the prophet Samuel to go to the house of Jesse in Bethlehem to anoint the new king. One by one the sons of Jesse are brought to the prophet. Seven sons are brought and none of them proves to be the Lord's choice (1 Samuel 16:6–7, 10). Samuel had thought, however, that one of these sons, Eliab, was the choice of God (16:6b). The appearance and commanding presence of this young man led him to this conclusion. But the Lord responds that there is a different set of divine criteria for judging people: "Do not judge from his appearance or from his lofty stature, because I have rejected him. Not as man sees does God see, because man sees the appearance but the LORD looks into the heart" (16:7).

Seven sons of Jesse receive no endorsement from God as the next king. David seems to be almost an afterthought. Samuel has to ask if Jesse has any other sons, and when Jesse says that there is still the youngest son, David has to be brought in from tending the sheep. Seven is a number of fullness, and David's being the eighth son suggests that God is working outside the boundaries of the expected.

It is David whom God confirms. Although David is described as handsome, it is clear from God's earlier words that the characteristic that God is looking for is David's interior disposition (16:7b, 12).

Many times in the Old Testament God chooses the younger son over the elder one as the means through which God's promises will be perpetuated. This is also the case, for example, when God chooses Isaac, Jacob, and Joseph. This biblical tradition, including today's passage, instructs us that the qualities that matter most are the internal ones.

❖ Reflecting on the Word

Today's first reading presents a seer who does not see. Samuel, the first of the great prophets, ruled as judge over Israel for many years. Then, at the Lord's direction, he anointed Saul as Israel's first king, a handsome young man who "stood head and shoulders above everyone else" (1 Samuel 9:2). Samuel grieved so much when God rejected Saul and sent Samuel to anoint another that God had to reprimand him.

When Samuel arrived in Bethlehem at the house of Jesse to anoint one of his sons as the next king, his eyes first fall on Eliab, the oldest. He was tall and handsome, just like Saul had been. Just as Samuel was about to uncap the vial of oil and pour it over Eliab's head, God shouts in his ear, "No, not that one! You are looking with human eyes, not with the Lord's. The Lord looks into the heart." In the end, Samuel had Jesse send for the youngest, out with the sheep. And, in time, David became the greatest king of Israel.

In the Gospel we have a blind man who comes to see more than anyone around him, not just physically, but with the eyes of faith. Jesus is off the scene before he begins to see, but we witness this man's vision sharpening as others challenge him, until finally he confesses Jesus as the Son of Man.

Faith is the gift that allows us to see Jesus for who he is. As we prepare to renew our baptismal promises on Easter, we pray for a deeper faith.

❖ Consider/Discuss:

- Have you had any experience of going from being blind to seeing?
- How do we see Jesus? What do we call him?

❖ Responding to the Word

We ask Jesus the light to come into our lives to help us see him as the image of the invisible God, the eternal Word who calls us to service, the one who calls us friend and sister or brother. Lord, help us to see your presence, hear your call, and do your will.

March 21, 2010

FIFTH SUNDAY OF LENT, YEAR C

Today's Focus: When a Stone Becomes a Boulder

The story of the woman caught in adultery is one of the most dramatic in the New Testament—one man standing up against a crowd, between them a woman they want to stone. The power of Jesus' words transforms the stones they have raised. Literally, these words save a life.

For pastoral reasons, the readings given for Year A may be used in place of these readings. See page 84.

FIRST READING
Isaiah 43:16–21

Thus says the LORD,
　who opens a way in the sea
　and a path in the mighty waters,
who leads out chariots and horsemen,
　a powerful army,
till they lie prostrate together, never to rise,
　snuffed out and quenched like a wick.
Remember not the events of the past,
　the things of long ago consider not;
see, I am doing something new!
　Now it springs forth, do you not perceive it?
In the desert I make a way,
　in the wasteland, rivers.
Wild beasts honor me,
　jackals and ostriches,
for I put water in the desert
　and rivers in the wasteland
　for my chosen people to drink,
the people whom I formed for myself,
　that they might announce my praise.

PSALM RESPONSE
Psalm 126:3

The Lord has done great things for us; we are filled with joy.

SECOND READING
Philippians 3: 8–14

Brothers and sisters: I consider everything as a loss because of the supreme good of knowing Christ Jesus my Lord. For his sake I have accepted the loss of all things and I consider them so much rubbish, that I may gain Christ and be found in him, not having any righteousness of my own based on the law but that which comes through faith in Christ, the righteousness from God, depending on faith to know him and the power of his resurrection and the sharing of his sufferings by being conformed to his death, if somehow I may attain the resurrection from the dead.

It is not that I have already taken hold of it or have already attained perfect maturity, but I continue my pursuit in hope that I may possess it, since I have indeed been taken possession of by Christ Jesus. Brothers and sisters, I for my part do not consider myself to have taken possession. Just one thing: forgetting what lies behind but straining forward to what lies ahead, I continue my pursuit toward the goal, the prize of God's upward calling, in Christ Jesus.

GOSPEL
John 8:1–11

Jesus went to the Mount of Olives. But early in the morning he arrived again in the temple area, and all the people started coming to him, and he sat down and taught them. Then the scribes and the Pharisees brought a woman who had been caught in adultery and made her stand in the middle. They said to him, "Teacher, this woman was caught in the very act of committing adultery. Now in the law, Moses commanded us to stone such women. So what do you say?" They said this to test him, so that they could have some charge to bring against him. Jesus bent down and began to write on the ground with his finger. But when they continued asking him, he straightened up and said to them, "Let the one among you who is without sin be the first to throw a stone at her." Again he bent down and wrote on the ground. And in response, they went away one by one, beginning with the elders. So he was left alone with the woman before him. Then Jesus straightened up and said to her, "Woman, where are they? Has no one condemned you?" She replied, "No one, sir." Then Jesus said, "Neither do I condemn you. Go, and from now on do not sin any more."

✢ Understanding the Word

The Gospel passage for today is the story of the woman caught in the act of adultery. In this passage we learn that people are never to be made the pawns of larger disputes.

The Pharisees have such a dispute with Jesus. They criticize their guards for not bringing in Jesus as they had told them to do. In the process the Pharisees say that the only ones who have been deceived by Jesus are the crowd "which does not know the law" and which is "accursed" (John 7:49).

In today's passage the scribes and the Pharisees bring a woman caught in adultery to Jesus and make "her stand in the middle" of the crowd that is listening to him (8:2–3). There they accuse her before everyone. Their purpose is to test Jesus. They tell him that the Law says that this woman should be stoned, and then ask him what he says about this (8:4–5). They make the woman a pawn in their attempt to prove that Jesus should be arrested. They show no concern for her plight; she is not only in danger of death but becomes the object of public scorn.

Jesus bends over and does not look at her, though (8:6). He does not subject her to his glance at a time when she is suffering the profound humiliation of being a public spectacle. What he does is advocate for her a broader mercy based on the knowledge of how fallible all of us are. His comment, "Let the one among you who is without sin be the first to throw a stone at her," compels everyone to leave the woman alone (8:7). It is then that Jesus straightens up and speaks to her, when looking at her does not add to the unbearable weight of scrutiny (8:10). His message to her is that he will not condemn her; rather, he exhorts her to sin no more (8:11).

The person is never to be sacrificed to political issues.

✣ Reflecting on the Word

The stone probably didn't feel that heavy when it was first picked up. But it was a stone, not a pebble, and there were many of them. They would do damage, especially when hurled in self-righteous anger. Perhaps it helped the people to believe that no one stone could be blamed for her death. This was an act of the community, all of them in it together, standing up for the Law of Moses, and bringing down God's wrath upon an adulteress.

While things were starting to heat up, no one was paying much attention to the woman. They were all watching Jesus. What was with the crouching down and drawing in the dirt? You really couldn't tell whether he was writing or drawing or maybe he was just stalling for time.

Some said he had tricked them, worked some kind of magic, proof that he was indeed in league with Beelzebub. The more thoughtful ones were silent. One even said he thought Jesus was praying. Where else could his words have come from, words that redirected their gaze from the woman to themselves, words that caused stones to drop and feet to shuffle off?

His words continue to echo any time we find ourselves about to cast stones of condemnation at one another: "Let the one among you who is without sin . . ." After taking these words to heart, we might hear more clearly Jesus' final words, meant not only for her, but for us: Go and sin no more.

- What do you think happened to this woman? What impact do you think this episode had on her life?
- Is there any particular sin or habit of sin that Jesus is asking you to leave behind?

❖ Responding to the Word

We pray that we might have the grace to see ourselves as we are, both graced by God and yet sometimes still sinful in thought, word, and deed. We pray that we might look on others with compassion and be given the power to forgive others who have harmed us, as God has forgiven us.

March 21, 2010

FIFTH SUNDAY OF LENT, YEAR A

Today's Focus: Coming Back from the Dead

Ezekiel's image of the dry bones coming back to life, given flesh and skin and sinews, witnesses to God's power to unclench the grip of death, whether it has a hold on our body or our spirit. The raising of Lazarus proclaims the power of the God of Israel now at work in Jesus, our Savior.

FIRST READING
Ezekiel 37: 12–14

Thus says the LORD GOD: O my people, I will open your graves and have you rise from them, and bring you back to the land of Israel. Then you shall know that I am the LORD, when I open your graves and have you rise from them, O my people! I will put my spirit in you that you may live, and I will settle you upon your land; thus you shall know that I am the LORD. I have promised, and I will do it, says the LORD.

PSALM RESPONSE
Psalm 130:7

With the Lord there is mercy and fullness of redemption.

SECOND READING
Romans 8:8–11

Brothers and sisters: Those who are in the flesh cannot please God. But you are not in the flesh; on the contrary, you are in the spirit, if only the Spirit of God dwells in you. Whoever does not have the Spirit of Christ does not belong to him. But if Christ is in you, although the body is dead because of sin, the spirit is alive because of righteousness. If the Spirit of the one who raised Jesus from the dead dwells in you, the one who raised Christ from the dead will give life to your mortal bodies also, through his Spirit dwelling in you.

GOSPEL
John 11:1–45 or 11:3–7, 17, 20–27, 33b–45

In the shorter version of the reading, the five passages in brackets are omitted.

[Now a man was ill, Lazarus from Bethany, the village of Mary and her sister Martha. Mary was the one who had anointed the Lord with perfumed oil and dried his feet with her hair; it was her brother Lazarus who was ill. So] the sisters sent word to him saying, "Master, the one you love is ill." When Jesus heard this he said, "This illness is not to end in death, but is for the glory of God, that the Son of God may be glorified through it." Now Jesus loved Martha and her sister and Lazarus. So when he heard that he was ill, he remained for two days in the place where he was. Then after this he said to his disciples, "Let us go back to Judea." [The disciples said to him, "Rabbi, the Jews were just trying to stone you, and you want to go back there?" Jesus answered, "Are there not twelve hours in a day? If one walks during the day, he does not stumble, because he sees the light of this world. But if one walks at night, he stumbles, because the light is not in him." He said this, and then told them, "Our friend Lazarus is asleep, but

I am going to awaken him." So the disciples said to him, "Master, if he is asleep, he will be saved." But Jesus was talking about his death, while they thought that he meant ordinary sleep. So then Jesus said to them clearly, "Lazarus has died. And I am glad for you that I was not there, that you may believe. Let us go to him." So Thomas, called Didymus, said to his fellow disciples, "Let us also go to die with him."]

When Jesus arrived, he found that Lazarus had already been in the tomb for four days. [Now Bethany was near Jerusalem, only about two miles away. And many of the Jews had come to Martha and Mary to comfort them about their brother.] When Martha heard that Jesus was coming, she went to meet him; but Mary sat at home. Martha said to Jesus, "Lord, if you had been here, my brother would not have died. But even now I know that whatever you ask of God, God will give you." Jesus said to her, "Your brother will rise." Martha said to him, "I know he will rise, in the resurrection on the last day." Jesus told her, "I am the resurrection and the life; whoever believes in me, even if he dies, will live, and everyone who lives and believes in me will never die. Do you believe this?" She said to him, "Yes, Lord. I have come to believe that you are the Christ, the Son of God, the one who is coming into the world."

[When she had said this, she went and called her sister Mary secretly, saying, "The teacher is here and is asking for you." As soon as she heard this, she rose quickly and went to him. For Jesus had not yet come into the village, but was still where Martha had met him. So when the Jews who were with her in the house comforting her saw Mary get up quickly and go out, they followed her, presuming that she was going to the tomb to weep there. When Mary came to where Jesus was and saw him, she fell at his feet and said to him, "Lord, if you had been here, my brother would not have died." When] Jesus [saw her weeping and the Jews who had come with her weeping, he] became perturbed and deeply troubled, and said, "Where have you laid him?" They said to him, "Sir, come and see." And Jesus wept. So the Jews said, "See how he loved him." But some of them said, "Could not the one who opened the eyes of the blind man have done something so that this man would not have died?"

So Jesus, perturbed again, came to the tomb. It was a cave, and a stone lay across it. Jesus said, "Take away the stone." Martha, the dead man's sister, said to him, "Lord, by now there will be a stench; he has been dead for four days." Jesus said to her, "Did I not tell you that if you believe you will see the glory of God?" So they took away the stone. And Jesus raised his eyes and said, "Father, I thank you for hearing me. I know that you always hear me; but because of the crowd here I have said this, that they may believe that you sent me."

And when he had said this, he cried out in a loud voice, "Lazarus, come out!" The dead man came out, tied hand and foot with burial bands, and his face was wrapped in a cloth. So Jesus said to them, "Untie him and let him go."

Now many of the Jews who had come to Mary and seen what he had done began to believe in him.

✤ Understanding the Word

The readings today help us to see signs of new life that open our hearts to the Christian message of the Resurrection.

The first two readings for today are about the connection between resurrection and righteousness. First is the culmination of Ezekiel's vision in 37:1–14. Ezekiel sees a plain filled with dry bones (37:1–2). The Lord asks Ezekiel to prophesy over them, and the result is that the bones are first covered with sinews and flesh and then with spirit so that they come to life (37:3–10). Today's first reading builds on these verses. In this reading God says that the bones in the graves are the house of Israel. The Lord will raise them from their graves and give them life (37:12–14).

In the context of the book of Ezekiel, the image of resurrection in 37:12–14 is a symbol of a new life of faithfulness to God. Chapters 3–24 of this book are about the sinfulness of the people, the problems to which this type of life leads, and the self-delusions they raise to protect themselves from admitting their wrongdoing. Beginning with chapter 33 the message of repentance is stressed. Chapter 37 shows the result of repentance. New life is possible for the people who repent, and this life is represented in terms of resurrection.

The second reading emphasizes that righteousness leads also to actual, not just metaphorical, resurrection. Ezekiel had spoken of the spirit as that which animates the flesh, allowing for new earthly life for the righteous. Paul writes that righteousness is only possible through living according to the Spirit of God. If one does so, then this Spirit "who raised Christ from the dead will give life to your mortal bodies also" (Romans 8:11).

Finally, the Gospel passage is about Jesus' raising of Lazarus (John 11:1–45). The restoration of Lazarus to life is the seventh sign in the Gospel of John and prepares for the Resurrection, which is also referred to as a sign (John 20:30).

Repentance, righteousness, and unexpected restorations of life signal God's intention of resurrection.

✥ Reflecting on the Word

Sometimes we are buried before we die. This can happen to nations as well as individuals. It happened to Israel back in the sixth century B.C. The people of Jerusalem had seen their king led off in chains, their army slaughtered, their young men and women put to the sword, and then most of Jerusalem was dragged off to Babylon to live in exile. After several decades there, the death Israel had experienced was not just death of the body but of the spirit. Then God spoke through the prophet Ezekiel: "I will put my spirit in you that you may live" (Ezekiel 37:14).

Skip ahead several centuries to a village outside Jerusalem and again God's spirit is put into one who was dead. A man named Lazarus is raised from the dead, called forth from his tomb where he has been lying for three days, and released from his burial garments to take up his life once again. Jesus of Nazareth, the Son of God, who called Lazarus his friend, had called him forth to take up life once again.

No word on whether Lazarus was happy about this, whether he might just as well have wanted to stay where he was. God did not consult with him. Both instances reveal that new life is always possible, even in the most seemingly Godforsaken situations. God's plan in sending the Son was that we might have life and have it abundantly—not just later, but now.

✥ Consider/Discuss:

- Have you ever had an experience of feeling dead inside? How did you come back to life?
- Can you say with Martha, "Yes, Lord, I believe that you are the resurrection and the life"?

✥ Responding to the Word

We pray that we will be faithful to God so that even when the forces of death threaten to overwhelm us, we will place our trust in the risen Lord who intercedes for us with the Father. We can always pray that God will put a new spirit in us, individually and as a community.

March 28, 2010

PALM SUNDAY OF THE LORD'S PASSION

Today's Focus: Jesus, the Divine Compassion

For Luke, Jesus is the prophet of God's compassion. We see this especially in the parables found only in Luke, like those of the prodigal son and the good Samaritan, and in certain events of Jesus' ministry also found only in Luke, like the raising of the widow's son at Nain. Today we encounter his compassion during his final hours.

FIRST READING
Isaiah 50:4–7

The Lord GOD has given me
    a well-trained tongue,
that I might know how to speak to the weary
    a word that will rouse them.
Morning after morning
    he opens my ear that I may hear;
and I have not rebelled,
    have not turned back.
I gave my back to those who beat me,
    my cheeks to those who plucked my beard;
my face I did not shield
    from buffets and spitting.

The Lord GOD is my help,
    therefore I am not disgraced;
I have set my face like flint,
    knowing that I shall not be put to shame.

PSALM RESPONSE
Psalm 22:2a

My God, my God, why have you abandoned me?

SECOND READING
Philippians 2: 6–11

Christ Jesus, though he was in the form of God,
    did not regard equality with God
    something to be grasped.
Rather, he emptied himself,
    taking the form of a slave,
    coming in human likeness;
    and found human in appearance,
    he humbled himself,
    becoming obedient to the point of death,
    even death on a cross.

Because of this, God greatly exalted him
and bestowed on him the name
which is above every name,
that at the name of Jesus
every knee should bend,
of those in heaven and on earth and under the earth,
and every tongue confess that
Jesus Christ is Lord,
to the glory of God the Father.

In the shorter form of the Passion, the passages in brackets are omitted.

GOSPEL
Luke 22:
14 — 23:56 or
23:1–49

[When the hour came, Jesus took his place at table with the apostles. He said to them, "I have eagerly desired to eat this Passover with you before I suffer, for, I tell you, I shall not eat it again until there is fulfillment in the kingdom of God." Then he took a cup, gave thanks, and said, "Take this and share it among yourselves; for I tell you that from this time on I shall not drink of the fruit of the vine until the kingdom of God comes." Then he took the bread, said the blessing, broke it, and gave it to them, saying, "This is my body, which will be given for you; do this in memory of me." And likewise the cup after they had eaten, saying, "This cup is the new covenant in my blood, which will be shed for you.

"And yet behold, the hand of the one who is to betray me is with me on the table; for the Son of Man indeed goes as it has been determined; but woe to that man by whom he is betrayed." And they began to debate among themselves who among them would do such a deed.

Then an argument broke out among them about which of them should be regarded as the greatest. He said to them, "The kings of the Gentiles lord it over them and those in authority over them are addressed as 'Benefactors'; but among you it shall not be so. Rather, let the greatest among you be as the youngest, and the leader as the servant. For who is greater: the one seated at table or the one who serves? Is it not the one seated at table? I am among you as the one who serves. It is you who have stood by me in my trials; and I confer a kingdom on you, just as my Father has conferred one on me, that you may eat and drink at my table in my kingdom; and you will sit on thrones judging the twelve tribes of Israel.

"Simon, Simon, behold Satan has demanded to sift all of you like wheat, but I have prayed that your own faith may not fail; and once you have turned back, you must strengthen your brothers." He said to him, "Lord, I am prepared to go to prison and to die with you." But he replied, "I tell you, Peter, before the cock crows this day, you will deny three times that you know me."

He said to them, "When I sent you forth without a money bag or a sack or sandals, were you in need of anything?" "No, nothing," they replied. He said to them, "But now one who has a money bag should take it, and likewise a sack, and one who does not have a sword should sell his cloak and buy one. For I tell you that this Scripture must be fulfilled in me, namely,

He was counted among the wicked;

and indeed what is written about me is coming to fulfillment." Then they said, "Lord, look, there are two swords here." But he replied, "It is enough!"

Then going out, he went, as was his custom, to the Mount of Olives, and the disciples followed him. When he arrived at the place he said to them, "Pray that you may not undergo the test." After withdrawing about a stone's throw from them and kneeling, he prayed, saying, "Father, if you are willing, take this cup away from me; still, not my will but yours be done." And to strengthen him an angel from heaven appeared to him. He was in such agony and he prayed so fervently that his sweat became like drops of blood falling on the ground. When he rose from prayer and returned to his disciples, he found them sleeping from grief. He said to them, "Why are you sleeping? Get up and pray that you may not undergo the test."

While he was still speaking, a crowd approached and in front was one of the Twelve, a man named Judas. He went up to Jesus to kiss him. Jesus said to him, "Judas, are you betraying the Son of Man with a kiss?" His disciples realized what was about to happen, and they asked, "Lord, shall we strike with a sword?" And one of them struck the high priest's servant and cut off his right ear. But Jesus said in reply, "Stop, no more of this!" Then he touched the servant's ear and healed him. And Jesus said to the chief priests and temple guards and elders who had come for him, "Have you come out as against a robber, with swords and clubs? Day after day I was with you in the temple area, and you did not seize me; but this is your hour, the time for the power of darkness."

After arresting him they led him away and took him into the house of the high priest; Peter was following at a distance. They lit a fire in the middle of the courtyard and sat around it, and Peter sat down with them. When a maid saw him seated in the light, she looked intently at him and said, "This man too was with him." But he denied it saying, "Woman, I do not know him." A short while later someone else saw him and said, "You too are one of them"; but Peter answered, "My friend, I am not." About an hour later, still another insisted, "Assuredly, this man too was with him, for he also is a Galilean." But Peter said, "My friend, I do not know what you are talking about." Just as he was saying this, the cock crowed, and the Lord turned and looked at Peter; and Peter remembered the word of the Lord, how he had said to him, "Before the cock crows today, you will deny me three times." He went out and began to weep bitterly. The men who held Jesus in custody were ridiculing and beating him. They blindfolded him and questioned him, saying, "Prophesy! Who is it that struck you?" And they reviled him in saying many other things against him.

When day came the council of elders of the people met, both chief priests and scribes, and they brought him before their Sanhedrin. They said, "If you are the Christ, tell us," but he replied to them, "If I tell you, you will not believe, and if I question, you will not respond. But from this time on the Son of Man will be seated at the right hand of the power of God." They all asked, "Are you then the Son of God?" He replied to them, "You say that I am." Then they said, "What further need have we for testimony? We have heard it from his own mouth."]

Then the whole assembly of them arose and brought him before Pilate. They brought charges against him, saying, "We found this man misleading our people; he opposes the payment of taxes to Caesar and maintains that he is the Christ, a king." Pilate asked him, "Are you the king of the Jews?" He said to him in reply, "You say so." Pilate then addressed the chief priests and the crowds, "I find this man not guilty." But they were adamant and said, "He is inciting the people with his teaching throughout all Judea, from Galilee where he began even to here."

On hearing this Pilate asked if the man was a Galilean; and upon learning that he was under Herod's jurisdiction, he sent him to Herod who was in Jerusalem at that time. Herod was very glad to see Jesus; he had been wanting to see him for a long time, for he had heard about him and had been hoping to see him perform some sign. He questioned him at length, but he gave him no answer. The chief priests and scribes, meanwhile, stood by accusing him harshly. Herod and his soldiers treated him contemptuously and mocked him, and after clothing him in resplendent garb, he sent him back to Pilate. Herod and Pilate became friends that very day, even though they had been enemies formerly. Pilate then summoned the chief priests, the rulers, and the people and said to them, "You brought this man to me and accused him of inciting the people to revolt. I have conducted my investigation in your presence and have not found this man guilty of the charges you have brought against him, nor did Herod, for he sent him back to us. So no capital crime has been committed by him. Therefore I shall have him flogged and then release him."

But all together they shouted out, "Away with this man! Release Barabbas to us."—Now Barabbas had been imprisoned for a rebellion that had taken place in the city and for murder.—Again Pilate addressed them, still wishing to release Jesus, but they continued their shouting, "Crucify him! Crucify him!" Pilate addressed them a third time, "What evil has this man done? I found him guilty of no capital crime. Therefore I shall have him flogged and then release him." With loud shouts, however, they persisted in calling for his crucifixion, and their voices prevailed. The verdict of Pilate was that their demand should be granted. So he released the man who had been imprisoned for rebellion and murder, for whom they asked, and he handed Jesus over to them to deal with as they wished.

As they led him away they took hold of a certain Simon, a Cyrenian, who was coming in from the country; and after laying the cross on him, they made him carry it behind Jesus. A large crowd of people followed Jesus, including many women who mourned and lamented him. Jesus turned to them and said, "Daughters of Jerusalem, do not weep for me; weep instead for yourselves and for your children, for indeed, the days are coming when people will say, 'Blessed are the barren, the wombs that never bore and the breasts that never nursed.' At that time people will say to the mountains, 'Fall upon us!' and to the hills, 'Cover us!' for if these things are done when the wood is green what will happen when it is dry?" Now two others, both criminals, were led away with him to be executed.

When they came to the place called the Skull, they crucified him and the criminals there, one on his right, the other on his left. Then Jesus said, "Father, forgive them, they know not what they do." They divided his garments by casting lots. The people stood by and watched; the rulers, meanwhile, sneered at him and said, "He saved others, let him save himself if he is the chosen one, the Christ of God." Even the soldiers jeered at him. As they approached to offer him wine they called out, "If you are King of the Jews, save yourself." Above him there was an inscription that read, "This is the King of the Jews."

Now one of the criminals hanging there reviled Jesus, saying, "Are you not the Christ? Save yourself and us." The other, however, rebuking him, said in reply, "Have you no fear of God, for you are subject to the same condemnation? And indeed, we have been condemned justly, for the sentence we received corresponds to our crimes, but this man has done nothing criminal." Then he said, "Jesus, remember me when you come into your kingdom." He replied to him, "Amen, I say to you, today you will be with me in Paradise."

It was now about noon and darkness came over the whole land until three in the afternoon because of an eclipse of the sun. Then the veil of the temple was torn down the middle. Jesus cried out in a loud voice, "Father, into your hands I commend my spirit"; and when he had said this he breathed his last.

The centurion who witnessed what had happened glorified God and said, "This man was innocent beyond doubt." When all the people who had gathered for this spectacle saw what had happened, they returned home beating their breasts; but all his acquaintances stood at a distance, including the women who had followed him from Galilee and saw these events.

[Now there was a virtuous and righteous man named Joseph who, though he was a member of the council, had not consented to their plan of action. He came from the Jewish town of Arimathea and was awaiting the kingdom of God. He went to Pilate and asked for the body of Jesus. After he had taken the body down, he wrapped it in a linen cloth and laid him in a rock-hewn tomb in which no one had yet been buried. It was the day of preparation, and the sabbath was about to begin. The women who had come from Galilee with him followed behind, and when they had seen the tomb and the way in which his body was laid in it, they returned and prepared spices and perfumed oils. Then they rested on the sabbath according to the commandment.]

✛ Understanding the Word

The three readings for today address the notion of service to others, what it entails, and what it accomplishes.

The first reading is one of the Suffering Servant Songs from Isaiah, and it talks about service in terms of a resolve to give testimony despite the hostility that such witness may engender. In these songs the prophet Isaiah shows how God acts through this faithful servant. Today's song emphasizes the faithful witness of the servant, whose testimony rouses the weary (Isaiah 50:4). Thus, the servant will inspire a greater religious zeal in the people by faithfully witnessing despite all the opposition that he experiences. This resistance is intense: people beat the servant, pluck his beard, strike him, and spit on him (50:6–7). Commitment despite opposition is a motivating force for others.

The second reading is the famous kenotic hymn in Philippians. "Kenotic" refers to the self-emptying of Jesus. In this hymn we learn the extent of Jesus' service and, by implication, what perspective on service we should have. Jesus not only did not grasp at equality with God, he became a servant who served even to the point of death, a most violent death on a cross (Philippians 2:6–11). As Jesus "did not regard equality with God something to be grasped," so, too, should we "humbly regard others as more important than" ourselves (2:3, 6). This is not an issue of low self-esteem. Rather, it means acting in the interests of others as a servant does for a master. As Jesus gave himself completely for us, so, too, should each of us be concerned "not for his own interests, but [also] everyone for those of others" (2:4).

The Gospel passage from Luke is the account of the acme of Jesus' self-giving in his passion and crucifixion and the covenant that it brings about. Here we have the vivid account that inspires all Christian service.

✛ Reflecting on the Word

We can find the compassion of Jesus not only on the cross, but throughout his passion. It begins at the Last Supper when he praises the apostles, saying, "It is you who have stood by me in my trials," and promises that they will eat and drink with him in his kingdom (Luke 22:28–30). And while he predicts that Simon will deny him, he also comforts him: "[O]nce you have turned back, you must strengthen your brothers" (22:32).

93

Later in the garden, when the mob comes for him and one of the disciples cuts off the right ear of the servant of the high priest, Jesus touches the servant and heals him. Jesus is tranquil before the Sanhedrin and Pilate and silent before Herod. On the way to Calvary, he stops to comfort women who are weeping for him, aware of what they themselves will have to face in days ahead.

But it is from the cross that we see Jesus as embodying God's compassion when Jesus prays, "Father, forgive them; they know not what they do" (23:34). Then, in one of the most tender scenes in the Gospels, in the final moments of his life, he turns to one of the criminals next to him who has asked that Jesus remember him and promises, "[T]oday you will be with me in Paradise" (23:43).

We take up the palms today and greet Jesus as our Savior, as Son of God, as the Compassion of God. When we look at his hands extended on the cross, we can see him embracing the world.

❖ Consider/Discuss:

- How does the compassion of Jesus speak to your life?
- How does the compassion of Jesus challenge you in your relationships with others?

❖ Responding to the Word

We pray to experience the compassionate love of Jesus and to be able to respond to it with all our heart and mind and soul. We ask that his spirit enter us in such a way that we will be able to pray each day as he prayed with his final breath: "Father, into your hands I commend my spirit" (Luke 23:46).

It's Time to Order
Living the Word 2011: Year A

By now you have discovered what a prayerful and valuable scriptural resource *Living the Word* provides for you each Sunday of the year.

Don't miss a single week! Subscribe to *Living the Word 2011* today for yourself, your staff, parishioners, family, and friends, and share the gift of God's Word.

Order now to receive the same low price as 2010:

100 or more copies	$6.95 each
25–99 copies	$8.95 each
10–24 copies	$9.95 each
2–9 copies	$10.95 each
Single copies..	$14.95

MAKE A COPY OF THIS ORDER FORM
AND FAX IT TODAY TO 888-957-3291.
(This will keep your current book intact!)

OR, CALL WLP CUSTOMER CARE AT
800-566-6150 TO PLACE YOUR ORDER.

[ ] Yes, I'd like to order *Living the Word 2011: Year A*. Please send me _____ copies at _____ each, plus shipping, handling and any applicable sales tax.

NAME _____ POSITION _____

PARISH/INSTITUTION _____

ADDRESS _____

CITY _____ STATE _____ ZIP _____

PHONE _____ FAX_____ E-MAIL_____

Please keep a copy of your order for reference.

Living the Word 2011 will be shipped and billed after October 1, 2010.

Add $6.00 for orders up to $20.00. Add 15% of total for orders over $20.00. Payment in U.S. currency only. No cash or stamps, please. Make checks payable to World Library Publications. Prices subject to change without notice. **Applicable sales tax will be added to orders based on individual state tax requirements.**

World Library Publications
3708 River Road, Suite 400, Franklin Park, IL 60131-2158
800 566-6150 Fax 888 957-3291
www.wlpmusic.com • wlpcs@jspaluch.com

LTWA11

The Easter readings reflect on how Resurrection faith becomes an integral, vibrant part of our lives, and how such faith should be witnessed in order for it to spread to others.

The Gospel of John heard on Easter Sunday guides us, through an unusual story about the Beloved Disciple, into the characteristics of beloved disciples. On the Second and Third Sundays of Easter the readings from the Acts of the Apostles inspire us with stories of the courageous witness of the apostles to the resurrected Lord. In the process, they also inform us about the faith-filled understandings that sustain this valor even in the face of intensified opposition.

For the Fourth and Fifth Sundays of Easter, two passages from the Gospel of John reflect on the love that grounds our salvation and the love that we are called to give to others. John 10:27–30 is the culmination of the Good Shepherd discourse. By connecting these verses with those that precede it, we find that our salvation is grounded in the secure love of God for us. To suggest the depth, intensity, and surety of this salvific love, John presents it in terms of love for a close family member. The Gospel for the Fifth Sunday of Easter provides us with the distinctive version of the commandment to love found in the Gospel of John. Although this command at first looks narrower in scope than that found in the synoptic Gospels, its value is that it encourages people to focus an extraordinary amount of personal resources on those who need them most.

Johannine readings for the Sixth and Seventh Sundays of Easter continue this focus on love and its concrete meaning in the lives of Christians. Both readings are from the final discourse of Jesus shortly before his crucifixion. On the Sixth Sunday of Easter we read about the extent of the Father's love for us as reflected in Jesus' love for the Father. On the Seventh Sunday of Easter we discover how we will be incorporated into this great love, with the responsibility of sharing it with others in order to increase the family of God.

Readings from Luke-Acts are heard on Ascension and Pentecost Sundays. Twice Luke writes about the Ascension in ways that show that the manner in which the Lord departs this world shapes the way that his followers live in it. For Luke, the Pentecost conferral of the Spirit on the disciples enables them to continue successfully the ministry of Jesus.

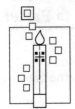

April 4, 2010

EASTER SUNDAY
THE RESURRECTION OF THE LORD

Today's Focus: In the Beginning, Darkness

New life often begins in the dark—the darkness of the earth where seed has been planted, the darkness of the bedroom where the love of a husband and wife brings life to the world, the darkness of the mind where a quest to seek the truth begins. Today we remember that morning when new life began in the darkness of a tomb.

FIRST READING
Acts 10:34a, 37–43

Peter proceeded to speak and said: "You know what has happened all over Judea, beginning in Galilee after the baptism that John preached, how God anointed Jesus of Nazareth with the Holy Spirit and power. He went about doing good and healing all those oppressed by the devil, for God was with him. We are witnesses of all that he did both in the country of the Jews and in Jerusalem. They put him to death by hanging him on a tree. This man God raised on the third day and granted that he be visible, not to all the people, but to us, the witnesses chosen by God in advance, who ate and drank with him after he rose from the dead. He commissioned us to preach to the people and testify that he is the one appointed by God as judge of the living and the dead. To him all the prophets bear witness, that everyone who believes in him will receive forgiveness of sins through his name.

PSALM RESPONSE
Psalm 118:24

This is the day the Lord has made; let us rejoice and be glad.

SECOND READING
Colossians 3: 1–4

Brothers and sisters: If then you were raised with Christ, seek what is above, where Christ is seated at the right hand of God. Think of what is above, not of what is on earth. For you have died, and your life is hidden with Christ in God. When Christ your life appears, then you too will appear with him in glory.

– or –

1 Corinthians 5: 6b–8

Brothers and sisters: Do you not know that a little yeast leavens all the dough? Clear out the old yeast, so that you may become a fresh batch of dough, inasmuch as you are unleavened. For our paschal lamb, Christ, has been sacrificed. Therefore, let us celebrate the feast, not with the old yeast, the yeast of malice and wickedness, but with the unleavened bread of sincerity and truth.

GOSPEL
John 20:1–9

On the first day of the week, Mary of Magdala came to the tomb early in the morning, while it was still dark, and saw the stone removed from the tomb. So she ran and went to Simon Peter and to the other disciple whom Jesus loved, and told them, "They have taken the Lord from the tomb, and we don't know where they put him." So Peter and the other disciple went out and came to the tomb. They both ran, but the other disciple ran faster than Peter and arrived at the tomb first; he bent down and saw the burial cloths there, but did not go in. When Simon Peter arrived after him, he went into the tomb and saw the burial cloths there, and the cloth that had covered his head, not with the burial cloths but rolled up in a separate place. Then the other disciple also went in, the one who had arrived at the tomb first, and he saw and believed. For they did not yet understand the Scripture that he had to rise from the dead.

✤ *Understanding the Word*

Today's Gospel passage is John's account of the empty tomb experienced first by Mary of Magdala and then by the Beloved Disciple and Simon Peter. The unique features of this version of the Easter story encourage us to wonder what makes the Beloved Disciple beloved and how we are all called to be beloved disciples.

The Beloved Disciple is not called such in this passage, but rather he is called "the other disciple," as he is in John 18:15–16. Upon hearing the message about the empty tomb from Mary Magdala, both he and Simon Peter run to see it (John 20:1–3). The Beloved Disciple outruns Peter but waits and allows Peter to enter the tomb first. But it is only the Beloved Disciple who at this time is said to believe (20:8). This is the more striking because right after this we read, "For they did not yet understand the Scripture that he had to rise from the dead" (20:9).

In this passage the Beloved Disciple appears to represent belief based on personal experience. After he sees the cloths in which the body of Jesus had been wrapped lying on the ground, he believes (20:6–8). His readiness to believe suggests a person whose faith arises out of reflection on the significance of his experiences. Jesus had previously told bystanders to take the cloths off the body of Lazarus when he raised Lazarus (11:44). Similar ideas and words in each passage suggest that the Beloved Disciple has learned from the Lazarus experience the power of God to effect resurrection.

Mature faith must remain rooted in the experience of God in our lives. Being able to observe and reflect on these experiences opens us to new types of experiences of God.

I can remember as a child being afraid of the dark. Not all the time—just usually after seeing a horror movie. For nights after, I would peer into the darkness, trying to make sure there was nothing out there. Even as an adult there have been times when I walked through a dark place feeling an uneasiness that was hard to shake.

Easter in the Gospel of John begins in the dark. Night still holds the earth in its embrace. Darkness also gripped the hearts of Jesus' followers—the darkness of grief, sorrow, and hopelessness. Jesus of Nazareth—who had preached in a way no one else ever had, who had worked deeds of great power by curing the sick, healing lepers, giving sight to the blind, lifting up the lame, and who had even called the dead back to life—had been crucified and laid in the tomb. A large stone had been rolled in front of the entrance, death's final punctuation mark.

Only John tells us there was a garden where he was crucified, and in the garden a new tomb in which no one had ever been laid. From this garden God decided to begin creation anew, so while it was still dark God breathed once again into a human figure, and the new Adam was raised up and would never die.

Not all darkness is to be feared. Sometimes it may even be necessary, summoning God to create once again, dispelling the shadow of death and despair that can settle over the human heart.

❖ *Consider/Discuss*:

- What are some of your experiences of darkness, external and internal?
- How does Easter bring light to our world?

❖ *Responding to the Word*

We pray to God on Easter "for the life that shall never again see darkness," asking God to "breathe on our minds and open our eyes that we may know him in the breaking of bread and follow him in his risen life" (*Sacramentary*, Alternative Opening Prayer for Easter Sunday).

April 11, 2010

SECOND SUNDAY OF EASTER

Today's Focus: Easter Gifts

Easter has always had a different "feel" from Christmas. Few Easter parties, practically no Easter "songs" on the radio, no Easter gifts to shop for and obsess over. This is not to say that there are no Easter gifts, just the ones brought by the risen Lord. Today's Gospel names them.

FIRST READING
Acts 5:12–16

Many signs and wonders were done among the people at the hands of the apostles. They were all together in Solomon's portico. None of the others dared to join them, but the people esteemed them. Yet more than ever, believers in the Lord, great numbers of men and women, were added to them. Thus they even carried the sick out into the streets and laid them on cots and mats so that when Peter came by, at least his shadow might fall on one or another of them. A large number of people from the towns in the vicinity of Jerusalem also gathered, bringing the sick and those disturbed by unclean spirits, and they were all cured.

PSALM RESPONSE
Psalm 118:1

Give thanks to the Lord for he is good, his love is everlasting.

SECOND READING
Revelation 1: 9–11a, 12–13, 17–19

I, John, your brother, who share with you the distress, the kingdom, and the endurance we have in Jesus, found myself on the island called Patmos because I proclaimed God's word and gave testimony to Jesus. I was caught up in spirit on the Lord's day and heard behind me a voice as loud as a trumpet, which said, "Write on a scroll what you see." Then I turned to see whose voice it was that spoke to me, and when I turned, I saw seven gold lampstands and in the midst of the lampstands one like a son of man, wearing an ankle-length robe, with a gold sash around his chest.

When I caught sight of him, I fell down at his feet as though dead. He touched me with his right hand and said, "Do not be afraid. I am the first and the last, the one who lives. Once I was dead, but now I am alive forever and ever. I hold the keys to death and the netherworld. Write down, therefore, what you have seen, and what is happening, and what will happen afterwards."

GOSPEL
John 20:19–31

On the evening of that first day of the week, when the doors were locked, where the disciples were, for fear of the Jews, Jesus came and stood in their midst and said to them, "Peace be with you." When he had said this, he showed them his hands and his side. The disciples rejoiced when they saw the Lord. Jesus said to them again, "Peace be with you. As the Father has sent me, so I send you." And when he had said this, he breathed on them and said to them, "Receive the Holy Spirit. Whose sins you forgive are forgiven them, and whose sins you retain are retained."

Thomas, called Didymus, one of the Twelve, was not with them when Jesus came. So the other disciples said to him, "We have seen the Lord." But he said to them, "Unless I see the mark of the nails in his hands and put my finger into the nailmarks and put my hand into his side, I will not believe."

Now a week later his disciples were again inside and Thomas was with them. Jesus came, although the doors were locked, and stood in their midst and said, "Peace be with you." Then he said to Thomas, "Put your finger here and see my hands, and bring your hand and put it into my side, and do not be unbelieving, but believe." Thomas answered and said to him, "My Lord and my God!" Jesus said to him, "Have you come to believe because you have seen me? Blessed are those who have not seen and have believed."

Now Jesus did many other signs in the presence of his disciples that are not written in this book. But these are written that you may come to believe that Jesus is the Christ, the Son of God, and that through this belief you may have life in his name.

✤ Understanding the Word

The first reading this Sunday provides an example of the courageous witness of the apostles to the resurrected Lord.

The reading is initially a bit ambiguous, and it is important to clarify who is involved and where they are located in order to appreciate the significance of the passage. Readers are told that the apostles did many miracles, and that "they were all together in Solomon's Portico" (Acts 5:12). Who was in Solomon's Portico? The prior verse speaks about the whole church. But it is unlikely that the whole church was in Solomon's Portico because as a result of the activity there we find out in verse 17 that the religious leaders arrest the apostles.

Solomon's Portico was in the temple in Jerusalem. It was in the temple that two of the apostles, Peter and John, had recently been arrested and sternly warned not to preach about Jesus again (Acts 3–4). The authorities do not want Christianity to spread among the people (4:17). Yet here are the apostles once more in the very spot that attracted this hostile reaction, doing the same thing that occasioned the leaders to threaten them: making many converts (5:14).

This explains the sentence that immediately follows the claim that "they were all together in Solomon's Portico" (5:12): "None of the others dared to join them, but the people esteemed them" (5:13). To be precise, none of the other Christians joined the apostles in the temple. For them, the place was simply too hot a spot to enter, given the current climate of intimidation.

By returning and witnessing despite the threats, the apostles provide the means for Resurrection faith to grow exponentially. They model for subsequent Christians the valor through which the Christian message reaches others.

Every year we get the same Gospel on the Sunday after Easter. Many times I have wished that we would continue from last week's Gospel with the touching story of Jesus appearing to Mary Magdalene. But perhaps we need to hear this Gospel every year because it gets to the heart of what Easter means for believers.

It tells us about the first Easter gift—indeed, the ongoing Easter gift. When the risen Lord suddenly appeared before that frightened group, he greeted them with one of the most important words in the Hebrew language before giving them the first Easter gift.

The word was *Shalom*, which means "Peace"—not just in the sense of not being at war, but meaning "I wish you all God's blessings, all good things, all that is needed to live upright in the sight of God." Then, after showing his hands and his side so they would know it was really him, he repeated his greeting: "*Shalom*." And then he breathed on them and said: "Receive the Holy Spirit" (John 20:22).

The Holy Spirit is the great gift of the risen Lord, given to us at baptism and confirmation, and whenever we gather to celebrate the Eucharist. Then the Spirit transforms bread and wine into the Body and Blood of Christ, so that by eating and drinking the sacrament, we may more fully become the body and blood of Christ. This Spirit brings the power to forgive, enabling the community of the risen Lord to both receive and give forgiveness.

✛ Consider/Discuss:

- When was the last time that I asked for or received forgiveness?
- What is the relationship between peace and forgiveness?

✛ Responding to the Word

The risen Christ is the head of his body, the church. We pray that we will be the instrument of Christ's peace in the world. We pray that we will be open to the Spirit working in our own lives, especially by our willingness to forgive others.

April 18, 2010

THIRD SUNDAY OF EASTER

Today's Focus: Yet More Easter Gifts

As we said last week, the risen Lord brought gracious gifts to his followers, beginning with the gift of the Holy Spirit and the power of forgiveness. Today we look to the Acts of the Apostles for an account of other gifts the apostles received.

FIRST READING
Acts 5:27–32, 40b–41

When the captain and the court officers had brought the apostles in and made them stand before the Sanhedrin, the high priest questioned them, "We gave you strict orders, did we not, to stop teaching in that name? Yet you have filled Jerusalem with your teaching and want to bring this man's blood upon us." But Peter and the apostles said in reply, "We must obey God rather than men. The God of our ancestors raised Jesus, though you had him killed by hanging him on a tree. God exalted him at his right hand as leader and savior to grant Israel repentance and forgiveness of sins. We are witnesses of these things, as is the Holy Spirit whom God has given to those who obey him."

The Sanhedrin ordered the apostles to stop speaking in the name of Jesus, and dismissed them. So they left the presence of the Sanhedrin, rejoicing that they had been found worthy to suffer dishonor for the sake of the name.

PSALM RESPONSE
Psalm 30:2a

I will praise you, Lord, for you have rescued me.

SECOND READING
Revelation 5: 11–14

I, John, looked and heard the voices of many angels who surrounded the throne and the living creatures and the elders. They were countless in number, and they cried out in a loud voice:

"Worthy is the Lamb that was slain
    to receive power and riches, wisdom and strength,
    honor and glory and blessing."

Then I heard every creature in heaven and on earth and under the earth and in the sea, everything in the universe, cry out:

"To the one who sits on the throne and to the Lamb
    be blessing and honor, glory and might,
    forever and ever."

The four living creatures answered, "Amen," and the elders fell down and worshiped.

In the shorter form of the reading, the passage in brackets is omitted.

GOSPEL
John 21:1–19 or
21:1–14

At that time, Jesus revealed himself again to his disciples at the Sea of Tiberias. He revealed himself in this way. Together were Simon Peter, Thomas called Didymus, Nathanael from Cana in Galilee, Zebedee's sons, and two others of his disciples. Simon Peter said to them, "I am going fishing." They said to him, "We also will come with you." So they went out and got into the boat, but that night they caught nothing. When it was already dawn, Jesus was standing on the shore; but the disciples did not realize that it was Jesus. Jesus said to them, "Children, have you caught anything to eat?" They answered him, "No." So he said to them, "Cast the net over the right side of the boat and you will find something." So they cast it, and were not able to pull it in because of the number of fish. So the disciple whom Jesus loved said to Peter, "It is the Lord." When Simon Peter heard that it was the Lord, he tucked in his garment, for he was lightly clad, and jumped into the sea. The other disciples came in the boat, for they were not far from shore, only about a hundred yards, dragging the net with the fish. When they climbed out on shore, they saw a charcoal fire with fish on it and bread. Jesus said to them, "Bring some of the fish you just caught." So Simon Peter went over and dragged the net ashore full of one hundred fifty-three large fish. Even though there were so many, the net was not torn. Jesus said to them, "Come, have breakfast." And none of the disciples dared to ask him, "Who are you?" because they realized it was the Lord. Jesus came over and took the bread and gave it to them, and in like manner the fish. This was now the third time Jesus was revealed to his disciples after being raised from the dead.

[When they had finished breakfast, Jesus said to Simon Peter, "Simon, son of John, do you love me more than these?" Simon Peter answered him, "Yes, Lord, you know that I love you." Jesus said to him, "Feed my lambs." He then said to Simon Peter a second time, "Simon, son of John, do you love me?" Simon Peter answered him, "Yes, Lord, you know that I love you." Jesus said to him, "Tend my sheep." Jesus said to him the third time, "Simon, son of John, do you love me?" Peter was distressed that Jesus had said to him a third time, "Do you love me?" and he said to him, "Lord, you know everything; you know that I love you." Jesus said to him, "Feed my sheep. Amen, amen, I say to you, when you were younger, you used to dress yourself and go where you wanted; but when you grow old, you will stretch out your hands, and someone else will dress you and lead you where you do not want to go." He said this signifying by what kind of death he would glorify God. And when he had said this, he said to him, "Follow me."]

◈ *Understanding the Word*

Last Sunday we saw the apostles' courage and the numerous conversions that resulted from it. Today we hear about the sustaining strength of their witness. The authorities decide to put into practice their threat against the apostles, should they continue to witness to the resurrected Lord. They put the proverbial thumb-screws to them. First, they claim that they had given the apostles "strict orders" to stop teaching about Jesus, orders that the apostles completely disobeyed (5:28). In response, the apostles not only deny the right of the leaders to tell them to do so, they even start teaching the leaders themselves about Jesus (5:29–32).

The reaction of the leaders is predictable. They want to kill the apostles (5:33). It is only the intervention of Rabbi Gamaliel that dissuades them from this plan (5:32–39). They do beat the apostles, however, before repeating their order and dismissing them (5:40).

Notice how the apostles meet the increase in pressure not to witness with an increase in witness. We have just seen that the leaders' claim that they had ordered the apostles not to teach anymore only caused the apostles to teach the leaders themselves. Now, after the apostles are beaten and ordered again not to teach, they return home and teach both there and in the temple "all day long" (5:42, not included in this Sunday's reading). Verse 42 tells us that they even increased their witness, adding that "they did not stop teaching and proclaiming the Messiah, Jesus."

Rather than break the apostles, the sufferings that they experienced were only goads for greater determination on their part. Supporting the commitment of the apostles is their knowledge that Jesus himself had been rejected and had suffered before he was raised (4:10–11). Courageous witness to Jesus is thus on the same trajectory from suffering to new life.

◈ *Reflecting on the Word*

When you compare the apostles before and after Jesus' death, you can see that not only did something special happen to Jesus at his resurrection, but a wonderful change took place in the apostles as well. Up until the death of Jesus, the apostles did not come off very well. When the chips were down, they ran.

But after the Lord has risen and appeared to them, we get a very different picture. In the Acts of the Apostles Luke gives us the most detailed description of what went on after the Holy Spirit descended upon this little community praying in the upper room.

The most obvious gift was courage, a word that has the same root as "heart." They were given a new heart. The Holy Spirit breathed new life into them and gave them a heart passionately in love with Christ, on fire to preach the gospel. And so they went to the heart of their city, the temple, and there they preached and taught about Jesus, witnessing to him as the Messiah, the Holy and Righteous One, the Author of Life.

106

They performed "many signs and wonders" (Acts 5:12), healing the sick and casting out unclean spirits. There they were arrested and taken to prison and beaten, only to return to the temple and do it all again, and be arrested again. Through all this they were joyful.

The philosopher Friedrich Nietzsche is remembered for saying that perhaps he would believe in our redeemer if we Christians looked a little more redeemed. Do you?

✤ Consider/Discuss:

- Have you been called upon in any way to witness to your faith in Jesus Christ?
- Have you asked the Holy Spirit for the gift of courage that you may be strong in witnessing to Christ in the world?

✤ *Responding to the Word*

We pray that we may grow in courage so that we can willingly and joyfully witness to the Lord, that we may be like Peter and the other apostles who followed Christ through suffering to glory, who were able to respond more than once to his call, "Follow me."

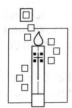

April 25, 2010

FOURTH SUNDAY OF EASTER

Today's Focus: Paul, a Jew, Called to Be Apostle to the Gentiles

Saint Paul was transformed from persecutor of Jesus' followers to the foremost preacher of the Good News of Jesus Christ. Today's first reading directs our attention to his dedication to preaching about Christ in the synagogues first, before turning to the Gentiles.

FIRST READING
Acts 13:14, 43–52

Paul and Barnabas continued on from Perga and reached Antioch in Pisidia. On the sabbath they entered the synagogue and took their seats. Many Jews and worshipers who were converts to Judaism followed Paul and Barnabas, who spoke to them and urged them to remain faithful to the grace of God.

On the following sabbath almost the whole city gathered to hear the word of the Lord. When the Jews saw the crowds, they were filled with jealousy and with violent abuse contradicted what Paul said. Both Paul and Barnabas spoke out boldly and said, "It was necessary that the word of God be spoken to you first, but since you reject it and condemn yourselves as unworthy of eternal life, we now turn to the Gentiles. For so the Lord has commanded us,

I have made you a light to the Gentiles,
that you may be an instrument of salvation
to the ends of the earth."

The Gentiles were delighted when they heard this and glorified the word of the Lord. All who were destined for eternal life came to believe, and the word of the Lord continued to spread through the whole region. The Jews, however, incited the women of prominence who were worshipers and the leading men of the city, stirred up a persecution against Paul and Barnabas, and expelled them from their territory. So they shook the dust from their feet in protest against them, and went to Iconium. The disciples were filled with joy and the Holy Spirit.

PSALM RESPONSE
Psalm 100:3c

We are his people, the sheep of his flock.

SECOND READING
Revelation 7:9, 14b–17

I, John, had a vision of a great multitude, which no one could count, from every nation, race, people, and tongue. They stood before the throne and before the Lamb, wearing white robes and holding palm branches in their hands.

Then one of the elders said to me, "These are the ones who have survived the time of great distress; they have washed their robes and made them white in the blood of the Lamb.

"For this reason they stand before God's throne
   and worship him day and night in his temple.
The one who sits on the throne will shelter them.
They will not hunger or thirst anymore,
   nor will the sun or any heat strike them.
For the Lamb who is in the center of the throne
   will shepherd them
   and lead them to springs of life-giving water,
   and God will wipe away every tear from their eyes."

GOSPEL
John 10:27–30

Jesus said: "My sheep hear my voice; I know them, and they follow me. I give them eternal life, and they shall never perish. No one can take them out of my hand. My Father, who has given them to me, is greater than all, and no one can take them out of the Father's hand. The Father and I are one."

✣ *Understanding the* Word

The Gospel passage today is the culmination of Jesus' discourse on the good shepherd in John's Gospel. In it, we hear that our salvation is grounded in the degree of commitment that Jesus has to us.

Jesus claims that his sheep follow him and that he gives them eternal life (John 10:27–28a). Then he says three times that no one can take the sheep from him or from the Father who is one with him (10:28b–30).

This emphasis on the security of Jesus' followers is the result of the danger in which they find themselves. Earlier in John 10 Jesus describes this danger with the image of a wolf coming upon the flock (10:12). Jesus' response is to meet the danger even to the extent of laying down his life for his sheep (10:11, 13, 17, 18).

Jesus presents security in terms of the love that will not run away when trouble comes. The instinct for self-preservation when the group is under attack is not present in Jesus, as it would be in the hired shepherd, because Jesus identifies us as his own (10:12–14). The sheep imagery shows the dangerous conditions in which people can find themselves. But it is the family imagery, found elsewhere in John's Gospel, that shows how close we are to Jesus and to the Father. Confidence in God's salvation should be the result of the Johannine notion that God's love will go to any extent to save a family member. What Jesus did for his disciples is what God always does through Jesus for us because of the unity of the Father and Son.

Chaos theorists often talk about how turbulence introduced into a stable physical system can result in chaos, undermining the stability of the whole system. Life can easily get out of control. John's Jesus introduces lasting stability into the always potentially chaotic situations that we experience. Ultimate stability is rooted in the greatest love that is always present to us when the wolf lurks nearby.

Our first reading ends with Paul and Barnabas shaking the dust from their feet, after the Jewish leaders drive them out of the town of Antioch. It would be easy to conclude that Paul and Barnabas were writing off the Jews and simply going over to the Gentiles. We can forget that both these leaders were Jews and did not cease to love their people. Paul continued to go first to the synagogues and preach to them about Jesus.

Years later in his Letter to the Romans, Paul wrote about his love for his people and acknowledged "great sorrow and constant anguish in my heart. For I could wish that I myself were accursed and separated from Christ for the sake of my [own people], my kin according to the flesh. They are Israelites; theirs the adoption, the glory, the covenants, the giving of the law, the worship, and the promises; theirs the patriarchs, and from them, according to the flesh, is the Messiah" (9:2–5).

We see how Paul modeled his life on Jesus Christ, who loved his own until the end, whose union with the Father moved him to see himself as the Good Shepherd, sent first to the house of Israel. We are called to recognize the Jewish people as the people of the first covenant, the people from whom the Messiah came. There can be no excuse for any kind of prejudice or disrespect between Christians and Jews, Christians and Muslims, Christians and any religious group that seeks God in integrity and sincerity of heart.

❖ Consider/Discuss:

- How do I think of the Jewish people?
- How does my calling as a follower of Christ lead me to relate to people of other faiths or no faith?

❖ Responding to the Word

We pray that all peoples will find their unity through faith in God, the Creator of all. We pray for our brothers and sisters in the Jewish faith. With them we share belief in one God, the Creator of heaven and earth; with them we acknowledge Abraham as our father in faith.

May 2, 2010

FIFTH SUNDAY OF EASTER

Today's Focus: The Call to Love

The last words of a loved one can linger in the memory for a long time. John's Gospel presents Jesus at the Last Supper leaving his disciples a final command: Love one another. Love begins with those at hand, those who join us at the table, but it cannot end there.

FIRST READING
Acts 14:21–27

After Paul and Barnabas had proclaimed the good news to that city and made a considerable number of disciples, they returned to Lystra and to Iconium and to Antioch. They strengthened the spirits of the disciples and exhorted them to persevere in the faith, saying, "It is necessary for us to undergo many hardships to enter the kingdom of God." They appointed elders for them in each church and, with prayer and fasting, commended them to the Lord in whom they had put their faith. Then they traveled through Pisidia and reached Pamphylia. After proclaiming the word at Perga they went down to Attalia. From there they sailed to Antioch, where they had been commended to the grace of God for the work they had now accomplished. And when they arrived, they called the church together and reported what God had done with them and how he had opened the door of faith to the Gentiles.

PSALM RESPONSE
Psalm 145:1

I will praise your name forever, my king and my God.

SECOND READING
Revelation 21: 1–5a

Then I, John, saw a new heaven and a new earth. The former heaven and the former earth had passed away, and the sea was no more. I also saw the holy city, a new Jerusalem, coming down out of heaven from God, prepared as a bride adorned for her husband. I heard a loud voice from the throne saying, "Behold, God's dwelling is with the human race. He will dwell with them and they will be his people and God himself will always be with them as their God. He will wipe every tear from their eyes, and there shall be no more death or mourning, wailing or pain, for the old order has passed away."

The One who sat on the throne said, "Behold, I make all things new."

GOSPEL
John 13: 31–33a, 34–35

When Judas had left them, Jesus said, "Now is the Son of Man glorified, and God is glorified in him. If God is glorified in him, God will also glorify him in himself, and God will glorify him at once. My children, I will be with you only a little while longer. I give you a new commandment: love one another. As I have loved you, so you also should love one another. This is how all will know that you are my disciples, if you have love for one another."

Today we hear a command by Jesus to love. It is not, however, the one with which we are probably most familiar: "You shall love the Lord, your God with all your heart, with all your being, with all your strength, and with all your mind, and your neighbor as yourself" (Luke 10:27). Today we read about the evangelist John's version of the love command: "[L]ove one another. As I have loved you, so you also should love one another. This is how all will know that you are my disciples, if you have love for one another" (John 13:34b–35).

At first glance one might prefer the version of this command found in Luke (and also in Matthew and Mark) on the grounds that it is the more expansive view. The synoptic command is to love all whereas this one in John's Gospel focuses on love of fellow Christians.

The significance of John's command, however, is to let those in special need be our special concern. The Johannine community is cut off from their larger social world; three times the evangelist speaks of them being "expelled from the synagogue" (9:22; 12:42; 16:2). They have been marginalized and are, therefore, particularly vulnerable.

For these the Johannine Jesus commands a heroic love. The very context in which Jesus gives this command suggests this intrepidness. It occurs right after Judas has left to betray Jesus (13:27–30). Moreover, John explicitly links the love command to this action of Judas by means of the transition, "When he had left, Jesus said . . ." (13:31). In John 15:12–13, Jesus elaborates on the phrase "As I have loved you" from verse 13:34b by observing that such love involves laying "down one's life for one's friends."

The Johannine love command is shocking in its intensity and orientation; those who are placed on the outside of the group should be supported with all that one has to give.

❖ *Reflecting on the Word*

Today's Gospel begins with the words, "When Judas had left them . . ." (John 13:31). We are at the Last Supper with Jesus, a few hours before he will be arrested, tried, and condemned to death. Immediately after this passage comes the prediction of Peter's denial. Between the move toward betrayal and the prediction of denial, in his darkest hour, Jesus speaks of his glorification and what that means for those who will follow him.

In all that follows, which includes his suffering, death, and resurrection, God will be glorified and God will glorify Jesus. This is the "hour" for which Jesus came—to be lifted up and to draw all to himself in an ultimate act of love. All is moving toward that moment when Jesus will say from the cross, "It is finished" (John 19:30).

Jesus' love is now to be found in the community that gathers in his name, in our love for each other, a love willing to give of itself completely for others, thereby mirroring the love that Jesus has for his disciples. The meaning of life is to be found in the giving and receiving of love.

In his encyclical *God Is Love*, Pope Benedict XVI writes that "the Church's deepest nature is expressed in her three-fold responsibility: proclaiming the word of God, celebrating the sacraments, and exercising the ministry of charity. These duties presuppose each other and are inseparable" (#25). Preaching Jesus, celebrating Jesus, and loving one another in Jesus—this is the circle of life in which we are caught up and that moves out to embrace the world.

❖ Consider/Discuss:

- When have you known the love of the other members of the community of disciples?
- Where do you feel called to bring the love of Christ at work in you to others?

❖ Responding to the Word

We pray that we may love as Jesus loved, especially those in our own community who are most in need of experiencing the love of God mediated through us. We pray that we may give glory to God in all that we say and do.

May 9, 2010

SIXTH SUNDAY OF EASTER

Today's Focus: The Spirit's Work Is Never Done

In its early days, the church faced great challenges. The first Christians were Jewish Christians, formed by the story of Israel's relationship with the God of the Mosaic covenant. But before long, Gentiles accepted Jesus as Lord. The gift of the Holy Spirit was essential to holding the church together, as it still is.

FIRST READING
Acts 15:1–2, 22–29

Some who had come down from Judea were instructing the brothers, "Unless you are circumcised according to the Mosaic practice, you cannot be saved." Because there arose no little dissension and debate by Paul and Barnabas with them, it was decided that Paul, Barnabas, and some of the others should go up to Jerusalem to the apostles and elders about this question.

The apostles and elders, in agreement with the whole church, decided to choose representatives and to send them to Antioch with Paul and Barnabas. The ones chosen were Judas, who was called Barsabbas, and Silas, leaders among the brothers. This is the letter delivered by them:

"The apostles and the elders, your brothers, to the brothers in Antioch, Syria, and Cilicia of Gentile origin: greetings. Since we have heard that some of our number who went out without any mandate from us have upset you with their teachings and disturbed your peace of mind, we have with one accord decided to choose representatives and to send them to you along with our beloved Barnabas and Paul, who have dedicated their lives to the name of our Lord Jesus Christ. So we are sending Judas and Silas who will also convey this same message by word of mouth: 'It is the decision of the Holy Spirit and of us not to place on you any burden beyond these necessities, namely, to abstain from meat sacrificed to idols, from blood, from meats of strangled animals, and from unlawful marriage. If you keep free of these, you will be doing what is right. Farewell.' "

PSALM RESPONSE
Psalm 67:4

O God, let all the nations praise you!

114

SECOND READING
Revelation 21: 10–14, 22–23

The angel took me in spirit to a great, high mountain and showed me the holy city Jerusalem coming down out of heaven from God. It gleamed with the splendor of God. Its radiance was like that of a precious stone, like jasper, clear as crystal. It had a massive, high wall, with twelve gates where twelve angels were stationed and on which names were inscribed, the names of the twelve tribes of the Israelites. There were three gates facing east, three north, three south, and three west. The wall of the city had twelve courses of stones as its foundation, on which were inscribed the twelve names of the twelve apostles of the Lamb.

I saw no temple in the city for its temple is the Lord God almighty and the Lamb. The city had no need of sun or moon to shine on it, for the glory of God gave it light, and its lamp was the Lamb.

GOSPEL
John 14:23–29

Jesus said to his disciples: "Whoever loves me will keep my word, and my Father will love him, and we will come to him and make our dwelling with him. Whoever does not love me does not keep my words; yet the word you hear is not mine but that of the Father who sent me.

"I have told you this while I am with you. The Advocate, the Holy Spirit, whom the Father will send in my name, will teach you everything and remind you of all that I told you. Peace I leave with you; my peace I give to you. Not as the world gives do I give it to you. Do not let your hearts be troubled or afraid. You heard me tell you, 'I am going away and I will come back to you.' If you loved me, you would rejoice that I am going to the Father; for the Father is greater than I. And now I have told you this before it happens, so that when it happens you may believe."

❖ Understanding the Word

There will always be disagreements in the church about what constitutes a Christian response to certain situations. Today's reading from the Acts of the Apostles helps us to see, however, the principle that should guide our practical considerations.

In the Acts of the Apostles Luke writes about a decision by a church council in Jerusalem regarding advice to send to new Gentile Christians. In the years c. 30–60 A.D. the major problem that confronted the church was the burgeoning numbers of Gentiles who were becoming Christians. At the beginning, Christians had been mostly Jewish.

The issue of the relation of Jewish law to Christianity came to the fore when Gentiles entered the church in large numbers. Both Paul and Luke write about this issue and about a council in Jerusalem that dealt with this matter. They differ, however, in what they say was decided. In the reading today the Gentiles are told to "abstain from meat sacrificed to idols, from blood, from meats of strangled animals, and from unlawful marriage" (Acts 15:29). In his Letter to the Galatians, Paul says that the only thing that the council decided was that Paul and his coworkers should "be mindful of the poor" (Galatians 2:10). The discrepancy between the accounts of what was required of the Gentiles is so great that some surmise that Luke and Paul were referring to different events.

The one thing similar in both accounts is the principle of gentleness that should underlie all practical advice. Thus, Paul wrote about considering the most vulnerable ("be mindful of the poor"). Similarly, Luke begins the council's letter to the Gentile Christians with the words, "It is the decision of the Holy Spirit and of us not to place on you any burden beyond these necessities" (Acts 15:28).

Differences will exist among Christians at times about what things are necessary. But by agreeing to the principle of not creating unnecessary burdens, the church lives into its God-filled future.

❖ Reflecting on the Word

Forming a community is never easy. This is true whether the community is made up of family members, citizens, or believers. Diversity can both enrich and divide. Jewish Christians were soon joined by Gentile believers. The church in Jerusalem was joined by the church in Antioch. While the Gentile Christians questioned whether they had to accept all the Jewish traditions and customs, Jewish Christians feared they would lose what had given them their identity.

Today's reading from Acts witnesses to the role of the Holy Spirit in helping to navigate a way through these sensitive issues. The leaders of the church in Jerusalem send a letter to the church in Antioch, proclaiming that the decision they reached came not just from human wisdom, but from working with the Holy Spirit.

Such testimony to the role of the Holy Spirit is also found in the Gospel of John. At the Last Supper, Jesus tells his disciples that the Holy Spirit will come from the Father and "teach you everything and remind you of all that I told you" (John 14:26). Because of this promise, we can have confidence that God will not abandon us. Indeed, the Trinity comes to dwell with those faithful to Jesus' word.

When we gather to celebrate the Eucharist, we call on the Holy Spirit both to open our minds to Jesus' word and to transform bread and wine so that we become more fully the body of Christ and the living temple of the Holy Spirit in the world.

Consider/Discuss:

- Have you had any experience in your community of diversity as both a gift and a burden?
- Have you ever had an experience of receiving help from the Holy Spirit?

❖ *Responding to the Word*

We pray that God will continue to send the Holy Spirit so that we might retain what is life-giving from the past and be open to any new initiatives that our loving God may offer in days ahead. We pray that our community may see in diversity a gift that can enrich, not a burden that will divide.

May 13, 2010

THE ASCENSION
OF THE LORD

Many dioceses in the United States celebrate the Ascension on May 16, replacing the Seventh Sunday of Easter

Today's Focus: Looking with the Eyes of Our Heart

The Ascension of the Lord announces the return of Jesus to the Father. What does it mean for us to say we believe that Jesus ascended into heaven and sits at the right hand of the Father? Jesus left us a legacy. It includes both a mission and a promise of a future beyond that mission.

FIRST READING
Acts 1: 1–11

In the first book, Theophilus, I dealt with all that Jesus did and taught until the day he was taken up, after giving instructions through the Holy Spirit to the apostles whom he had chosen. He presented himself alive to them by many proofs after he had suffered, appearing to them during forty days and speaking about the kingdom of God. While meeting with them, he enjoined them not to depart from Jerusalem, but to wait for "the promise of the Father about which you have heard me speak; for John baptized with water, but in a few days you will be baptized with the Holy Spirit."

When they had gathered together they asked him, "Lord, are you at this time going to restore the kingdom to Israel?" He answered them, "It is not for you to know the times or seasons that the Father has established by his own authority. But you will receive power when the Holy Spirit comes upon you, and you will be my witnesses in Jerusalem, throughout Judea and Samaria, and to the ends of the earth." When he had said this, as they were looking on, he was lifted up, and a cloud took him from their sight. While they were looking intently at the sky as he was going, suddenly two men dressed in white garments stood beside them. They said, "Men of Galilee, why are you standing there looking at the sky? This Jesus who has been taken up from you into heaven will return in the same way as you have seen him going into heaven."

PSALM RESPONSE
Psalm 47:6

God mounts his throne to shouts of joy: a blare of trumpets for the Lord.

Brothers and sisters: May the God of our Lord Jesus Christ, the Father of glory, give you a Spirit of wisdom and revelation resulting in knowledge of him. May the eyes of your hearts be enlightened, that you may know what is the hope that belongs to his call, what are the riches of glory in his inheritance among the holy ones, and what is the surpassing greatness of his power for us who believe, in accord with the exercise of his great might: which he worked in Christ, raising him from the dead and seating him at his right hand in the heavens, far above every principality, authority, power, and dominion, and every name that is named not only in this age but also in the one to come. And he put all things beneath his feet and gave him as head over all things to the church, which is his body, the fullness of the one who fills all things in every way.

– or –

Christ did not enter into a sanctuary made by hands, a copy of the true one, but heaven itself, that he might now appear before God on our behalf. Not that he might offer himself repeatedly, as the high priest enters each year into the sanctuary with blood that is not his own; if that were so, he would have had to suffer repeatedly from the foundation of the world. But now once for all he has appeared at the end of the ages to take away sin by his sacrifice. Just as it is appointed that men and women die once, and after this the judgment, so also Christ, offered once to take away the sins of many, will appear a second time, not to take away sin but to bring salvation to those who eagerly await him.

Therefore, brothers and sisters, since through the blood of Jesus we have confidence of entrance into the sanctuary by the new and living way he opened for us through the veil, that is, his flesh, and since we have "a great priest over the house of God," let us approach with a sincere heart and in absolute trust, with our hearts sprinkled clean from an evil conscience and our bodies washed in pure water. Let us hold unwaveringly to our confession that gives us hope, for he who made the promise is trustworthy.

GOSPEL
Luke 24:46–53

Jesus said to his disciples: "Thus it is written that the Christ would suffer and rise from the dead on the third day and that repentance, for the forgiveness of sins, would be preached in his name to all the nations, beginning from Jerusalem. You are witnesses of these things. And behold I am sending the promise of my Father upon you; but stay in the city until you are clothed with power from on high."

Then he led them out as far as Bethany, raised his hands, and blessed them. As he blessed them he parted from them and was taken up to heaven. They did him homage and then returned to Jerusalem with great joy, and they were continually in the temple praising God.

❖ Understanding the Word

The only New Testament author who describes the Ascension itself is Luke. For him the Ascension is so important that he writes about it twice: once in today's Gospel reading and once in the second part of his work, the Acts of the Apostles (Acts 1:1–11). Both times the Lukan Jesus tells his disciples not to leave Jerusalem after he has ascended, but rather to wait there for the Holy Spirit (Luke 24:49; Acts 1:4–5). Jesus' departure is tied to the renewal of divine presence to the disciples through the Holy Spirit.

What is interesting is where the disciples are called to wait for the Spirit. In Luke's Gospel, Jerusalem has become a dangerous place to preach. Only in Luke's Gospel do we read that the reason that the Jewish leaders plot to kill Jesus is that he won't stop preaching in the temple in Jerusalem. In the Gospel of Mark the impression is that Jesus' final days in Jerusalem were about a week. In Luke, however, one gets the sense that Jesus was in the city for quite some time (Luke 20:1; 21:37).

When the Lukan Jesus is in Jerusalem, he does one thing: teach in the temple. There are no miracles in the Jerusalem area and no teaching right outside of Jerusalem on the Mount of Olives, as found in Mark's Gospel. It is his continual teaching in the temple that leads to the plans to kill him. Thus, only in Luke's Gospel are these plans preceded by the notice, "And every day he was teaching in the temple area" (19:47). The Lukan Jesus goes where he can do the most good: the temple area, which would be packed with people for the Passover festival. There he teaches.

Correspondingly, Luke ends his Gospel with Jesus telling his disciples to remain in Jerusalem. They follow his advice and are "continually in the temple praising God" (24:53). They continue the witness of Jesus where it can do the most good.

God meets people in powerful ways when they remain where they can do the most good.

❧ *Reflecting on the Word*

In the first account of the Ascension today, after Jesus was lifted up and a cloud had taken him from sight, suddenly two men dressed in white stood beside the disciples and asked them why they were looking up at the sky. Jesus was gone. There were things to do, like witnessing to Jesus not only in Jerusalem, but in Judea and Samaria and to the ends of the earth.

Luke was writing his Gospel nearly fifty years after Jesus had ascended. The hope that Jesus would be returning soon was beginning to fade. The disciples had heeded Jesus' last words. They had readjusted their vision from looking up in expectation of a quick return to looking outward and seeing all that had to be done. Given that the number of people declaring themselves atheists and agnostics has doubled, according to a recent survey, the mission of making Jesus known still remains.

In the Letter to the Ephesians, the author prays: "May the eyes of your hearts be enlightened" (1:18). Then he asks for three things for the community: "[T]hat you may know what is the hope that belongs to his call, what are the riches of glory in his inheritance among the holy ones, and what is the surpassing greatness of his power for us who believe" (1:18–19).

This knowledge is the lasting legacy of the ascended Jesus, now sitting at the right hand of the Father, interceding for us: that we have knowledge of hope, of glory, and of God's power at work in all who believe.

❧ *Consider/Discuss*:

- What does it mean for us to pray that the eyes of our hearts be enlightened?
- What is the darkness that can blind our hearts?
- What are the riches of glory that are the inheritance of God's holy ones? How do you imagine them?

❧ *Responding to the Word*

We praise God that we have the hope of following where Jesus has led. We thank God for giving us the gift of faith that calls us beyond any darkness that threatens us to share in the glory that Christ has won for all who believe in him.

May 16, 2010

SEVENTH SUNDAY OF EASTER

Today's Focus: The Rest of the Story

Today's readings draw our attention to the prayer of Jesus and the prayer of Stephen, the first martyr. We hear some of their last words. These words, along with the vision from the book of Revelation, remind us that we have a destiny, that God has planned a happy ending to our story.

FIRST READING
Acts 7:55–60

Stephen, filled with the Holy Spirit, looked up intently to heaven and saw the glory of God and Jesus standing at the right hand of God, and Stephen said, "Behold, I see the heavens opened and the Son of Man standing at the right hand of God." But they cried out in a loud voice, covered their ears, and rushed upon him together. They threw him out of the city, and began to stone him. The witnesses laid down their cloaks at the feet of a young man named Saul. As they were stoning Stephen, he called out, "Lord Jesus, receive my spirit." Then he fell to his knees and cried out in a loud voice, "Lord, do not hold this sin against them"; and when he said this, he fell asleep.

PSALM RESPONSE
Psalm 97:1a, 9a

The Lord is king, the most high over all the earth.

SECOND READING
Revelation 22: 12–14, 16–17, 20

I, John, heard a voice saying to me: "Behold, I am coming soon. I bring with me the recompense I will give to each according to his deeds. I am the Alpha and the Omega, the first and the last, the beginning and the end."

Blessed are they who wash their robes so as to have the right to the tree of life and enter the city through its gates.

"I, Jesus, sent my angel to give you this testimony for the churches. I am the root and offspring of David, the bright morning star."

The Spirit and the bride say, "Come." Let the hearer say, "Come." Let the one who thirsts come forward, and the one who wants it receive the gift of life-giving water.

The one who gives this testimony says, "Yes, I am coming soon." Amen! Come, Lord Jesus!

GOSPEL
John 17:20–26

Lifting up his eyes to heaven, Jesus prayed, saying: "Holy Father, I pray not only for them, but also for those who will believe in me through their word, so that they may all be one, as you, Father, are in me and I in you, that they also may be in us, that the world may believe that you sent me. And I have given them the glory you gave me, so that they may be one, as we are one, I in them and you in me, that they may be brought to perfection as one, that the world may know that you sent me, and that you loved them even as you loved me. Father, they are your gift to me. I wish that where I am they also may be with me, that they may see my glory that you gave me, because you loved me before the foundation of the world. Righteous Father, the world also does not know you, but I know you, and they know that you sent me. I made known to them your name and I will make it known, that the love with which you loved me may be in them and I in them."

❖ Understanding the Word

Today's reading from the Acts of the Apostles is about the death of the church's first martyr, Stephen. In this passage Luke articulates an important theme of his writings: that one can depend on God's sustaining and saving presence during suffering.

Our passage today begins with the immediate consequences of Stephen's extended speech to the Jewish council. Stephen had been performing miracles and debating successfully with Jews in Jerusalem (Acts 6:8–10). Some then brought false accusations against Stephen and he had to defend himself before the Jewish council (Acts 6:11–15). Stephen's long speech is filled with criticisms that enrage his audience (Acts 7:2–54). This leads to today's passage.

While his listeners are still fuming, Stephen looks and sees "the heavens opened and the Son of man standing at the right hand of God" (7:56). This is a reference to Psalm 110:1, that says, "The LORD says to you, my lord, / 'Take your throne at my right hand, / while I make your enemies your footstool.' " In other New Testament uses of this verse the Lord is sitting. Only in Stephen's vision is Jesus standing.

Stephen is sustained by this vision during the stoning; as they are stoning him he prays, "Lord Jesus, receive my spirit" (Acts 7:59). This is the first time that Stephen calls Jesus "Lord," and it is significant that it occurs after his vision of the "Son of man standing at the right hand of God" (7:56). Elsewhere in the Acts of the Apostles, Luke uses another reference to Psalm 110:1 to prove that Jesus is Lord (2:34–36). This shows that when Stephen calls Jesus "Lord" as he is being stoned, he is still sustained by the vision of Jesus "standing at the right hand of God."

The first martyr does not die alone. There is for him a sustaining divine presence that saves him through his suffering.

The late Paul Harvey was famous for his stories on the radio. He would tell only part of a story, then announce that, after the commercials, he would be back with "the rest of the story." Then he would come back with a surprising or satisfying wrap-up. The word of God reminds us that, no matter what has already happened in our lives or what will happen in future days, God will provide us "the rest of the story."

John does not have Jesus praying in the garden of Gethsemane but at the Last Supper. Jesus prays to the Father for his disciples and for all who will hear their words about him. He prays that all may be one. The ending that God has planned for all who believe in Jesus is that we enter into unity with Jesus and the Father and the Holy Spirit.

Today we also witness the end of the story of one of the first preachers of the gospel, Stephen the deacon. As he was being stoned, he prayed that the Lord Jesus receive his spirit and that those stoning him be forgiven. The end of his story on this earth echoes the final words of Jesus on the cross in Luke's Gospel.

Finally, the author of Revelation holds up an image of Jesus as the beginning and the end of the human story. He will return at the end of time and bring a recompense that he "will give to each according to [our] deeds" (Revelation 22:12). At the end, then, is God's plan for unity, forgiveness, and glory. And that's the rest of the story.

✥ Consider/Discuss:

- What does Jesus' prayer mean when he asks that "all be one, as you, Father, are in me and I in you, that they also may be in us" (John 17:21)?
- How did Stephen find the ability to pray to God to forgive those who were stoning him?

✥ Responding to the Word

Today's readings offer us different reasons to pray: for the unity of all believers, for Jesus to receive our spirit at the end of our life, for the ability to forgive any who have done us harm, and for Jesus to come at the end of our days with a reward for our good deeds.

May 23, 2010

PENTECOST SUNDAY

Today's Focus: The Power of One

Recently someone referred to the Holy Spirit as the "Cinderella" of the Trinity, working quietly in the background while the Father and Son get all the credit. The Holy Spirit is the great gift of the Father and the Son. Today's feast invites us to recognize the wonderful ways that God continues to work among us.

FIRST READING
Acts 2:1–11

When the time for Pentecost was fulfilled, they were all in one place together. And suddenly there came from the sky a noise like a strong driving wind, and it filled the entire house in which they were. Then there appeared to them tongues as of fire, which parted and came to rest on each one of them. And they were all filled with the Holy Spirit and began to speak in different tongues, as the Spirit enabled them to proclaim.

Now there were devout Jews from every nation under heaven staying in Jerusalem. At this sound, they gathered in a large crowd, but they were confused because each one heard them speaking in his own language. They were astounded, and in amazement they asked, "Are not all these people who are speaking Galileans? Then how does each of us hear them in his native language? We are Parthians, Medes, and Elamites, inhabitants of Mesopotamia, Judea and Cappadocia, Pontus and Asia, Phrygia and Pamphylia, Egypt and the districts of Libya near Cyrene, as well as travelers from Rome, both Jews and converts to Judaism, Cretans and Arabs, yet we hear them speaking in our own tongues of the mighty acts of God."

PSALM RESPONSE
Psalm 104:30

Lord, send out your Spirit, and renew the face of the earth.

SECOND READING
1 Corinthians 12:3b–7, 12–13

Brothers and sisters: No one can say, "Jesus is Lord," except by the Holy Spirit. There are different kinds of spiritual gifts but the same Spirit; there are different forms of service but the same Lord; there are different workings but the same God who produces all of them in everyone. To each individual the manifestation of the Spirit is given for some benefit.

As a body is one though it has many parts, and all the parts of the body, though many, are one body, so also Christ. For in one Spirit we were all baptized into one body, whether Jews or Greeks, slaves or free persons, and we were all given to drink of one Spirit.

Romans 8:8–17 Brothers and sisters: Those who are in the flesh cannot please God. But you are not in the flesh; on the contrary, you are in the spirit, if only the Spirit of God dwells in you. Whoever does not have the Spirit of Christ does not belong to him. But if Christ is in you, although the body is dead because of sin, the spirit is alive because of righteousness. If the Spirit of the one who raised Jesus from the dead dwells in you, the one who raised Christ from the dead will give life to your mortal bodies also, through his Spirit that dwells in you. Consequently, brothers and sisters, we are not debtors to the flesh, to live according to the flesh. For if you live according to the flesh, you will die, but if by the Spirit you put to death the deeds of the body, you will live.

For those who are led by the Spirit of God are sons of God. For you did not receive a spirit of slavery to fall back into fear, but you received a Spirit of adoption, through whom we cry, "Abba, Father!" The Spirit himself bears witness with our spirit that we are children of God, and if children, then heirs, heirs of God and joint heirs with Christ, if only we suffer with him so that we may also be glorified with him.

GOSPEL
John 20:19–23 On the evening of that first day of the week, when the doors were locked, where the disciples were, for fear of the Jews, Jesus came and stood in their midst and said to them, "Peace be with you." When he had said this, he showed them his hands and his side. The disciples rejoiced when they saw the Lord. Jesus said to them again, "Peace be with you. As the Father has sent me, so I send you." And when he had said this, he breathed on them and said to them, "Receive the Holy Spirit. Whose sins you forgive are forgiven them, and whose sins you retain are retained."

– or –

John 14:15–16, Jesus said to his disciples: "If you love me, you will keep my com-
23b–26 mandments. And I will ask the Father, and he will give you another Advocate to be with you always.

"Whoever loves me will keep my word, and my Father will love him, and we will come to him and make our dwelling with him. Those who do not love me do not keep my words; yet the word you hear is not mine but that of the Father who sent me.

"I have told you this while I am with you. The Advocate, the Holy Spirit whom the Father will send in my name, will teach you everything and remind you of all that I told you."

The reading from Acts of the Apostles today is Luke's account of the first Pentecost. It presents the Spirit as the source of power for witness.

The first manifestations of the Spirit are a "noise like a strong driving wind" and "tongues of fire" resting on each of the disciples (Acts 2:2–3). They are then able to speak in other languages so that all present could understand them (2:4–12).

Immediately their speech takes the form of preaching to the thousands of people who are in the city. Peter speaks to the crowd and testifies to Jesus (2:14–36, 38–40). What they are hearing is prophecy that results from the Spirit being poured out upon people (2:17–18). Thus, the witness is said to be a message from God. This is important because it makes the message all the more cutting to its auditors when Peter says that they killed Jesus. What is worse, he says that they used "lawless men to crucify him" (2:23). The message leads to a crescendo of condemnation as Peter culminates: "Therefore, let the whole house of Israel know for certain that God has made him both Lord and Messiah, this Jesus whom you crucified" (2:36).

It is evident that this is a power that allows Peter to witness courageously before such a large throng. The effectiveness of this power is shown through the three thousand people who accept Peter's message and become Christians (2:41). This power remains effective through witness as "every day the Lord added to their number those who were being saved" (2:47).

For Luke, Pentecost is the celebration of the Spirit as the force for Christian growth. The force expresses itself through the willingness of Christians to stand up and witness to their faith. This growth is always the product of courageously moving beyond ourselves toward others with the message of life that we have been given.

✦ Reflecting on the Word

Years ago, I read a wonderful novel called *The Power of One* by South African novelist Bryce Courtenay, a mesmerizing story about the difference one person could make in the world. Today's readings remind us of the power of one when that one is under the influence of the Holy Spirit. This same Spirit who came upon Jesus at his baptism and worked through him during his ministry came upon the disciples.

We see the Spirit at work in Peter today, as he courageously preaches Jesus as risen Lord before a multitude from all over the Mediterranean world. The Spirit is also at work in Paul, giving him a vision that continues to inflame us so many centuries later. And as we celebrate the birthday of the church today, we can also recognize the work of the Holy Spirit in the lives of hundreds of thousands of men and women over the centuries.

The Spirit works in different ways, sometimes moving us out of our comfortable places into a world of uncertainty and danger. Sometimes the Spirit fires our minds and hearts to say and do things we never would have thought possible. And sometimes the Spirit works in quiet ways through gifts given to each of us for the good of the community.

The power of one is ultimately the power of our one God, whom we acknowledge as Father, Son, and Holy Spirit. It is one in many, unity in diversity. And we are to mirror that unity in diversity by allowing the power of the Spirit to work in us as a community.

✦ Consider/Discuss:

- Have you had any experiences of the Holy Spirit at work in your life, either as an individual or within a community?
- How do you like to think of the Holy Spirit? As fire, mighty wind, giver of gifts, or some other way?

✦ Responding to the Word

We can pray to the Holy Spirit to bestow the gift that we most need to bring the presence and power of God into our world. We ask the Holy Spirit to guide us to the truth, to inflame our hearts with love for Jesus, and to lead us to act in our world to do the Father's will.

We begin with the solemnities of the Most Holy Trinity and the Most Holy Body and Blood of Christ before returning to Ordinary Time Sundays for the remainder of the liturgical year. The Letter to the Romans on Trinity Sunday clarifies how the response of the Trinity to humanity is the basis for peace in human life. In the Gospel reading on the following Sunday, we find that remembering Jesus' saving deeds for us opens us to the spiritual nourishment of the Eucharist.

The Gospel readings for the Sundays in Ordinary Time in Year C are taken from the Gospel of Luke. The section of Luke heard on the remaining Sundays this year is mainly the part in which Jesus is on a journey to Jerusalem (Luke 9:51 — 19:44), with a few passages just before and just following. What is distinctive about this section and its adjoining passages is that the speaking of Jesus predominates. Only a few miracles are found at this point in Luke's Gospel, and in some of these occurrences the miracles serve as a springboard for his message.

As we read these passages it is helpful to keep some points in mind. First, Jesus' speech is directed at any of three groups of people: the crowd, the religious leaders, and the disciples. Second, different types of words are delivered to each group. The crowds are called to conversion. The religious leaders are criticized. The disciples are instructed. Jesus speaks in these ways even before he journeys to Jerusalem, but once the journey begins and once he arrives in Jerusalem he concentrates on these types of speech to these particular groups.

The reason is that Jerusalem is the place where the first Christian community will be formed. So calling the crowds to conversion takes on a new urgency. The religious authority of the church will be the apostles, and so preparing them through instructions becomes important. Finally, the criticism of the leaders becomes more pointed because the apostles will constitute an alternate religious leadership.

So when we read these passages from the Eleventh through the Thirty-third Sundays in Ordinary Time, an overarching perspective for appreciating them is that their message is urgent. People pay special attention to what happens in such situations because they realize that the speaker approaching his final moments must focus on what is essential.

May 30, 2010

THE MOST HOLY TRINITY

Today's Focus: Wonder-full Triune God, Giver of Life

Often the Trinity becomes an intellectual puzzle that we try to figure out, rather than an invitation to live into the very being of God, the God who is Fullness-of-Being. The God revealed to us in scripture is always reaching out to draw us into relationship—through creating us, redeeming us, and making us holy.

FIRST READING
Proverbs 8: 22–31

Thus says the wisdom of God:
"The LORD possessed me, the beginning of his ways,
    the forerunner of his prodigies of long ago;
from of old I was poured forth,
    at the first, before the earth.
When there were no depths I was brought forth,
    when there were no fountains or springs of water;
before the mountains were settled into place,
    before the hills, I was brought forth;
while as yet the earth and fields were not made,
    nor the first clods of the world.

"When the Lord established the heavens I was there,
    when he marked out the vault over the face of the deep;
when he made firm the skies above,
    when he fixed fast the foundations of the earth;
when he set for the sea its limit,
    so that the waters should not transgress his command;
then was I beside him as his craftsman,
    and I was his delight day by day,
playing before him all the while,
    playing on the surface of his earth;
    and I found delight in the human race."

PSALM RESPONSE
Psalm 8:2a

O Lord, our God, how wonderful your name in all the earth!

SECOND READING
Romans 5:1–5

Brothers and sisters: Therefore, since we have been justified by faith, we have peace with God through our Lord Jesus Christ, through whom we have gained access by faith to this grace in which we stand, and we boast in hope of the glory of God. Not only that, but we even boast of our afflictions, knowing that affliction produces endurance, and endurance, proven character, and proven character, hope, and hope does not disappoint, because the love of God has been poured out into our hearts through the Holy Spirit that has been given to us.

GOSPEL
John 16:12–15 Jesus said to his disciples: "I have much more to tell you, but you cannot bear it now. But when he comes, the Spirit of truth, he will guide you to all truth. He will not speak on his own, but he will speak what he hears, and will declare to you the things that are coming. He will glorify me, because he will take from what is mine and declare it to you. Everything that the Father has is mine; for this reason I told you that he will take from what is mine and declare it to you."

❖ Understanding the Word

The reading from the Letter to the Romans that we hear today is about how the life of the Trinity leads to peace for people in all situations. Christ showed his love for us by dying for us while we were still sinners. It wasn't because we were living sterling moral lives that Christ gave himself for us. So there is something about our very beings that God loves greatly (Romans 5:6–8).

Our reading says that this divine love "has been poured out into our hearts through the Holy Spirit that has been given to us" (5:5). For Paul this means that our hope is well founded. Everything in life is a means to good. As Paul says, affliction leads to endurance, endurance to proven character, and proven character to hope. Paul concludes that this hope is secure because of the divine love "poured out into our hearts through the Holy Spirit." Later on in this letter Paul will describe the effects of the Spirit in us as enabling us to live a godly life (8:2, 4–5, 10–13). Thus, Paul is saying today that all situations lead to a proven character because God has enabled us through the Spirit to live a godly life.

This leads to a deep peace, according to Paul. We have been given the divine life that keeps us close to God. Because of this there need be no fear that any situation can separate us from God. The love of God is stronger than anything else, and its power in us enables us to keep living good lives no matter what. This grace leads to a very specific hope "of the glory of God" (Romans 5:2).

For Paul God's actions through Christ and the sending of the Spirit to us have enabled all situations in life to lead to the glory of God. The fickleness of chance is replaced by the security of divine love.

131

Call to mind— or "Google," if you have access to the Internet—the famous ceiling painting of creation by Michelangelo in the Vatican's Sistine Chapel. God the Creator's right hand is extended to touch the fingers of the first human creature, Adam. Often forgotten or overlooked are the other figures there. Besides a dozen infant angels, you can find a beautiful woman in the crook of the Creator's left arm. That is Wisdom, who speaks to us in our first reading today.

Proverbs tells us that at the dawn of creation, when all was being marked out, made firm, and fixed fast, Wisdom was in on the act. When the Creator set the limits of the sea and the borders of the sky and the foundation of the firmament, she was there, beside God as God's craftsperson, delighting God, playing before God all the while, playing on the surface of the earth (see Proverbs 8:30–31). Then those wonderful words: "and I found delight in the human race" (8:31).

The Creator loved the world and all of creation from the beginning, so much that in the fullness of time God's only Son was sent by God to redeem us, and then the Holy Spirit was sent to dwell within us. Into the life of this Trinity we were baptized in the name of the Father and of the Son and of the Holy Spirit.

Today's feast calls us to joy because our living God continues to lead us to the truth of who God is, and to pour the love that is the very life of the Trinity into our own hearts, enabling us to love as God loves.

✦ Consider/Discuss:

- Does you see God as rejoicing in all that has been made?
- Do you understand God as continuing to reach out to fill us with a love that gives both life and communion with the Trinity: Creator, Redeemer, and Sanctifier?

✦ Responding to the Word

Join in singing during this day:

Praise God, from whom all blessings flow;
Praise God, all creatures here below;
Praise God above, you heavenly host;
Praise Father, Son, and Holy Ghost.

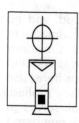

June 6, 2010

THE MOST HOLY BODY AND BLOOD OF CHRIST

Today's Focus: A "B and B" for the Soul

Today's celebration reminds us of the mystery of the presence of the Body and Blood of Christ in the Eucharist, the major source of ongoing nourishment and strength for all believers. In this sacrament, the Lord continues to meet us, dwell with us, and fulfill God's promise to be with us always.

FIRST READING
Genesis 14: 18–20

In those days, Melchizedek, king of Salem, brought out bread and wine, and being a priest of God Most High, he blessed Abram with these words:

"Blessed be Abram by God Most High,
  the creator of heaven and earth;
and blessed be God Most High,
  who delivered your foes into your hand."
Then Abram gave him a tenth of everything.

PSALM RESPONSE
Psalm 110:4b

You are a priest for ever, in the line of Melchizedek.

SECOND READING
1 Corinthians 11: 23–26

Brothers and sisters: I received from the Lord what I also handed on to you, that the Lord Jesus, on the night he was handed over, took bread, and, after he had given thanks, broke it and said, "This is my body that is for you. Do this in remembrance of me." In the same way also the cup, after supper, saying, "This cup is the new covenant in my blood. Do this, as often as you drink it, in remembrance of me." For as often as you eat this bread and drink the cup, you proclaim the death of the Lord until he comes.

GOSPEL
Luke 9:11b–17   Jesus spoke to the crowds about the kingdom of God, and he healed those who needed to be cured. As the day was drawing to a close, the Twelve approached him and said, "Dismiss the crowd so that they can go to the surrounding villages and farms and find lodging and provisions; for we are in a deserted place here." He said to them, "Give them some food yourselves." They replied, "Five loaves and two fish are all we have, unless we ourselves go and buy food for all these people." Now the men there numbered about five thousand. Then he said to his disciples, "Have them sit down in groups of about fifty." They did so and made them all sit down. Then taking the five loaves and the two fish, and looking up to heaven, he said the blessing over them, broke them, and gave them to the disciples to set before the crowd. They all ate and were satisfied. And when the leftover fragments were picked up, they filled twelve wicker baskets.

✤ Understanding the Word

Today's Gospel is about Eucharist as spiritual sustenance.

Jesus had just sent the disciples out to continue his ministry of preaching and healing. This they had done and returned to him, so he took them away from the crowd in private to the town of Bethsaida (Luke 9:1–6, 10), perhaps in order to provide time to restore and refresh themselves spiritually, as Jesus will soon be praying with them away from the crowds (9:18).

Spiritual sustenance is also the theme of today's reading, which is placed in the middle of this attempt of Jesus and his disciples to seek some privacy (9:10, 18). The crowds find Jesus, who proceeds to teach and to heal them (9:11). By the end of the day the disciples approach Jesus and suggest dismissing the crowds so that they can go and procure food and find a place to lodge (9:12). Jesus responds that the disciples themselves should provide sustenance for them. He then proceeds to multiply five loaves and two fishes so that it feeds the five thousand people (9:13–17).

Jesus does so in a manner that shows clearly that this miracle is a sign of the Eucharist. In 9:16 Luke writes that Jesus took the bread and fish, "and looking up to heaven, he said the blessing over them, broke them, and gave them to the disciples to set before the crowd." Similarly, in 22:19 Jesus "took the bread, said the blessing, broke it, and gave it to them saying, 'This is my body which will be given for you; do this in memory of me.' "

Luke embeds the miracle of the loaves and fishes between verses about seeking spiritual refreshment to show that the miracle relates to nourishment of the soul, and he describes Jesus' actions in the miracle in a way that reveals that it is a sign of the Eucharist. By so doing, Luke presents the Eucharist as an act in which the memory of Jesus' self-gift opens us to receive food for our soul.

✤ Reflecting on the Word

I came across a little book not too long ago that offered a selection of "B and Bs" ("Bed and Breakfast" residences) where travelers could stay in a certain state. The promise of a good "B and B" is a clean place, a good night's sleep, and a good meal to begin the day. In short, rest and sustenance.

Is it too irreverent to propose that today's feast is a reminder that we believers have available the "B and B" of all "B and Bs" in the Eucharist? This sacrament of the Body and Blood of Christ offers an ongoing opportunity for rest and sustenance with the Lord.

Today's scriptures all deal with offering sustenance, beginning with Melchizedek presenting Abraham a little bread and wine along with a blessing. Then there is Paul reminding the fractious Corinthians how eating the bread and wine sustains them as they proclaim the death of the Lord until he comes. Finally, Jesus provides rest and sustenance for his disciples, along with five thousand others who show up.

My late stepfather worked off a truck, checking gas meters and doing repairs for the Baltimore Gas and Electric Company. He used to stop in church and have his lunch there. He said it provided him a chance to talk to the Lord and rest for a few moments in the Lord's presence. It sustained him over the years. Again, rest and sustenance.

God's ongoing hospitality in the Eucharist has continued over generations to offer rest and sustenance. What could be better than having the Lord coming to dwell within us, giving us the nourishment necessary to sustain us on our journey?

✤ Consider/Discuss:

- What does the sacrament of the Eucharist mean to you?
- How does the reality of the Eucharist sustain you in your life?

✤ Responding to the Word

When you go to church this week, read the sequence for today's solemnity in the Missalette®. You can find it after the second reading. It includes these words:

"Very bread, good shepherd, tend us, / Jesu, of your love befriend us, / You refresh us, you defend us, / Your eternal goodness send us / In the land of life to see" (*Laud, O Zion*, from the English translation of *The Roman Missal*, USCCB, 1964).

June 13, 2010

ELEVENTH SUNDAY IN ORDINARY TIME

Today's Focus: Extravagant Love

Forgiveness is a gift. You can't earn it; it must always be received as a gift. In today's readings, God's forgiveness is given to a king, to a nameless woman known throughout the city as a sinner, and to all of us who have been made "right" with God through our faith in the Son of God. There's just no end to it in sight.

FIRST READING
2 Samuel 12: 7–10, 13

Nathan said to David: "Thus says the LORD God of Israel: 'I anointed you king of Israel. I rescued you from the hand of Saul. I gave you your lord's house and your lord's wives for your own. I gave you the house of Israel and of Judah. And if this were not enough, I could count up for you still more. Why have you spurned the Lord and done evil in his sight? You have cut down Uriah the Hittite with the sword; you took his wife as your own, and him you killed with the sword of the Ammonites. Now, therefore, the sword shall never depart from your house, because you have despised me and have taken the wife of Uriah to be your wife.' " Then David said to Nathan, "I have sinned against the LORD." Nathan answered David: "The LORD on his part has forgiven your sin: you shall not die."

PSALM RESPONSE
Psalm 32:5c

Lord, forgive the wrong I have done.

SECOND READING
Galatians 2:16, 19–21

Brothers and sisters: We who know that a person is not justified by works of the law but through faith in Jesus Christ, even we have believed in Christ Jesus that we may be justified by faith in Christ and not by works of the law, because by works of the law no one will be justified. For through the law I died to the law, that I might live for God. I have been crucified with Christ; yet I live, no longer I, but Christ lives in me; insofar as I now live in the flesh, I live by faith in the Son of God who has loved me and given himself up for me. I do not nullify the grace of God; for if justification comes through the law, then Christ died for nothing.

In the shorter form of the reading, the passage in brackets is omitted.

GOSPEL
Luke 7:36—8:3
or 7:36–50

A Pharisee invited Jesus to dine with him, and he entered the Pharisee's house and reclined at table. Now there was a sinful woman in the city who learned that he was at table in the house of the Pharisee. Bringing an alabaster flask of ointment, she stood behind him at his feet weeping and began to bathe his feet with her tears. Then she wiped them with her hair, kissed them, and anointed them with the ointment. When the Pharisee who had invited him saw this he said to himself, "If this man were a prophet, he would know who and what sort of woman this is who is touching him, that she is a sinner." Jesus said to him in reply, "Simon, I have something to say to you." "Tell me, teacher," he said. "Two people were in debt to a certain creditor; one owed five hundred days' wages and the other owed fifty. Since they were unable to repay the debt, he forgave it for both. Which of them will love him more?" Simon said in reply, "The one, I suppose, whose larger debt was forgiven." He said to him, "You have judged rightly."

Then he turned to the woman and said to Simon, "Do you see this woman? When I entered your house, you did not give me water for my feet, but she has bathed them with her tears and wiped them with her hair. You did not give me a kiss, but she has not ceased kissing my feet since the time I entered. You did not anoint my head with oil, but she anointed my feet with ointment. So I tell you, her many sins have been forgiven because she has shown great love. But the one to whom little is forgiven, loves little." He said to her, "Your sins are forgiven." The others at table said to themselves, "Who is this who even forgives sins?" But he said to the woman, "Your faith has saved you; go in peace."

[Afterward he journeyed from one town and village to another, preaching and proclaiming the good news of the kingdom of God. Accompanying him were the Twelve and some women who had been cured of evil spirits and infirmities, Mary, called Magdalene, from whom seven demons had gone out, Joanna, the wife of Herod's steward Chuza, Susanna, and many others who provided for them out of their resources.]

The Gospel passage today contains two distinct accounts, both of which show that awareness of how much debt God has forgiven leads to a great love on the part of the one who has been forgiven.

The first account is about a woman who washes Jesus' feet with her tears, dries them with her hair, and then anoints them with oil while Jesus is eating at the home of Simon, a Pharisee (Luke 7:36–50). The woman has a reputation for being a sinner, and so Simon doubts that Jesus can be a prophet or he would have known "what sort of woman this is who is touching him, that she is a sinner" (7:39).

Jesus tells Simon a parable about a creditor who forgives two debtors who owed, respectively, five hundred and fifty days' wages. In response to Jesus' question as to who will love the creditor more, Simon correctly responds that it is the one who owed him more. From this, Jesus draws the conclusion that this woman must have had her sins forgiven because she has done the courteous acts of washing, drying, and anointing Jesus' feet, acts which Simon had not done (7:40–47).

The second account is a brief note on those who accompanied Jesus. It ends with, and so highlights, many women whom Jesus had healed and who responded generously by providing for Jesus and the apostles out of their resources (8:1–3).

Luke's message at this point of his Gospel is that all have been forgiven much, although some think that they have only little that needs to be forgiven (7:47). The idea of forgiveness as debt removal is a way of helping people to see how forgiveness takes them out of a deep hole in which they find themselves because of their former actions. Those who realize how much they have been forgiven and what a great burden this forgiveness has lifted from their shoulders will respond with a greater love.

❖ *Reflecting on the Word*

Kings are not easily cornered. Hamlet has to put on a play to catch the conscience of the king, his own uncle, who has killed his (Hamlet's) father and married his mother. In the passage just prior to today's first reading, the prophet Nathan catches the conscience of Israel's King David by telling the story of a rich man who takes a poor man's beloved and only lamb and serves it up in a stew. When David angrily demands to know who this man is, Nathan replies: "That man is you." David repents. And God forgives.

Jesus catches the conscience of a Pharisee—perhaps. We don't really know if there is any change in Simon after hearing the story. But it is hard to conceive that he did not "get it." Those who know their need for God's mercy receive God's mercy and love in return. Those who do not recognize their need for mercy live their lives refusing to love others.

The woman had already known God's forgiveness; she walked in freedom and acted in freedom. No judgments could stop her from honoring the one who had brought her this freedom. So she stood weeping tears of gratitude, trying to mirror the extravagant love she had received. Simon, dry-eyed and dry-hearted, can only denigrate Jesus ("if this man were a prophet") and the woman ("he would know who and what sort of woman this is who is touching him" [7:39]). Simon saw only "a sort of woman."

The heart that has been forgiven is deep enough to hold the love of God and to share it with others. Extravagance begets extravagance. Ask for the gift of a forgiven and forgiving heart.

❖ Consider/Discuss:

- Have you experienced the forgiveness of another as a gift?
- Have you offered forgiveness to another as a gift?

❖ Responding to the Word

Sometimes we need to pray to God for forgiveness for ourselves, at other times that we can forgive others. Not to forgive can be a great burden, doing more harm to the one who won't—or, can't—forgive than to the one who did the harm. So maybe we should pray, "Forgive us our sins and help us forgive those who sin against us."

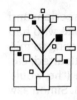

June 20, 2010

TWELFTH SUNDAY IN ORDINARY TIME

Today's Focus: Not Their Grandmother's Messiah

There comes a point in each of the first three Gospels when Jesus turns to the disciples and asks, "Who do you say that I am?" Peter comes up with, "The Christ of God." Jesus goes on to explain how he sees himself and what that means for them, and for us.

FIRST READING
Zechariah 12: 10–11; 13:1

Thus says the LORD: I will pour out on the house of David and on the inhabitants of Jerusalem a spirit of grace and petition; and they shall look on him whom they have pierced, and they shall mourn for him as one mourns for an only son, and they shall grieve over him as one grieves over a firstborn.

On that day the mourning in Jerusalem shall be as great as the mourning of Hadadrimmon in the plain of Megiddo.

On that day there shall be open to the house of David and to the inhabitants of Jerusalem, a fountain to purify from sin and uncleanness.

PSALM RESPONSE
Psalm 63:2b

My soul is thirsting for you, O Lord my God.

SECOND READING
Galatians 3: 26–29

Brothers and sisters: Through faith you are all children of God in Christ Jesus. For all of you who were baptized into Christ have clothed yourselves with Christ. There is neither Jew nor Greek, there is neither slave nor free person, there is not male and female; for you are all one in Christ Jesus. And if you belong to Christ, then you are Abraham's descendant, heirs according to the promise.

GOSPEL
Luke 9:18–24

Once when Jesus was praying in solitude, and the disciples were with him, he asked them, "Who do the crowds say that I am?" They said in reply, "John the Baptist; others, Elijah; still others, 'One of the ancient prophets has arisen.' " Then he said to them, "But who do you say that I am?" Peter said in reply, "The Christ of God." He rebuked them and directed them not to tell this to anyone.

He said, "The Son of Man must suffer greatly and be rejected by the elders, the chief priests, and the scribes, and be killed and on the third day be raised."

Then he said to all, "If anyone wishes to come after me, he must deny himself and take up his cross daily and follow me. For whoever wishes to save his life will lose it, but whoever loses his life for my sake will save it."

❖ Understanding the Word

Discipleship is a journey like the Exodus or like Jesus carrying his cross.

In today's Gospel, while praying in a certain place Jesus uses the opportunity for reflection to inform the disciples about his and their identity. Jesus clarifies what it means to be God's messiah. It means to "suffer greatly," to be rejected, and then to be killed. The disciples also must be willing to take up their crosses if they wish to follow Jesus.

The positioning of these events is instructive. Right before them we read that Jesus had sent the disciples out on a mission during which they had preached and healed (9:1–6). Upon their return they witnessed Jesus' multiplication of the five loaves and two fishes so that it fed five thousand people. Moreover, Jesus had told the disciples that they were to do the same: "Give them some food yourselves" (9:13). Thus, the disciples are filled with examples of the power of the ministry that they are to undertake. Lest they think that ministry is a move from power to power, Jesus takes the opportunity to tell them that the way of ministry is the path that he will take from suffering to glory.

The section that follows today's Gospel reading is about the transfiguration of Jesus, and it is also helpful for determining the significance of today's reading. Only in the Lukan account of the Transfiguration do we hear that Moses and Elijah were speaking with Jesus about "his exodus that he was going to accomplish in Jerusalem" (9:31). These words of theirs pick up Jesus' exhortation to the disciples that they must come after him by denying themselves and following him (9:23).

Luke would have the disciples realize that they are to exercise a powerful ministry for others while participating in their own exodus following Jesus. The images of the Exodus and of taking up the cross and following Jesus imply the rigors of a difficult time filled with suffering. They also imply, however, that the end of the journey is the Promised Land and resurrection.

The apostles were probably not very different from the rest of their families or their friends. They were not very different from any other Jew of their day. Indeed, given our expectations and hopes for our own leaders, we would not have answered Jesus much differently ourselves. They were waiting for the Messiah to come, and once he came, happy days would be here again.

They expected the Messiah or "Anointed One" to come in power and might; he was going to be a liberator like Moses, who led God's people out of slavery, and he was going to be a great king like David, who brought the people of the northern kingdom of Israel and the people of the southern kingdom of Judah into one nation. The Messiah would usher in a new era. It was going to be great!

Imagine their surprise when Jesus rebukes Peter for saying that he is "The Christ [Messiah] of God" (Luke 9:20). Then Jesus goes on to say that he must suffer greatly, be rejected by their religious leaders, and be killed—"and on the third day be raised" (9:22). (I wonder if they even heard the last part about being raised.) But worse yet, he goes on to say that they must be willing to deny themselves, take up their cross daily, and follow him.

This Messiah would not get many votes, even now. But it is through faith in Christ Jesus, Anointed One of God, that we have become children of God. And we are called to "clothe ourselves with Christ" (see Galatians 3:27). Which is a more pleasant way of saying, "take up [your] cross daily" (Luke 9:23).

✣ Consider/Discuss:

- If Jesus asked you, "Who do you do say that I am?" what would you answer?
- What form does the daily cross take in your life? What form does it take in the life of the Church today?

✣ *Responding to the Word*

We pray that we may walk the way of Christ together with Christ, taking up our cross today. We pray to understand what it means to "put on Christ" and to live "in Christ," and to have that faith that allows us to know God as a loving, gracious God.

June 27, 2010

THIRTEENTH SUNDAY IN ORDINARY TIME

Today's Focus: Following His Lead

As much as we might think that the life of faith is only about "letting go and letting God (take over)," it is equally true that the life of faith is about our getting up and getting going. God has expectations, too. To take seriously the life of discipleship means following Jesus' lead, as he reminds us today.

FIRST READING
1 Kings 19:16b, 19–21

The LORD said to Elijah: "You shall anoint Elisha, son of Shaphat of Abel-meholah, as prophet to succeed you."

Elijah set out and came upon Elisha, son of Shaphat, as he was plowing with twelve yoke of oxen; he was following the twelfth. Elijah went over to him and threw his cloak over him. Elisha left the oxen, ran after Elijah, and said, "Please, let me kiss my father and mother goodbye, and I will follow you." Elijah answered, "Go back! Have I done anything to you?" Elisha left him, and taking the yoke of oxen, slaughtered them; he used the plowing equipment for fuel to boil their flesh, and gave it to his people to eat. Then Elisha left and followed Elijah as his attendant.

PSALM RESPONSE
Psalm 16:5a

You are my inheritance, O Lord.

SECOND READING
Galatians 5:1, 13–18

Brothers and sisters: For freedom Christ set us free; so stand firm and do not submit again to the yoke of slavery.

For you were called for freedom, brothers and sisters. But do not use this freedom as an opportunity for the flesh; rather, serve one another through love. For the whole law is fulfilled in one statement, namely, *You shall love your neighbor as yourself.* But if you go on biting and devouring one another, beware that you are not consumed by one another.

I say, then: live by the Spirit and you will certainly not gratify the desire of the flesh. For the flesh has desires against the Spirit, and the Spirit against the flesh; these are opposed to each other, so that you may not do what you want. But if you are guided by the Spirit, you are not under the law.

GOSPEL
Luke 9:51-62

When the days for Jesus' being taken up were fulfilled, he resolutely determined to journey to Jerusalem, and he sent messengers ahead of him. On the way they entered a Samaritan village to prepare for his reception there, but they would not welcome him because the destination of his journey was Jerusalem. When the disciples James and John saw this they asked, "Lord, do you want us to call down fire from heaven to consume them?" Jesus turned and rebuked them, and they journeyed to another village.

As they were proceeding on their journey someone said to him, "I will follow you wherever you go." Jesus answered him, "Foxes have dens and birds of the sky have nests, but the Son of Man has nowhere to rest his head."

And to another he said, "Follow me." But he replied, "Lord, let me go first and bury my father." But he answered him, "Let the dead bury their dead. But you, go and proclaim the kingdom of God." And another said, "I will follow you, Lord, but first let me say farewell to my family at home." To him Jesus said, "No one who sets a hand to the plow and looks to what was left behind is fit for the kingdom of God."

✥ Understanding the Word

Today's Gospel is Luke's version of the beginning of Jesus' journey to Jerusalem. In it Luke provides a model of the focus and the resolution to remain focused that discipleship requires.

Matthew, Mark, and Luke all tell of a certain point in Jesus' ministry when he journeys from Galilee to Jerusalem. Mark's Gospel presents it as a simple move from one area toward the next. In Luke's Gospel, however, it is clear that something momentous is occurring. Only Luke writes about Jesus deciding to go to Jerusalem "when the days for his being taken up were fulfilled" (Luke 9:51). These days refer to the time when Jesus will be lifted up on the cross, raised from the dead, and ascend to the Father. Only the Lukan Jesus shows an iron will at this point in the narrative in the face of his knowledge that the time to depart from this world is near: "When the days for his being taken up were fulfilled, he resolutely determined to journey to Jerusalem" (9:51).

This determination to go to Jerusalem provides an example for the disciples of a willingness to take up the cross that awaits Jesus there. The disciples need such an example because they have chosen to focus on other aspects of discipleship. Following Jesus' announcement that the disciples need to take up their cross and follow him, the disciples have been focusing on the glory of ministry rather than its strenuous requirements. Thus, although Moses and Elijah at the Transfiguration talk about the journey that Jesus is to make, Peter suggests that the journey halt; that they make tents for Jesus and these Old Testament figures because "it is good that we are here" (9:33). The disciples have also argued about which of them is the greatest, and they have tried to limit exorcisms only to those who are one of their company (9:46-50).

144

Even after Jesus begins the journey to Jerusalem they ask if they should "call down fire" on a city that does not accept them (9:54). Jesus shows them what real discipleship is about by simply rebuking them, continuing on the journey, and talking about the rigors and sufferings of discipleship (9:55 — 10:62).

❖ Reflecting on the Word

Today Jesus is teaching his disciples what it means to follow him. For one thing it means renouncing the way of violence, that is, of responding to the violence of others by our own form of violence, whether in word or deed. The hatred between Jews and Samaritans shows itself here in the Samaritans' refusal to let Jesus and his disciples pass through their town on their way to Jerusalem. When James and John want to call down fire on them, Jesus rebukes them.

Following Jesus on the way does not allow for repaying contempt or unkindness in kind, much less with escalated violence. Jesus goes on to teach what it means to be his disciple: being willing to put the kingdom of God above everything else—possessions, family, even one's security. It means putting the kingdom of God first.

As a further example, in today's first reading we see Elisha responding to the call to be a prophet when Elijah throws his cloak over him. Not only does Elisha burn his bridges behind him, he burns his plow and slaughters twelve oxen. One wonders how his family felt about this.

Jesus asks much but gives even more in response to our generosity. "For freedom Christ set us free," Paul writes to the Galatians, "so stand firm and do not submit again to the yoke of slavery" (Galatians 5:1). Following Christ gives us freedom from being enslaved by our anger, our desire for vengeance, our being held captive to anything other than Christ. In him is our freedom; in him, the life of the Spirit.

❖ Consider/Discuss:

- What does Christ call you to leave behind so that you can walk with him in freedom?
- What does Christ free you for?

❖ Responding to the Word

We ask God to free us from anything that enslaves us; even more, we ask God to help us recognize the more subtle addictions and habits that prevent us from living in the freedom of the children of God. We pray that we may follow Christ wholeheartedly.

July 4, 2010

FOURTEENTH SUNDAY IN ORDINARY TIME

Today's Focus: God Who Comforts

God works to gather together all people. God's will is that we find joy in God our Savior. God comforts by bringing the people home to Jerusalem to be nursed there, and Jesus sends out disciples to proclaim that the kingdom is at hand in their midst.

FIRST READING
Isaiah 66: 10–14c

Thus says the LORD:
Rejoice with Jerusalem and be glad because of her,
    all you who love her;
exult, exult with her,
    all you who were mourning over her!
Oh, that you may suck fully
    of the milk of her comfort,
that you may nurse with delight
    at her abundant breasts!
For thus says the LORD:
Lo, I will spread prosperity over Jerusalem like a river,
    and the wealth of the nations like an overflowing torrent.
As nurslings, you shall be carried in her arms,
    and fondled in her lap;
as a mother comforts her child,
    so will I comfort you;
in Jerusalem you shall find your comfort.
When you see this, your heart shall rejoice
    and your bodies flourish like the grass;
the LORD's power shall be known to his servants.

PSALM RESPONSE
Psalm 66:1

Let all the earth cry out to God with joy.

SECOND READING
Galatians 6: 14–18

Brothers and sisters: May I never boast except in the cross of our Lord Jesus Christ, through which the world has been crucified to me, and I to the world. For neither does circumcision mean anything, nor does uncircumcision, but only a new creation. Peace and mercy be to all who follow this rule and to the Israel of God.

From now on, let no one make troubles for me; for I bear the marks of Jesus on my body.

The grace of our Lord Jesus Christ be with your spirit, brothers and sisters. Amen.

GOSPEL
Luke 10:1–12,
17–20 or 10:1–9

At that time the Lord appointed seventy-two others whom he sent ahead of him in pairs to every town and place he intended to visit. He said to them, "The harvest is abundant but the laborers are few; so ask the master of the harvest to send out laborers for his harvest. Go on your way; behold, I am sending you like lambs among wolves. Carry no money bag, no sack, no sandals; and greet no one along the way. Into whatever house you enter, first say, 'Peace to this household.' If a peaceful person lives there, your peace will rest on him; but if not, it will return to you. Stay in the same house and eat and drink what is offered to you, for the laborer deserves his payment. Do not move about from one house to another. Whatever town you enter and they welcome you, eat what is set before you, cure the sick in it and say to them, 'The kingdom of God is at hand for you.' [Whatever town you enter and they do not receive you, go out into the streets and say, 'The dust of your town that clings to our feet, even that we shake off against you.' Yet know this: the kingdom of God is at hand. I tell you, it will be more tolerable for Sodom on that day than for that town."

The seventy-two returned rejoicing, and said, "Lord, even the demons are subject to us because of your name." Jesus said, "I have observed Satan fall like lightning from the sky. Behold, I have given you the power to 'tread upon serpents' and scorpions and upon the full force of the enemy and nothing will harm you. Nevertheless, do not rejoice because the spirits are subject to you, but rejoice because your names are written in heaven."]

❖ Understanding the Word

All vital Christian life needs periodic renewal with reflection, quiet, and continuing education.

In the Gospel of Luke, Jesus sends out another group besides the Twelve. The apostles had just exhibited an excessive concern for their position, as first manifested in their concern about which of them was the greatest, and then in their efforts to exclude from the ministry of exorcisms those who were not part of their group (Luke 9:46–50). They had also asked if they should destroy a city whose citizens had rejected them (9:52–54). From these events Jesus discerns that the Twelve are in need of more quality time with Jesus in order to help them solidify healthy perspectives that will sustain them over the long haul.

So Jesus sends out another seventy-two to go and prepare the way for him in the towns to which he will be going. This action has two goals. First, it gives the Twelve an example that rejection in ministry needs the response of even greater preparation for ministry. Second, it enables the Twelve to have more time with Jesus so that they can develop a better perspective on what Christian life is all about. Jesus wants to make sure that their ministry does not outrun the values that undergird it.

147

We see from the reaction of the seventy-two to their ministries that getting caught up in the power of God working through them is a danger that affects all. The seventy-two return from their journeys rejoicing, saying, "Lord, even the demons are subject to us because of your name" (10:17). Jesus has to remind them, too, that their focus should be on where they are going rather than on the flattering portraits of themselves that their ministry may be evoking in their minds: "Do not rejoice because the spirits are subject to you, but rejoice because your names are written in heaven" (10:20).

We must always make time to immerse ourselves in the Christian vision so that our Christian ministry may be properly ordered.

✤ Reflecting on the Word

It is not often that we are invited to think of God as mother. Two occasions can be found in the book of the prophet Isaiah. First, we hear God speaking the beautiful words: "Can a mother forget her infant, / be without tenderness for the child of her womb? / Even should she forget, / I will never forget you" (Isaiah 49:15).

Then, today we hear words of comfort addressed to the exiles in Babylon, calling them to rejoice with Jerusalem, to exult with her. God will make a new Jerusalem and all her children will be nursed at her breasts. Then suddenly the image shifts from Jerusalem as mother and the peoples as nurslings to God as mother: "As a mother comforts her child, so will I comfort you" (66:13).

Jesus sends out the seventy-two disciples to bring comfort by proclaiming that "The kingdom of God is at hand for you" (Luke 10:9). The first words of the disciples when they enter a house are to be "Peace to this household" (10:5). The God who comforts wishes to dwell with us in peace.

In concluding his fiery letter to the Galatians, Paul wishes peace and mercy to all who follow him in boasting in the cross of our Lord Jesus Christ. Through Christ's dying on the cross a new creation is coming into being.

We are always free to reject this peace, to refuse God's comfort, to avoid entering into the dying and rising of Christ. Yet Eucharist offers us the opportunity to open our hearts once again to God doing new things in and through us.

✤ Consider/Discuss:

- When has God given you comfort?
- Do you see yourself as continuing the work of the seventy-two disciples by bringing God's peace and healing into the world?

✤ Responding to the Word

We ask God to bring us to a new Jerusalem where we can find delight and comfort. We also ask God to comfort us in our sorrows and to bring our hearts to the new joy to be found by those who recognize Jesus as the embodiment of the kingdom of God.

July 11, 2010

FIFTEENTH SUNDAY IN ORDINARY TIME

Today's Focus: Holding All Things Together

The Letter to the Colossians offers us one of the great hymns to Jesus, proclaiming that "in him all things hold together" (Colossians 1:17). Jesus offers a lawyer a way to move through life that will hold things together. The story of the Good Samaritan is one that calls us to live motivated by God's compassion.

FIRST READING
Deuteronomy 30:10–14

Moses said to the people: "If only you would heed the voice of the LORD, your God, and keep his commandments and statutes that are written in this book of the law, when you return to the LORD, your God, with all your heart and all your soul.

"For this command that I enjoin on you today is not too mysterious and remote for you. It is not up in the sky, that you should say, 'Who will go up in the sky to get it for us and tell us of it, that we may carry it out?' Nor is it across the sea, that you should say, 'Who will cross the sea to get it for us and tell us of it, that we may carry it out?' No, it is something very near to you, already in your mouths and in your hearts; you have only to carry it out."

PSALM RESPONSE
Psalm 69:33

Turn to the Lord in your need, and you will live.

SECOND READING
Colossians 1: 15–20

Christ Jesus is the image of the invisible God,
　　the firstborn of all creation.
For in him were created all things in heaven and on earth,
　　the visible and the invisible,
　　　whether thrones or dominions or principalities or powers;
　　all things were created through him and for him.
He is before all things,
　　and in him all things hold together.
He is the head of the body, the church.
He is the beginning, the firstborn from the dead,
　　that in all things he himself might be preeminent.
For in him all the fullness was pleased to dwell,
　　and through him to reconcile all things for him,
　　making peace by the blood of his cross
　　through him, whether those on earth or those in heaven.

GOSPEL
Luke 10:25–37

There was a scholar of the law who stood up to test Jesus and said, "Teacher, what must I do to inherit eternal life?" Jesus said to him, "What is written in the law? How do you read it?" He said in reply,

> You shall love the Lord, your God,
> with all your heart,
> with all your being,
> with all your strength,
> and with all your mind,
> and your neighbor as yourself.

He replied to him, "You have answered correctly; do this and you will live."

But because he wished to justify himself, he said to Jesus, "And who is my neighbor?" Jesus replied, "A man fell victim to robbers as he went down from Jerusalem to Jericho. They stripped and beat him and went off leaving him half-dead. A priest happened to be going down that road, but when he saw him, he passed by on the opposite side. Likewise a Levite came to the place, and when he saw him, he passed by on the opposite side. But a Samaritan traveler who came upon him was moved with compassion at the sight. He approached the victim, poured oil and wine over his wounds and bandaged them. Then he lifted him up on his own animal, took him to an inn, and cared for him. The next day he took out two silver coins and gave them to the innkeeper with the instruction, 'Take care of him. If you spend more than what I have given you, I shall repay you on my way back.' Which of these three, in your opinion, was neighbor to the robbers' victim?" He answered, "The one who treated him with mercy." Jesus said to him, "Go and do likewise."

❖ Understanding the Word

The evangelist Luke today provides an explanation for what can limit or foster the command to "love . . . your neighbor as yourself" (Luke 10:27).

In Luke's Gospel, a lawyer, not Jesus, gives the command in response to his own question of what is necessary for him "to inherit eternal life" (10:25, 27). Love functions for the lawyer as a means to an end, albeit an admirable end. He is concerned about his own eternal future.

This self-focus continues after Jesus approves of his response. The lawyer then asks Jesus, "Who is my neighbor?" (10:29). He raises the question "because he wished to justify himself." Thus, the lawyer's question is a doubly limiting one, asking who should be the object of his love for the sake of improving his own image.

The lawyer's self-absorption leads Jesus to reply with the parable of the Good Samaritan. What we might not have realized about this well-known parable is the relation of the question that Jesus asks the lawyer to the question about the identity of his neighbor that the lawyer had asked: "Which of the three . . . was neighbor to the robbers' victim?" (10:36). Notice that Jesus says that the real question with which love is concerned is not who one's neighbor is, but rather, who lives like a neighbor.

Jesus invites the lawyer to look beyond his self-concern because love is primarily directed toward others. There are examples of these two outlooks in the three figures in the parable who have an opportunity to aid the injured man. A priest and a Levite see the man but pass by "on the opposite side" (10:31–32). They have sacrificial jobs that would be imperiled if they were to come into contact with a dead body. There would have to be a period of purification before they could resume their cultic work. They cannot be certain if the injured person is dead or will soon die; Luke describes him as "half-dead" (10:30). So they are careful for themselves. The Samaritan who helps him is moved, however, by compassion (10:33). This leads him to the selfless care that is the hallmark of love.

❖ Reflecting on the Word

Being a "good Samaritan" has entered our language as a call to be helpful to those in need, whether we know them or not. Certainly this is a wonderful thing, since we all have depended at times on the kindness of strangers. But the point of Jesus' story goes beyond the admonition to "be nice to strangers."

The setting for this story is a conversation between a lawyer, a specialist in the law of Moses, and Jesus the teacher. Jesus is on the road to Jerusalem and his death that will lead to resurrection life. The lawyer asks, "[W]hat must I do to inherit eternal life?" (Luke 10:25). Jesus refers him to the law and its call to love God and neighbor, but being pressed further about the identity of one's neighbor, he answers with a road story.

A man is left for dead on the road. Priest and Levite pass by "on the opposite side" (10:31, 32), not going near. Touching a dead man would make them unfit for temple worship according to the law. Along comes a Samaritan, a member of a group hated by the Jews, a mutual hatred centuries old. But this man is "moved with compassion" (10:33), crosses the road, and not only touches but takes the man left for dead to an inn and pays for his recovery.

God's compassion moves in and through us when we cross boundaries to reach out to others in need; it burns away all hatred or indifference. And it moves us into eternal life, beginning now. To love God is to love neighbor is to love God.

❖ Consider/Discuss:

- What do you think is necessary "to inherit eternal life"?
- Who is your neighbor? Does God want you to add anyone, any group to your list?

❖ Responding to the Word

Let us pray for compassion that can move us across the barriers erected by fear, anger, hatred, a desire for vengeance, or indifference. Let us pray for compassion that makes us willing to suffer even rejection of our help. Let us pray for compassion that allows us to taste eternal life even now.

July 18, 2010

SIXTEENTH SUNDAY IN ORDINARY TIME

Today's Focus: A Tale of Two Sisters

The story of Jesus visiting Martha and Mary is one of the most well known and frequently used stories in the New Testament. Often the two sisters are contrasted, with Mary getting the praise and Martha the putdown. But it may not be that simple. Remember, "Jesus loved Martha and her sister" (John 11:5).

FIRST READING
Genesis 18: 1–10a

The LORD appeared to Abraham by the terebinth of Mamre, as he sat in the entrance of his tent, while the day was growing hot. Looking up, Abraham saw three men standing nearby. When he saw them, he ran from the entrance of the tent to greet them; and bowing to the ground, he said: "Sir, if I may ask you this favor, please do not go on past your servant. Let some water be brought, that you may bathe your feet, and then rest yourselves under the tree. Now that you have come this close to your servant, let me bring you a little food, that you may refresh yourselves; and afterward you may go on your way." The men replied, "Very well, do as you have said."

Abraham hastened into the tent and told Sarah, "Quick, three measures of fine flour! Knead it and make rolls." He ran to the herd, picked out a tender, choice steer, and gave it to a servant, who quickly prepared it. Then Abraham got some curds and milk, as well as the steer that had been prepared, and set these before the three men; and he waited on them under the tree while they ate.

They asked Abraham, "Where is your wife Sarah?" He replied, "There in the tent." One of them said, "I will surely return to you about this time next year, and Sarah will then have a son."

PSALM RESPONSE
Psalm 15:1a

He who does justice will live in the presence of the Lord.

SECOND READING
Colossians 1:
24–28

Brothers and sisters: Now I rejoice in my sufferings for your sake, and in my flesh I am filling up what is lacking in the afflictions of Christ on behalf of his body, which is the church, of which I am a minister in accordance with God's stewardship given to me to bring to completion for you the word of God, the mystery hidden from ages and from generations past. But now it has been manifested to his holy ones, to whom God chose to make known the riches of the glory of this mystery among the Gentiles; it is Christ in you, the hope for glory. It is he whom we proclaim, admonishing everyone and teaching everyone with all wisdom, that we may present everyone perfect in Christ.

GOSPEL
Luke 10:38–42

Jesus entered a village where a woman whose name was Martha welcomed him. She had a sister named Mary who sat beside the Lord at his feet listening to him speak. Martha, burdened with much serving, came to him and said, "Lord, do you not care that my sister has left me by myself to do the serving? Tell her to help me." The Lord said to her in reply, "Martha, Martha, you are anxious and worried about many things. There is need of only one thing. Mary has chosen the better part and it will not be taken from her."

❖❖ Understanding the Word

Last week we focused on the Lukan approach to the command to love your neighbor as yourself. Today's story about Martha and Mary is Luke's way of clarifying the other love command that is linked to the love of neighbor: the love of God (Luke 10:27).

Jesus arrives during his journey at the house of Martha and Mary. Martha busies herself with preparing a meal for them, but her sister, Mary, "sat beside the Lord at his feet listening to him speak" (10:39). This provokes Martha, who complains to Jesus that Mary has left all the work to her (10:40). Jesus responds, "Martha, Martha, you are anxious and worried about many things. There is need of only one thing. Mary has chosen the better part and it will not be taken from her" (10:41–42).

Did not Martha have a point? Did not Jesus, after all, preach about service to others?

The key to appreciating Jesus' response appears to be that this story follows immediately after the twofold command to love God and others and the explication of the love of others by the parable of the Good Samaritan (10:25–37). The focus of Mary mirrors the singleness of purpose in the command to love God "with all your heart, with all your being, with all your strength, and with all your mind" (10:27).

This is why Jesus responds to Martha as he does. Mary has made room for the love of God, which, for Luke, is manifested in her listening to Jesus' words. His observations that Martha is "anxious and troubled about many things" and that "there is a need of only one thing" are his way of talking about the room that must be made for the love of God among many possible, even worthwhile, activities.

Love of God expresses itself in the desire to hear God and in actually making time to do so.

Our readings pair up the story of Jesus coming to dine at Martha and Mary's house with God coming to dine with Abraham and Sarah. And just as Abraham turned to Sarah for help in preparing the meal, Martha turns to her sister for a hand. After all, why should one person bear the burden of serving the Lord?

But Mary does not come into the kitchen, even after hearing her sister banging things around in there, perhaps a little more loudly than usual. Instead, she stays sitting at the foot of the Lord, listening to him. Martha, not one to keep her thoughts to herself, addresses directly the cause of her sister's prolonged delay: "Lord, do you not care that my sister has left me by myself to do the serving?" (Luke 10:40).

As a matter of fact, Jesus didn't care. What he did care about was that Martha was all "anxious and worried about many things"(10:41). Jesus did not care about busy Martha but about worried and anxious Martha. Even more simply, what he cared about was Martha. Not the meal, not the table, not the time they ate, or whatever else was bothering her. He just cared about Martha—and Mary, too, of course. But he didn't have to worry as much about Mary.

Perhaps we could consider this simply a story about Jesus visiting two very dear friends and wanting some time with them both, together. And if that was true then, why wouldn't it be true now? If you find yourself worried and anxious these days, give yourself some time with the Lord.

❖ Consider/Discuss:

- What might Jesus want to call you from? Will you answer?
- What might he say to you when you sit at his feet, listening to him?

❖ Responding to the Word

We can pray that we find that balance between serving the Lord in our brothers and sisters and spending time in the presence of the Lord, both as members of the community of believers and as individuals whom Jesus loves very much.

July 25, 2010

SEVENTEENTH SUNDAY IN ORDINARY TIME

Today's Focus: He Prayed, So We Pray

Prayer is one of the most important things we do, an action that keeps us in touch with God. Saint Paul thought it so important that he wrote to the Thessalonians, "Pray without ceasing" (1 Thessalonians 5:17). Jesus taught his disciples to pray, then added some motivating stories to keep them praying. The prayer and the motives are still in play.

FIRST READING
Genesis 18: 20–32

In those days, the LORD said: "The outcry against Sodom and Gomorrah is so great, and their sin so grave, that I must go down and see whether or not their actions fully correspond to the cry against them that comes to me. I mean to find out."

While Abraham's visitors walked on farther toward Sodom, the LORD remained standing before Abraham. Then Abraham drew nearer and said: "Will you sweep away the innocent with the guilty? Suppose there were fifty innocent people in the city; would you wipe out the place, rather than spare it for the sake of the fifty innocent people within it? Far be it from you to do such a thing, to make the innocent die with the guilty so that the innocent and the guilty would be treated alike! Should not the judge of all the world act with justice?" The LORD replied, "If I find fifty innocent people in the city of Sodom, I will spare the whole place for their sake." Abraham spoke up again: "See how I am presuming to speak to my Lord, though I am but dust and ashes! What if there are five less than fifty innocent people? Will you destroy the whole city because of those five?" He answered, "I will not destroy it, if I find forty-five there." But Abraham persisted, saying "What if only forty are found there?" He replied, "I will forbear doing it for the sake of the forty." Then Abraham said, "Let not my Lord grow impatient if I go on. What if only thirty are found there?" He replied, "I will forbear doing it if I can find but thirty there." Still Abraham went on, "Since I have thus dared to speak to my Lord, what if there are no more than twenty?" The LORD answered, "I will not destroy it, for the sake of the twenty." But he still persisted: "Please, let not my Lord grow angry if I speak up this last time. What if there are at least ten there?" He replied, "For the sake of those ten, I will not destroy it."

PSALM RESPONSE
Psalm 138:3a

Lord, on the day I called for help, you answered me.

SECOND READING
Colossians 2: 12–14

Brothers and sisters: You were buried with him in baptism, in which you were also raised with him through faith in the power of God, who raised him from the dead. And even when you were dead in transgressions and the uncircumcision of your flesh, he brought you to life along with him, having forgiven us all our transgressions; obliterating the bond against us, with its legal claims, which was opposed to us, he also removed it from our midst, nailing it to the cross.

GOSPEL
Luke 11:1–13

Jesus was praying in a certain place, and when he had finished, one of his disciples said to him, "Lord, teach us to pray just as John taught his disciples." He said to them, "When you pray, say:
Father, hallowed be your name,
your kingdom come.
Give us each day our daily bread
and forgive us our sins
for we ourselves forgive everyone in debt to us,
and do not subject us to the final test."

And he said to them, "Suppose one of you has a friend to whom he goes at midnight and says, 'Friend, lend me three loaves of bread, for a friend of mine has arrived at my house from a journey and I have nothing to offer him,' and he says in reply from within, 'Do not bother me; the door has already been locked and my children and I are already in bed. I cannot get up to give you anything.' I tell you, if he does not get up to give the visitor the loaves because of their friendship, he will get up to give him whatever he needs because of his persistence.

"And I tell you, ask and you will receive; seek and you will find; knock and the door will be opened to you. For everyone who asks, receives; and the one who seeks, finds; and to the one who knocks, the door will be opened. What father among you would hand his son a snake when he asks for a fish? Or hand him a scorpion when he asks for an egg? If you then, who are wicked, know how to give good gifts to your children, how much more will the Father in heaven give the Holy Spirit to those who ask him?"

❖ Understanding the Word

The version of the Lord's Prayer that people most often pray is the one found in the Gospel of Matthew (Mattew 6:9–13).

Today's Gospel reading is Luke's version of the Lord's Prayer and the two passages that immediately follow it. This version is significantly shorter than Matthew's. Though the prayer is shorter, Luke provides rich advice on it in the succeeding passages.

The first is about a man whose guest arrives in the middle of the night. He has no bread to offer him, so he goes to his friend's house and asks to borrow some bread. The friend protests that it is too late and he is already in bed. But Jesus assures the man that if he persists the neighbor will give him what he wants (Luke 11:5–8).

The next passage moves from a man requesting a gift from a friend to a child requesting the basic necessities of life from his father. This passage ends by contrasting the human fathers with "how much more" can be expected when making a request of "the Father in heaven" (11:13).

There are movements in these passages from the outside to the inside with consequent greater expectations for having a request granted. The man asks bread of a friend who responds that his gate is already locked and his children are with him in bed. The man who made the request is characterized as an outsider by these words. The children are insiders: members of the same household. When the next passage first takes us to children making a request of their father and then—with exaggeration to make a point about how good God is—contrasts earthly fathers to the heavenly Father, we can see how close we are to God.

For Luke, trust in prayer is supported by realizing how close we are to God; how we are children on the inside of God's household.

✤ Reflecting on the Word

Prayer has always been part of the Christian heritage. The book of Psalms long ago became the prayer book of the church, along with some hymns and canticles from other books of the Bible, both Old and New Testaments. Among the most beautiful prayers we have are the Magnificat of Mary, the Benedictus of Zechariah, and the Nunc Dimittis of Simeon, all in the Gospel of Luke (Luke 1:46–55; 1:68–79; 2:29–32).

Most importantly, Jesus prayed. Think about that for a moment. Jesus, the Son of God, the Word made flesh, the only begotten Son, prayed. We know that he went off by himself to pray. He did this before some of the most important moments in his ministry, like before he chose those who would be with him. But it is safe to assume that he did it as a habit.

So when one of the disciples asked him to teach them to pray and Jesus responded with the Our Father, it deserves our attention. This prayer reveals the heart of Jesus, and tells us how we should speak to the Father. The prayer has two parts: blessing the Father and calling for God's presence in the world, then turning God for our basic needs of food, forgiveness, and fidelity.

The parables that follow call us to persevere and persist in prayer because God is a Father who will give us his life-blood, in this case, the Holy Spirit, to all who ask. Continue to knock, continue to ask. God will respond.

- Do you think of the Our Father as a prayer that Jesus has given to you?
- Do you relate more to God as a friend you have to wake up or a father who gives his children good gifts—or both?

✛ Responding to the Word

Pray Luke's version of the Our Father, then pray Matthew's version (Matthew 6:9–13.) Linger over each phrase as you say them. Take one of these phrases with you throughout the day and repeat it when you have a chance, like a mantra. Let it dwell in your heart.

August 1, 2010

EIGHTEENTH SUNDAY IN ORDINARY TIME

Today's Focus: We, Not Me

We hear the voice of the teacher in today's readings. "Qoheleth" (which means "Teacher") and Jesus remind us of the passing nature of life and what we often value greatly—our property and possessions. Paul instructs us to redirect our minds to things above, that is, our relationship with God in Christ.

FIRST READING
Ecclesiastes 1:2; 2:21–23

Vanity of vanities, says Qoheleth,
    vanity of vanities! All things are vanity!
Here is one who has labored with wisdom and knowledge and skill, and yet to another who has not labored over it, he must leave property. This also is vanity and a great misfortune. For what profit comes to man from all the toil and anxiety of heart with which he has labored under the sun? All his days sorrow and grief are his occupation; even at night his mind is not at rest. This also is vanity.

PSALM RESPONSE
Psalm 90:1

If today you hear his voice, harden not your hearts.

SECOND READING
Colossians 3: 1–5, 9–11

Brothers and sisters: If you were raised with Christ, seek what is above, where Christ is seated at the right hand of God. Think of what is above, not of what is on earth. For you have died, and your life is hidden with Christ in God. When Christ your life appears, then you too will appear with him in glory.

Put to death, then, the parts of you that are earthly: immorality, impurity, passion, evil desire, and the greed that is idolatry. Stop lying to one another, since you have taken off the old self with its practices and have put on the new self, which is being renewed, for knowledge, in the image of its creator. Here there is not Greek and Jew, circumcision and uncircumcision, barbarian, Scythian, slave, free; but Christ is all and in all.

GOSPEL
Luke 12:13–21

Someone in the crowd said to Jesus, "Teacher, tell my brother to share the inheritance with me." He replied to him, "Friend, who appointed me as your judge and arbitrator?" Then he said to the crowd, "Take care to guard against all greed, for though one may be rich, one's life does not consist of possessions."

Then he told them a parable. "There was a rich man whose land produced a bountiful harvest. He asked himself, 'What shall I do, for I do not have space to store my harvest?' And he said, 'This is what I shall do: I shall tear down my barns and build larger ones.

There I shall store all my grain and other goods and I shall say to myself, "Now as for you, you have so many good things stored up for many years, rest, eat, drink, be merry!" ' But God said to him, 'You fool, this night your life will be demanded of you; and the things you have prepared, to whom will they belong?' Thus will it be for all who store up treasure for themselves but are not rich in what matters to God."

✤ Understanding the Word

What sustains life? Physically we know that we must have adequate food, drink, and shelter from the elements. In today's Gospel reading Luke weaves together several passages to comment on how a person should deal with these physical needs in the light of faith in God. Through three distinct passages Luke lets us know who is in control of every aspect of life and how this should affect the way that we live.

Everything begins when someone asks Jesus to tell his brother to share the inheritance with him. Behind this question Jesus discerns the presupposition that life is secured by possessions (12:15). Jesus proceeds to illustrate how this is not the case. He tells the crowd a parable about a rich man who enlarged his granaries so that he would be comfortable for a long time. On that very night, the man died. From this parable Jesus wishes his hearers to take away the point that rather than attempting to "store up treasure" for oneself, a person should seek to be "rich in what matters to God" (12:16–21).

In the verses following today's reading Jesus turns from the crowd to his disciples to give them the secrets of how to be rich in God's sight. The advice is twofold: (1) do not worry about food, drink, and clothing and (2) seek the reign of God. Disciples need not worry for several reasons. First, they are so much more valuable than the birds and the flowers that God takes care of. Therefore, God will provide for them much more (12:24, 27–28). Second, worrying cannot add one moment to their lives and is therefore pointless (12:25–26, 29). Jesus concludes with the promise that if disciples "seek the kingdom," then God will take care of the rest.

The natural drive for security can easily become all-consuming. Jesus provides the perspectives so that life can be properly ordered and not hijacked by this unruly drive.

✣ *Reflecting on the Word*

At some point in their development, children go through the "me" phase. Everything is about "me." This is when "No" becomes a frequent word in their vocabulary. Sometimes the "me" phase extends into adulthood, with everything continuing to be about "me, me, me."

Take the man in the parable. His inner dialogue is all about "me." "What shall I do?" he asks himself in the face of a plentiful harvest. Then we hear his thoughts: "This is what I shall do," since I don't have space. "I shall tear down my barns and build . . . I shall store all my grain . . . I shall say to myself" (Luke 12:17, 18), and so on. The only time "you " enters into the conversation is when he is talking to himself.

Jesus tells this story to a man who wants Jesus to advise his brother to share an inheritance with him. Another "me" person. Jesus' warning to the man and those standing around is to guard against greed, that life is not about things. Qoheleth, too, warns about being preoccupied with all that is passing.

The author of Colossians calls us to "seek what is above" (Colossians 3:1), attend to what lasts, put on Christ, live in intimacy with the Father as Jesus did. Be a "we" person, rather than a "me" person. When we gather for Mass on Sunday, we come together as a "we" people. We say or sing together the great hymn of Glory to God in the highest; we profess our faith as a community; we pray "Our Father." It's about We, not Me.

✣ *Consider/Discuss*:

- Can you think of something that was so very important for your happiness at one time but now barely survives as a memory?
- How do I live most of my life—as a "me" or a "we" person?

✣ *Responding to the Word*

When we pray the Our Father, we focus first on God, then on our life as a community. The second half of the prayer is said as a community, asking God to give us our daily bread, forgive us our trespasses, lead us not into temptation. We pray as a family, God's family.

August 8, 2010

NINETEENTH SUNDAY IN ORDINARY TIME

Today's Focus: A Future Built on Promises

What does it mean to live a life of faith? The Letter to the Hebrews tells us that faith is the realization of what is hoped for and evidence of things not seen. In the meantime we live in expectation, trusting God to be true to the promises made, trusting Jesus to return.

FIRST READING
Wisdom 18:6–9

The night of the passover was known beforehand to our fathers,
    that, with sure knowledge of the oaths in which they put
        their faith,
  they might have courage.
Your people awaited the salvation of the just
  and the destruction of their foes.
For when you punished our adversaries,
  in this you glorified us whom you had summoned.
For in secret the holy children of the good were offering sacrifice
  and putting into effect with one accord the divine institution.

PSALM RESPONSE
Psalm 33:12b

Blessed the people the Lord has chosen to be his own.

In the shorter form of the reading, the passage in brackets is omitted.

SECOND READING
Hebrews 11: 1–2, 8–19 or 11:1–2, 8–12

Brothers and sisters: Faith is the realization of what is hoped for and evidence of things not seen. Because of it the ancients were well attested.

By faith Abraham obeyed when he was called to go out to a place that he was to receive as an inheritance; he went out, not knowing where he was to go. By faith he sojourned in the promised land as in a foreign country, dwelling in tents with Isaac and Jacob, heirs of the same promise; for he was looking forward to the city with foundations, whose architect and maker is God. By faith he received power to generate, even though he was past the normal age—and Sarah herself was sterile—for he thought that the one who had made the promise was trustworthy. So it was that there came forth from one man, himself as good as dead, descendants as numerous as the stars in the sky and as countless as the sands on the seashore.

[All these died in faith. They did not receive what had been promised but saw it and greeted it from afar and acknowledged themselves to be strangers and aliens on earth, for those who speak thus show that they are seeking a homeland. If they had been thinking of the land from which they had come, they would have had opportunity to return. But now they desire a better homeland, a heavenly one. Therefore, God is not ashamed to be called their God, for he has prepared a city for them.

By faith Abraham, when put to the test, offered up Isaac, and he who had received the promises was ready to offer his only son, of whom it was said, "Through Isaac descendants shall bear your name." He reasoned that God was able to raise even from the dead, and he received Isaac back as a symbol.]

In the shorter form of the reading, the passages in brackets are omitted.

GOSPEL
*Luke 12:32–48
or 12:35–40*

Jesus said to his disciples: ["Do not be afraid any longer, little flock, for your Father is pleased to give you the kingdom. Sell your belongings and give alms. Provide money bags for yourselves that do not wear out, an inexhaustible treasure in heaven that no thief can reach nor moth destroy. For where your treasure is, there also will your heart be.]

"Gird your loins and light your lamps and be like servants who await their master's return from a wedding, ready to open immediately when he comes and knocks. Blessed are those servants whom the master finds vigilant on his arrival. Amen, I say to you, he will gird himself, have them recline at table, and proceed to wait on them. And should he come in the second or third watch and find them prepared in this way, blessed are those servants. Be sure of this: if the master of the house had known the hour when the thief was coming, he would not have let his house be broken into. You also must be prepared, for at an hour you do not expect, the Son of Man will come."

[Then Peter said, "Lord, is this parable meant for us or for everyone?" And the Lord replied, "Who, then, is the faithful and prudent steward whom the master will put in charge of his servants to distribute the food allowance at the proper time? Blessed is that servant whom his master on arrival finds doing so. Truly, I say to you, the master will put the servant in charge of all his property. But if that servant says to himself, 'My master is delayed in coming,' and begins to beat the menservants and the maidservants, to eat and drink and get drunk, then that servant's master will come on an unexpected day and at an unknown hour and will punish the servant severely and assign him a place with the unfaithful. That servant who knew his master's will but did not make preparations nor act in accord with his will shall be beaten severely; and the servant who was ignorant of his master's will but acted in a way deserving of a severe beating shall be beaten only lightly. Much will be required of the person entrusted with much, and still more will be demanded of the person entrusted with more."]

163

The Gospel today is about the freedom that God has given us to focus our lives on living toward God's kingdom and how we can do so.

The passage begins with the assurance that the kingdom of God is God's gift to us (Luke 12:32). Just prior to this passage we read that everything else that people need will also be granted by God to those who seek the kingdom (12:31). Therefore, everything that we need in this life and in the next has been provided for us as a gift.

What should follow from this gift is liberality on our part: a generous open-handedness that is the result of having our needs already attended to by God. Thus, we are first encouraged to give alms and then to be as committed to the service of others as a servant is to a master.

In fact, Jesus says that having had our needs for this life and the next taken care of by God should lead us disciples to act as zealous servants for others. The degree of our commitment to service should be like one who is even ready to help in the middle of the night (12:38): someone willing to do overtime work for others.

The justification for this attitude of service is that others depend upon us. God intends disciples to attend to the need of others: "Who, then, is the faithful and prudent steward whom the master will put in charge of his servants to distribute [the] food allowance at the proper time" (12:42)?

The problem with zealous, sustained service is that as time progresses we may become lax in such service (12:45). So Jesus provides a perspective that will help counter this tendency. While it is true that the future stretches out beyond us, a view whose undetermined length can lead us to be less energetic than we should be in service, we never know how much time we have left, says Jesus; so we should be prepared that at the end we are serving others, for such is our call (12:46).

❖   *Reflecting on the Word*

Sometimes the future looks grim. Will there ever be a time when some country in the world is not at war? Or a time when no children are dying of starvation or lacking the security of a home and the promise of a future? Will there ever be a time when people will not resort to violence to solve their problems?

The words of Jesus today are directed to a community already waiting half a century for Jesus to return. He has not yet arrived—at least, not in glory. The parable of the master who will return from the wedding feast when you least expect him refers to Jesus, who is presently at the wedding banquet in the kingdom of heaven.

Luke calls the church to think of itself as a community of servants, taking care of one another, with one eye on the door for the master's return. The image suddenly switches to a thief coming in the night. A bit jarring—thieves come to steal. But this master/thief will only come to steal our hearts.

The Letter to the Hebrews is thought to be a sermon. The preacher is exhorting a community that is tired of waiting, saying that their faith in God will be generously met, as Abraham's faith was. God will be faithful. Trust God and endure.

Jesus returns to us at every Eucharist. He comes as the master who proceeds to wait on us at the table and feed us with his body and blood. This food is meant to nourish our hope in God, who will not let us down.

✤ Consider/Discuss:

- Do you see the future as the place from which Christ will return to fulfill the promises made to those who are faithful?
- Do you see in your life the signs of a faithful and prudent servant? Does anything need to change for this to be true?

✤ Responding to the Word

We can pray to the Lord who will return to let us live in a way that looks to the future with hope. We ask the Lord that whether we are servants at home or people like Abraham and Sara sent out on a journey, we will trust in the goodness of our God.

August 15, 2010

THE ASSUMPTION OF
THE BLESSED VIRGIN MARY

Today's Focus: Looking Good by Living Well

Pius XII defined the Assumption as a doctrine of the faith in 1950, saying that "the Immaculate Mother of God, having completed the course of her earthly life, was assumed body and soul into heavenly glory." This solemnity calls us to trust in God's plan that all who believe in Jesus will share in his resurrection.

FIRST READING
Revelation 11: 19a; 12:1–6a, 10ab

God's temple in heaven was opened, and the ark of his covenant could be seen in the temple.

A great sign appeared in the sky, a woman clothed with the sun, with the moon beneath her feet, and on her head a crown of twelve stars. She was with child and wailed aloud in pain as she labored to give birth. Then another sign appeared in the sky; it was a huge red dragon, with seven heads and ten horns, and on its heads were seven diadems. Its tail swept away a third of the stars in the sky and hurled them down to the earth. Then the dragon stood before the woman about to give birth, to devour her child when she gave birth. She gave birth to a son, a male child, destined to rule all the nations with an iron rod. Her child was caught up to God and his throne. The woman herself fled into the desert where she had a place prepared by God.

Then I heard a loud voice in heaven say:
"Now have salvation and power come,
   and the kingdom of our God
   and the authority of his Anointed One."

PSALM RESPONSE
Psalm 45:10bc

The queen stands at your right hand, arrayed in gold.

SECOND READING
1 Corinthians 15:20–27

Brothers and sisters: Christ has been raised from the dead, the firstfruits of those who have fallen asleep. For since death came through man, the resurrection of the dead came also through man. For just as in Adam all die, so too in Christ shall all be brought to life, but each one in proper order: Christ the firstfruits; then, at his coming, those who belong to Christ; then comes the end, when he hands over the kingdom to his God and Father, when he has destroyed every sovereignty and every authority and power. For he must reign until he has put all his enemies under his feet. The last enemy to be destroyed is death, for "he subjected everything under his feet."

GOSPEL
Luke 1:39–56

Mary set out and traveled to the hill country in haste to a town of Judah, where she entered the house of Zechariah and greeted Elizabeth. When Elizabeth heard Mary's greeting, the infant leaped in her womb, and Elizabeth, filled with the Holy Spirit, cried out in a loud voice and said, "Blessed are you among women, and blessed is the fruit of your womb. And how does this happen to me, that the mother of my Lord should come to me? For at the moment the sound of your greeting reached my ears, the infant in my womb leaped for joy. Blessed are you who believed that what was spoken to you by the Lord would be fulfilled."

And Mary said:

"My soul proclaims the greatness of the Lord;
　my spirit rejoices in God my Savior
　for he has looked upon his lowly servant.
From this day all generations will call me blessed:
　the Almighty has done great things for me,
　and holy is his Name.
He has mercy on those who fear him
　in every generation.
He has shown the strength of his arm,
　and has scattered the proud in their conceit.
He has cast down the mighty from their thrones,
　and has lifted up the lowly.
He has filled the hungry with good things,
　and the rich he has sent away empty.
He has come to the help of his servant Israel
　for he has remembered his promise of mercy,
　the promise he made to our fathers,
　to Abraham and his children for ever."

Mary remained with her about three months and then returned to her home.

✛ *Understanding the Word*

In the Gospel of Luke, Mary is a model for giving God credit for what God does. Today's Gospel reading is about Mary's visit to her elderly pregnant cousin, Elizabeth. Having heard of Elizabeth's pregnancy, Mary goes to help. She stays until the end of Elizabeth's pregnancy, as can be seen in the observation that Elizabeth is in her sixth month when Mary goes to her, and remains with Elizabeth "about three months" (1:36, 56).

While Mary is there, Elizabeth praises her: "Blessed are you among women" (1:42). Elizabeth continues later by saying that Mary is "blessed" because she "believed that what was spoken" to her by God "would be fulfilled" (1:45). Mary's response is the Magnificat. In it she attributes to God everything that is good and identifies herself with the lowly who are the recipients of the gifts of God. Thus, she speaks about God's greatness and calls God her savior (1:46b, 47a). God is "the Mighty One" who does great things for Mary and for others (1:49, 52b, 53a–55).

These great deeds of God come to the lowly with whom Mary identifies herself (1:48a, 52b). Behind all this love is God's mercy, further focusing the gifts on the giver rather than on the recipients (1:54). It is not power or status that enables one to merit the greatest gifts in life. Thus, the divine beneficence comes not to the proud, to rulers, or to the rich (1:1:51b, 52a, 53b). Pride, power, and wealth cannot attract God's help. Rather, it is reverence for God (sometimes called "fear of God") that opens one up to God's powerful works (1:50).

Mary points the way to living in the presence of the self-giving God. The Magnificat is a declaration that all important gifts are from God. We cannot attain them by our own power and capabilities.

✤ Reflecting on the Word

Today's celebration can challenge some of our fears. First and foremost is the fear of death. The Assumption of Mary calls us to trust that God who "raised the sinless Virgin Mary . . . body and soul to the glory of heaven" will also raise us from the dead. "In Christ shall all be brought to life," Paul writes (1 Corinthians 15:22).

This solemnity can also challenge the fear of growing old, of aging, of seeing our body change and weaken, losing its ability to do what it wants when it wants. Our culture puts a premium on "looking good," which becomes equated with looking youthful and not showing our years. The idea of growing old, of maturing into a deeper, wiser, more fully human version of who God created does not seem to be on many agendas.

This feast calls us to focus on looking good in the sense of reflecting the very goodness of God, living a life that embodies the grace of our relationship with God in Jesus Christ. We truly "look good" when our soul "proclaims the greatness of the Lord" by recognizing the important gifts that God has given us: the gifts of faith in Jesus Christ, hope in Jesus Christ, and the ability to love in Jesus Christ.

Life can be lived in response to our fears of dying, sickness, aging, fear of the loss of our physical, mental, and even spiritual abilities. But looking good has more to do with those qualities that show the Spirit of the Lord alive in us, shining through our words and deeds, or even through our simply being.

✜ Consider/Discuss:

- Is there any fear that governs my attitude toward life and limits my actions for good in the world?
- Can I join with Mary in her prayer of praise, recognizing that God can do great things in us and will be faithful to us as God has been with Jesus and Mary?

✜ Responding to the Word

The words of Mary's prayer, the Magnificat, are said every evening by those who pray the Evening Prayer of the Church. Take some time praying it this week. Pause after each phrase, and consider how this prayer can truly become your prayer. See Luke 1:46–55.

169

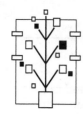

August 22, 2010

TWENTY-FIRST SUNDAY IN ORDINARY TIME

Today's Focus: Getting Through the Gate—
A Tough Squeeze!

There is not much comfort in today's readings. God is imagined as a disciplining father who "scourges every son he acknowledges" (Hebrews 12:6). In the Gospel reading, Jesus cautions his listeners about the difficulty of being saved: "Strive to enter through the narrow gate" (Luke 13:24); then he says that many will not make it. A rod-swinging father who makes it difficult to get into the kingdom—where's the good news?

FIRST READING
Isaiah 66:18-21

Thus says the Lord: I know their works and their thoughts, and I come to gather nations of every language; they shall come and see my glory. I will set a sign among them; from them I will send fugitives to the nations: to Tarshish, Put and Lud, Mosoch, Tubal and Javan, to the distant coastlands that have never heard of my fame, or seen my glory; and they shall proclaim my glory among the nations. They shall bring all your brothers and sisters from all the nations as an offering to the Lord, on horses and in chariots, in carts, upon mules and dromedaries, to Jerusalem, my holy mountain, says the Lord, just as the Israelites bring their offering to the house of the Lord in clean vessels. Some of these I will take as priests and Levites, says the Lord.

PSALM RESPONSE
Mark 16:15

Go out to all the world and tell the Good News.

SECOND READING
Hebrews 12: 5–7, 11–13

Brothers and sisters, You have forgotten the exhortation addressed to you as children:

"My son, do not disdain the discipline of the Lord
    or lose heart when reproved by him;
for whom the Lord loves, he disciplines;
    he scourges every son he acknowledges."

Endure your trials as "discipline"; God treats you as sons. For what "son" is there whom his father does not discipline? At the time, all discipline seems a cause not for joy but for pain, yet later it brings the peaceful fruit of righteousness to those who are trained by it.

So strengthen your drooping hands and your weak knees. Make straight paths for your feet, that what is lame may not be disjointed but healed.

GOSPEL
Luke 13:22–30

Jesus passed through towns and villages, teaching as he went and making his way to Jerusalem. Someone asked him, "Lord, will only a few people be saved?" He answered them, "Strive to enter through the narrow gate, for many, I tell you, will attempt to enter but will not be strong enough. After the master of the house has arisen and locked the door, then will you stand outside knocking and saying, 'Lord, open the door for us.' He will say to you in reply, 'I do not know where you are from.' And you will say, 'We ate and drank in your company and you taught in our streets.' Then he will say to you, 'I do not know where you are from. Depart from me, all you evildoers!' And there will be wailing and grinding of teeth when you see Abraham, Isaac, and Jacob and all the prophets in the kingdom of God and you yourselves cast out. And people will come from the east and the west and from the north and the south and will recline at table in the kingdom of God. For behold, some are last who will be first, and some are first who will be last."

❖ Understanding the Word

Although the kingdom is a gift from God to us, we must respond appropriately to this gift with generous service to others. The gift is free, but the response requires much effort. To encourage this effort Jesus says that many will struggle to enter through the narrow door that leads to the kingdom of God but be unable to do so (Luke 13:24).

The kind of effort that is required is implicit in the way that Jesus describes those who will not be able to gain entrance. Matthew writes that this group is made up of those who will say, " 'Lord, Lord, did we not prophesy in your name? Did we not drive out demons in your name? Did we not do mighty deeds in your name?' " (Matthew 7:22). Luke writes, however, that this group will say, " 'We ate and drank in your company and you taught in our streets' " (Luke 13:26). Luke's wording is instructive. The last time Luke wrote about eating and drinking was when Jesus taught that the "faithful and wise steward" was the one who gave the household "the food allowance at the proper time." The unfaithful steward was the one who began to "beat the menservants and the maidservants, to eat and drink and get drunk" (12:42, 45). The eating and drinking connection suggests both that the many who will not be able to enter the kingdom are those who have not focused on service of others rather than on service of self, and that those who have continued to live their lives by the principle of serving others are the few who will be able to enter through the narrow door.

The reason that the unfaithful servant began to eat, get drunk, and beat the servants was because of the delay in the Lord's return (12:45). To encourage prompt service Luke presents an image of a contest to see who will win and be allowed access to the kingdom. The verb *agonizomai* ("to strive") in verse 24 is used in contests in the sense of struggling against other competitors. The image in Luke 13:24 is of people struggling through their service to others to reach the "narrow door" and enter the kingdom before the throng comes and clogs the entrance.

I was lucky to get a ticket to get through the "purple gate" at President Obama's inauguration. Many did not. Thousands, some from far away, found themselves watching it back in their hotel rooms because they could not get through the gate. It was truly an experience of trying to get through a very narrow gate. Those of us who did knew the crush of the crowd as people became impatient to enter.

What is Jesus trying to tell us in this troubling image given in response to someone asking how many will be saved? Is this God's plan? That we have this hunger for heaven, but too bad, only a few are going to get in? Will even the next world be handed over to a privileged few with the right credentials?

And what is this image of God as a father who scourges his children to get them to shape up? What is God's word trying to tell us this week? Is there good news to be found in a message that the kingdom is not for the weak, the sinners, those with less than perfect records?

We must remember that God's grace and mercy carry us through the narrow gate. Like Jesus, we do our best to discern God's will while trusting in the Father's love for us. Trust God to be God. Know that Jesus will walk with us and guide us through that narrow gate. We need to do all we can to gain entrance. We have a part to play.

❖ *Consider/Discuss*:

- What is the narrow gate that Jesus is calling you to go through to enter the kingdom?
- If eating and drinking with Jesus (even at the Eucharist) is not enough to have Jesus recognize us, then what is needed?

❖ *Responding to the Word*

We pray that God will shepherd us through the gate into the kingdom, and that we will not presume on God's mercy and goodness without living a life shaped by and reflecting that mercy and goodness. Rather than having drooping hands, we hold up our hands in praise to our God, whose only Son stretched out his hands on the cross for our sake.

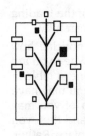

August 29, 2010

TWENTY-SECOND SUNDAY IN ORDINARY TIME

Today's Focus: Next to the Food,
Put a Little Humility on Your Plate

Table etiquette used to be part of having "good manners." Jesus himself offered some words on this matter. His words continue to instruct, even in a world of fast food, carry-out, and microwave meals. But his suggestions apply to those hoping to dine in the kingdom of God one day.

FIRST READING
Sirach 3:17–18, 20, 28–29

My child, conduct your affairs with humility,
    and you will be loved more than a giver of gifts.
Humble yourself the more, the greater you are,
    and you will find favor with God.
What is too sublime for you, seek not,
    into things beyond your strength search not.
The mind of a sage appreciates proverbs,
    and an attentive ear is the joy of the wise.
Water quenches a flaming fire,
    and alms atone for sins.

PSALM RESPONSE
Psalm 68:11b

God, in your goodness, you have made a home for the poor.

SECOND READING
Hebrews 12: 18–19, 22–24a

Brothers and sisters: You have not approached that which could be touched and a blazing fire and gloomy darkness and storm and a trumpet blast and a voice speaking words such that those who heard begged that no message be further addressed to them. No, you have approached Mount Zion and the city of the living God, the heavenly Jerusalem, and countless angels in festal gathering, and the assembly of the firstborn enrolled in heaven, and God the judge of all, and the spirits of the just made perfect, and Jesus, the mediator of a new covenant, and the sprinkled blood that speaks more eloquently than that of Abel.

GOSPEL
Luke 14:1, 7–14

On a sabbath Jesus went to dine at the home of one of the leading Pharisees, and the people there were observing him carefully.

He told a parable to those who had been invited, noticing how they were choosing the places of honor at the table. "When you are invited by someone to a wedding banquet, do not recline at table in the place of honor. A more distinguished guest than you may have been invited by him, and the host who invited both of you may approach you and say, 'Give your place to this man,' and then you would proceed with embarrassment to take the lowest place. Rather, when you are invited, go and take the lowest place so that when the host comes to you he may say, 'My friend, move up to a higher position.' Then you will enjoy the esteem of your companions at the table. For everyone who exalts himself will be humbled, but the one who humbles himself will be exalted." Then he said to the host who invited him, "When you hold a lunch or a dinner, do not invite your friends or your brothers or your relatives or your wealthy neighbors, in case they may invite you back and you have repayment. Rather, when you hold a banquet, invite the poor, the crippled, the lame, the blind; blessed indeed will you be because of their inability to repay you. For you will be repaid at the resurrection of the righteous."

✤ Understanding the Word

The Gospel message today is that need trumps ease. In the passage that precedes today's reading from Luke, Jesus exemplifies this by healing a man on the Sabbath while he is eating in the home of a Pharisee (Luke 14:1–6). In doing so, Jesus obliterates two cultural incentives to rest: the situation of being a guest and the command to rest on the Sabbath. For Jesus they are unimportant in the light of the present need.

To help his fellow diners perceive the relative weight of distress and comfort in the balance, Jesus provides those at table with an image of a son or an ox of theirs falling into a well on the Sabbath. Would any leave them in this distress for a day while they remained at rest (14:5)? Clearly, the answer is no. Of course, Jesus worded the question in such a way as to encourage the priority of service. First, the listeners are persuaded to view the one in distress as they would view their own child in this situation. This perspective elevates need over ease. Second, moving from "son" to "ox" reminds the guests that they would even help their farm animals when they are in trouble. These observations should goad the guests to see that the need of any person should be one's priority.

There are different forms of ease. For example, honor provides inner contentment. In the Gospel passage that we hear today (Luke 14:1, 7–14), Jesus, still using the image of a dinner, advises against seeking honor. Implicit is the call to focus on service rather than this type of ease. At first it may seem that his instruction not to seek honor is just practical advice about how others treat a humble person. But in the light of Jesus' upcoming teachings about a host being rewarded at the resurrection and about guests being rewarded at a heavenly banquet, Jesus' advice is that God will honor the one who seeks service rather than personal privilege (14:14b–24).

Jesus also advises the hosts not to invite family, friends, and neighbors to dinner but instead to invite outcasts (14:12–14). The former group can repay the host, but the latter group is in need. He uses the hyperbole about not inviting family and friends to show again that the real focus of one's life should be on serving others rather than on serving oneself.

✤ Reflecting on the Word

Jesus is not just taking a turn as Emily Post in today's Gospel. At first sight, this Gospel can simply seem to be a case of calling people to be more respectful of others of higher station. To the guests he says: Don't rush for the best places near the host, the seats of honor. You might end up embarrassed if someone else has a better claim to that seat. So be humble, take a lesser place, and let the host bring you higher. Such advice can really sound like a call to a more calculating kind of self-interest.

In a similar vein, he says to the host: Don't just invite the same old crowd all the time—your family, your friends, the ones who can either do something for you or who will invite you back in return. Instead, Jesus says, invite those who do not belong at any "respectable" Sabbath dinner—the ones who are outsiders, those considered beyond the bounds of society because of their physical, social, or religious impediments.

What is all this about? It is about being children of the kingdom of God, about being humble before the table of the Lord and about inviting the needy to that table, just as God did when God began to form a people out of a lowly group of slaves in Egypt. This people God called to be the chosen people. So be generous now as God has been generous with you. "Humble yourself the more, the greater you are, / and you will find favor with God" (Sirach 3:18).

✤ Consider/Discuss:

- What are the "table manners" that you find active in your own family, among your friends, when you gather for a meal? Who gets "honored"?
- Jesus calls all who approach his table to have humility before one another and to provide room for the weak and those often judged to be unworthy. How might this come into play at the Eucharist?

✤ Responding to the Word

We pray that we might rejoice with all who join us at the table of the Lord and be satisfied with the very fact that we are there. We ask the Lord to draw to this holy place a gathering that excels in serving one another and reaching out to those who have known rejection and exclusion.

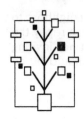

September 5, 2010

TWENTY-THIRD SUNDAY IN ORDINARY TIME

Today's Focus: Choices That Define a Disciple

Getting things straight in our own minds is not easy, as Wisdom reminds us: "For the deliberations of mortals are timid, / and unsure are our plans. / For the corruptible body burdens the soul / and the earthen shelter weighs down the mind that has many concerns"(Wisdom 9:14–15). Jesus has confidence that we can make a commitment to him, responding to the demands he asks of his disciples.

FIRST READING
Wisdom 9: 13–18b

Who can know God's counsel,
   or who can conceive what the LORD intends?
For the deliberations of mortals are timid,
   and unsure are our plans.
For the corruptible body burdens the soul
   and the earthen shelter weighs down the mind
      that has many concerns.
And scarce do we guess the things on earth,
   and what is within our grasp we find with difficulty;
      but when things are in heaven, who can search them out?
Or who ever knew your counsel, except you had given wisdom
   and sent your holy spirit from on high?
And thus were the paths of those on earth made straight.

PSALM RESPONSE
Psalm 90:1

In every age, O Lord, you have been our refuge.

SECOND READING
Philemon 9–10, 12–17

I, Paul, an old man, and now also a prisoner for Christ Jesus, urge you on behalf of my child Onesimus, whose father I have become in my imprisonment; I am sending him, that is, my own heart, back to you. I should have liked to retain him for myself, so that he might serve me on your behalf in my imprisonment for the gospel, but I did not want to do anything without your consent, so that the good you do might not be forced but voluntary. Perhaps this is why he was away from you for a while, that you might have him back forever, no longer as a slave but more than a slave, a brother, beloved especially to me, but even more so to you, as a man and in the Lord. So if you regard me as a partner, welcome him as you would me.

GOSPEL
Luke 14:25–33

Great crowds were traveling with Jesus, and he turned and addressed them, "If anyone comes to me without hating his father and mother, wife and children, brothers and sisters, and even his own life, he cannot be my disciple. Whoever does not carry his own cross and come after me cannot be my disciple. Which of you wishing to construct a tower does not first sit down and calculate the cost to see if there is enough for its completion? Otherwise, after laying the foundation and finding himself unable to finish the work the onlookers should laugh at him and say, 'This one began to build but did not have the resources to finish.' Or what king marching into battle would not first sit down and decide whether with ten thousand troops he can successfully oppose another king advancing upon him with twenty thousand troops? But if not, while he is still far away, he will send a delegation to ask for peace terms. In the same way, anyone of you who does not renounce all his possessions cannot be my disciple."

❖❖ Understanding the Word

Today's Gospel reading from Luke contains four radical images to express the degree of service that Jesus expects his disciples to render to others. Luke makes the first image even more radical than its use in Matthew. Whereas Matthew warns against loving family more than Jesus, Luke says hyperbolically that one must hate family members and even one's own life (Matthew 10:37; Luke 14:25).

These four extreme images stress that one must place service of others above personal ease and comfort. Constructing a tower is a difficult enterprise. Battling twenty thousand with only ten thousand is exponentially much more difficult. Carrying one's cross makes the sacrifice even more personal.

Today's passage connects to the preceding section, Luke 14:15–24, to develop its message. The connection is established by Jesus treating in verses 15–24 the invitation to come to the banquet in the kingdom of God and how three people refused this invitation, the last saying that the reason for his refusal is that he has "just married a woman" (14:20). In today's Gospel the images are used to show what is necessary in order to come to Jesus (14:26). The first thing that Jesus says is that one must hate one's family and oneself. This links to the last person in the parable in verses 15–24 who refused to come to the banquet because he had just married.

Last week's Gospel stressed the importance of service to others versus ease for oneself. What today's Gospel shows is that the service of others that enables one to enter the kingdom of God entails the making of radical sacrifices, as demonstrated by the four difficult scenarios. With hyperbole Luke stresses that even the legitimate duties to family and work, as all-consuming as these can seem to be at times, must not be allowed to outweigh service to others.

✦ Reflecting on the Word

Old Dumbledore, the wise headmaster of Hogwarts, tells young Harry Potter that the choices that we make define us far more than our abilities. Choice is at the heart of Jesus' words to the crowds in today's Gospel. He outlines three decisions that define a disciple:

1) Putting Jesus first, above all other persons, plans, and possessions. Before family, before friends, even before one's own life, a disciple chooses Jesus. This choice had to be made by the apostles, by the other first disciples, and by all who have come after, down to our own day, faithfully living out a commitment to Jesus in all the circumstances of life.

2) Carrying one's own cross and following after Jesus. This means taking up whatever duty calls us to lay down our life in service for the sake of others. It involves making a realistic appraisal of the resources that we have at our disposal, just like the builder and the king in the two parables today. Count the cost before committing.

3) Finally, he asks for a renunciation of all possessions, allowing no thing, just as there is to be no person, to take the place in our hearts that belongs to Christ.

An example of this commitment is found in Saint Paul's request in his letter to Philemon, whose slave had run away and sought refuge with Paul. Paul asks Philemon to take his slave Onesimus back into his household, not simply as a slave, but as a brother in Christ. We do not know what Philemon chose. We do know that it would have cost him.

✦ Consider/Discuss:

- How do you experience the cost of discipleship in your own life?
- Which of the three decisions has been the most demanding in your own response as a disciple of Jesus Christ?

✦ Responding to the Word

We pray for the strength to commit ourselves fully to the Lord, that we might say with Saint Paul: "Whatever gains I had, these I have come to consider a loss because of Christ. More than that, I even consider everything as a loss because of the supreme good of knowing Christ Jesus my Lord" (Philippians 3:7).

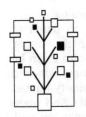

September 12, 2010

TWENTY-FOURTH SUNDAY IN ORDINARY TIME

Today's Focus: The Face of Mercy

Three of the most famous parables are set before us today: the shepherd searching for his sheep, the woman searching for her coin, and the father "searching" to bring back together his two sons. Through them, Jesus shows us the face of our searching God, the face of divine mercy.

FIRST READING
Exodus 32: 7–11, 13–14

The LORD said to Moses, "Go down at once to your people, whom you brought out of the land of Egypt, for they have become depraved. They have soon turned aside from the way I pointed out to them, making for themselves a molten calf and worshiping it, sacrificing to it and crying out, 'This is your God, O Israel, who brought you out of the land of Egypt!' I see how stiff-necked this people is," continued the LORD to Moses. "Let me alone, then, that my wrath may blaze up against them to consume them. Then I will make of you a great nation."

But Moses implored the LORD, his God, saying, "Why, O LORD, should your wrath blaze up against your own people, whom you brought out of the land of Egypt with such great power and with so strong a hand? Remember your servants Abraham, Isaac, and Israel, and how you swore to them by your own self, saying, 'I will make your descendants as numerous as the stars in the sky; and all this land that I promised, I will give your descendants as their perpetual heritage.' " So the LORD relented in the punishment he had threatened to inflict on his people.

PSALM RESPONSE
Luke 15:18

I will rise and go to my father.

SECOND READING
1 Timothy 1: 12–17

Beloved: I am grateful to him who has strengthened me, Christ Jesus our Lord, because he considered me trustworthy in appointing me to the ministry. I was once a blasphemer and a persecutor and arrogant, but I have been mercifully treated because I acted out of ignorance in my unbelief. Indeed, the grace of our Lord has been abundant, along with the faith and love that are in Christ Jesus. This saying is trustworthy and deserves full acceptance: Christ Jesus came into the world to save sinners. Of these I am the foremost. But for that reason I was mercifully treated, so that in me, as the foremost, Christ Jesus might display all his patience as an example for those who would come to believe in him for everlasting life. To the king of ages, incorruptible, invisible, the only God, honor and glory forever and ever. Amen.

GOSPEL
Luke 15:1–32 or
15:1–10

Tax collectors and sinners were all drawing near to listen to Jesus, but the Pharisees and scribes began to complain, saying, "This man welcomes sinners and eats with them." So to them he addressed this parable. "What man among you having a hundred sheep and losing one of them would not leave the ninety-nine in the desert and go after the lost one until he finds it? And when he does find it, he sets it on his shoulders with great joy and, upon his arrival home, he calls together his friends and neighbors and says to them, 'Rejoice with me because I have found my lost sheep.' I tell you, in just the same way there will be more joy in heaven over one sinner who repents than over ninety-nine righteous people who have no need of repentance.

"Or what woman having ten coins and losing one would not light a lamp and sweep the house, searching carefully until she finds it? And when she does find it, she calls together her friends and neighbors and says to them, 'Rejoice with me because I have found the coin that I lost.' In just the same way, I tell you, there will be rejoicing among the angels of God over one sinner who repents."

[Then he said, "A man had two sons, and the younger son said to his father, 'Father give me the share of your estate that should come to me.' So the father divided the property between them. After a few days, the younger son collected all his belongings and set off to a distant country where he squandered his inheritance on a life of dissipation. When he had freely spent everything, a severe famine struck that country, and he found himself in dire need. So he hired himself out to one of the local citizens who sent him to his farm to tend the swine. And he longed to eat his fill of the pods on which the swine fed, but nobody gave him any. Coming to his senses he thought, 'How many of my father's hired workers have more than enough food to eat, but here am I, dying from hunger. I shall get up and go to my father and I shall say to him, "Father, I have sinned against heaven and against you. I no longer deserve to be called your son; treat me as you would treat one of your hired workers." ' So he got up and went back to his father. While he was still a long way off, his father caught sight of him, and was filled with compassion. He ran to his son, embraced him and kissed him. His son said to him, 'Father, I have sinned against heaven and against you; I no longer deserve to be called your son.' But his father ordered his servants, 'Quickly bring the finest robe and put it on him; put a ring on his finger and sandals on his feet. Take the fattened calf and slaughter it. Then let us celebrate with a feast, because this son of mine was dead, and has come to life again; he was lost, and has been found.' Then the celebration began. Now the older son had been out in the field and, on his way back, as he neared the house, he heard the sound of music and dancing. He called one of the servants and asked what this might mean. The servant said to him, 'Your brother has returned and your father has slaughtered the fattened calf because he has him back safe and sound.' He became angry, and when he refused to enter the house, his father came out and pleaded with him. He said to his father in reply, 'Look, all these years I served you and not once did I disobey your orders; yet you never gave me even a young goat to feast on with my friends. But when your son returns, who swallowed up your property with prostitutes, for him you slaughter the fattened calf.' He said to him, 'My son, you are here with me always; everything I have is yours. But now we must celebrate and rejoice, because your brother was dead and has come to life again; he was lost and has been found.' " |

❖ Understanding the Word

Nothing tells us more viscerally how much we care about someone or something than the flood of emotion that fills us when who or what we have feared lost is found. The poet Kay Ryan speaks about this feeling poignantly in her poem "Relief." This feeling and what it shows about what matters most to us are behind today's Gospel reading from Luke.

The initial verses tell about the complaint of the religious leaders that Jesus "welcomes sinners and eats with them." The last part of the reading is the parable of the lost son (Luke 15:11–32). Intervening between these sections are two other parables. All three parables evoke the experiences of loss, recovery, and the sense of blessing that the recovery brings.

The first parable is about a man who has lost one of his hundred sheep and then finds it (15:3–6). The second is about a woman who has lost one of her ten coins and then finds it (15:8–9). In both cases the people search thoroughly for what is lost and then invite people to rejoice with them when they have found it. The point is that there will be great rejoicing in heaven over those who repent (15:7, 10). The idea presented in both parables is that we are lost and that by repenting we allow God to find us.

These parables prepare the way for the parable of the lost son (15:11–32). What this final parable accomplishes is to show people that no actions can place them beyond the possibility of return to God because God considers their return an overwhelming blessing. The son has squandered his inheritance on a dissolute life; his older brother claims that the money went to prostitutes (15:13, 30). For the father, however, the young man's return is a movement from death to life (15:32).

Together the different parts of Luke 15 encourage repentance by presenting the relief that is the outcome of return.

✥ Reflecting on the Word

I am not sure whether our first reading today is a help or a hindrance. Here's the problem. While Moses is up on Mount Sinai talking with God, the people, fresh out of slavery in Egypt, have set up an image of a molten calf and are worshiping it. God is angry enough to want to annihilate them. Moses uses all his skill to calm God down and turn away the divine wrath. This story might reinforce an image of an angry God who needs someone to turn aside the divine anger. Some have understood Jesus as doing this by dying for our sins.

Thank God for Paul and the three parables that Jesus tells today! Paul uses his own life as a story of sin offset by mercy, telling us he was once a blasphemer, a persecutor, and arrogant, "but I have been mercifully treated . . . Indeed, the grace of our Lord has been abundant" (1 Timothy 1:13, 14). Paul proclaims that Christ came into the world to save us. The Father sent him so that we might know God's mercy.

Jesus' parables are about getting lost, whether wandering off like sheep, accidentally getting lost like a coin, deliberately getting lost like that young son who thought freedom to do as he pleased was all that mattered, or stubbornly getting lost like that older brother who won't make his way into the party. In all these cases, someone searches out what's gotten lost and celebrates with a party when it is found. That someone is God, revealed in Jesus Christ, a searching God passionately in love with us.

✥ Consider/Discuss:

- Why did Jesus tell these stories to the Pharisees and the scribes? How do they offer insight as to why Jesus kept company with tax collectors and sinners?
- Have you experienced in your own life God's merciful love for you?
- Do you see in Jesus the image of the living God who searches us out?

✥ Responding to the Word

We pray to God, our creator and guide, in the opening prayer this week that "we may serve you with all our heart and know your forgiveness in our lives" (*Sacramentary*, Twenty-fourth Sunday in Ordinary Time). When we see Jesus crucified we are to recognize in Jesus the face of God fully revealed, not appeasing divine anger but revealing merciful love.

September 19, 2010

TWENTY-FIFTH SUNDAY IN ORDINARY TIME

Today's Focus: Money—Seducer or Sacrament?

More than any other Gospel, the Gospel of Luke calls his listeners to consider the role that money plays in the life of a disciple. Today we find a parable, followed by three shorter sections, all focusing our attention on our attitude toward and our use of money.

FIRST READING
Amos 8:4–7

Hear this, you who trample upon the needy
    and destroy the poor of the land!
"When will the new moon be over," you ask,
    "that we may sell our grain,
    and the sabbath, that we may display the wheat?
We will diminish the ephah,
    add to the shekel,
    and fix our scales for cheating!
We will buy the lowly for silver,
    and the poor for a pair of sandals;
    even the refuse of the wheat we will sell!"
The Lord has sworn by the pride of Jacob:
    Never will I forget a thing they have done!

PSALM RESPONSE
*Psalm 113:
1a, 7b*

Praise the Lord who lifts up the poor.

SECOND READING
*1 Timothy 2:
1–8*

Beloved: First of all, I ask that supplications, prayers, petitions, and thanksgivings be offered for everyone, for kings and for all in authority, that we may lead a quiet and tranquil life in all devotion and dignity. This is good and pleasing to God our savior, who wills everyone to be saved and to come to knowledge of the truth.
    For there is one God.
    There is also one mediator between God and men,
    the man Christ Jesus,
    who gave himself as ransom for all.
This was the testimony at the proper time. For this I was appointed preacher and apostle—I am speaking the truth, I am not lying—, teacher of the Gentiles in faith and truth.

It is my wish, then, that in every place the men should pray, lifting up holy hands, without anger or argument.

In the shorter form of the reading, the passage in brackets is omitted.

GOSPEL
Luke 16:1–13 or
16:10–13

Jesus said to his disciples, ["A rich man had a steward who was reported to him for squandering his property. He summoned him and said, 'What is this I hear about you? Prepare a full account of your stewardship, because you can no longer be my steward.' The steward said to himself, 'What shall I do, now that my master is taking the position of steward away from me? I am not strong enough to dig and I am ashamed to beg. I know what I shall do so that, when I am removed from the stewardship, they may welcome me into their homes.' He called in his master's debtors one by one. To the first he said, 'How much do you owe my master?' He replied, 'One hundred measures of olive oil.' He said to him, 'Here is your promissory note. Sit down and quickly write one for fifty.' Then to another the steward said, 'And you, how much do you owe?' He replied, 'One hundred kors of wheat.' The steward said to him, 'Here is your promissory note; write one for eighty.' And the master commended that dishonest steward for acting prudently.

"For the children of this world are more prudent in dealing with their own generation than are the children of light. I tell you, make friends for yourselves with dishonest wealth, so that when it fails, you will be welcomed into eternal dwellings.] The person who is trustworthy in very small matters is also trustworthy in great ones; and the person who is dishonest in very small matters is also dishonest in great ones. If, therefore, you are not trustworthy with dishonest wealth, who will trust you with true wealth? If you are not trustworthy with what belongs to another, who will give you what is yours? No servant can serve two masters. He will either hate one and love the other, or be devoted to one and despise the other. You cannot serve both God and mammon."

❖ Understanding the Word

Last week, we heard how the prodigal son wasted his father's resources in a life of dissipation. Today's Gospel story is also about wasting the resources of another. Jesus tells it in order to guide us in how we think about and spend our money.

In the story, a steward wastes the resources of his master ("squander" is the word used in the translation heard at Mass). The verb for "waste" is the same verb used of the prodigal son when he wasted his father's goods on loose living (Luke 15:13). The master finds out and is about to dismiss him. The servant changes the bills of his master's debtors, however, so that they can pay the master less than they owe him. When the master finds out he commends the prudence of this action, which was designed by the steward to secure him friends when he is discharged. Jesus concludes from this parable that his disciples should also "make friends for yourselves with dishonest wealth, so that when it fails, you will be welcomed into eternal dwellings" (16:9).

There are two unexpected twists in the parable: first, when the master praises the steward and second, when Jesus bases his advice to the disciples on what this steward did. Jesus explains the parable by advising the disciples to be trustworthy with what they have been given (16:10–12). For Jesus, being trustworthy with money means using it to lighten the load of others. This is why he told them the parable about the steward who reduces the debt of his master's debtors.

Jesus claims that by using money in this way the disciple will be received "into eternal dwellings" (16:9). This parallels the unjust steward's attempt at reducing bills to make sure that people "may welcome me into their homes" (16:4). But 16:9 also seems to point to Jesus' words, "If you are not trustworthy with what belongs to another, who will give you what is yours?" (16:12). In other words, the "eternal dwellings," the heavenly life, is what is really ours, and money ought to be used in a way that shows that we are worthy of such dwellings.

❖❖ Reflecting on the Word

When Jacob Marley appears to Ebenezer Scrooge at the beginning of A Christmas Carol, he wears a long chain, clasped around his middle, "made of cash-boxes, keys, padlocks, ledgers, deeds, and heavy purses wrought in steel." He tells Scrooge that he wears the chain he forged in life, and now he wanders the earth because in life his spirit never went beyond "the narrow limits of our money-changing hole." Old Marley's life had been about money until it ended; now he pays the price.

Luke calls on his community to consider its use of money. In today's parable a steward has been caught squandering his master's property. Seeing that his days are numbered, the steward acts quickly to assure that he will have friends at the end. Surprisingly, the master commends him for "acting prudently." Jesus then comments that that the children of this world have more gumption than the children of light, using their money to make friends.

Three other comments follow: use money to make friends for eternity; being trustworthy in small matters and earthly wealth will lead to being trusted with true wealth, God's kingdom; and you have to choose between God and "mammon" (whatever you put your deepest trust in other than God). In a nutshell, use your money to serve; allow God to save.

Jesus is in line with the prophet Amos, who castigates the businessmen of his day for cheating the poor and needy. God is on the side of these little ones. They are the ones we are to befriend by using our money for their good. Jesus, who came as a "ransom for all" (1 Timothy 2:4), is our true wealth.

- Is there such a thing as a "holy use of money"?
- Who is your "master"? In whom do you put your deepest trust?

❖ Responding to the Word

We pray for the wisdom to live justly, that is, in a way that we keep ourselves in proper relationship with God, with each other, and with the earth. We pray that we will have the wisdom to use our financial resources to help bring about such "just living."

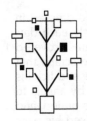

September 26, 2010

TWENTY-SIXTH SUNDAY IN ORDINARY TIME

Today's Focus: Bridging the Gap

God's word again calls us to consider what we do with our money. First the prophet Amos and then Jesus address the fate of those whose wealth insulates them from caring for those with less. First Timothy describes how a disciple is to live in order to "[l]ay hold of eternal life" (1 Timothy 6:12).

FIRST READING
Amos 6:1a, 4–7

Thus says the LORD the God of hosts:
Woe to the complacent in Zion!
Lying upon beds of ivory,
    stretched comfortably on their couches,
they eat lambs taken from the flock,
    and calves from the stall!
Improvising to the music of the harp,
    like David, they devise their own accompaniment.
They drink wine from bowls
    and anoint themselves with the best oils;
    yet they are not made ill by the collapse of Joseph!
Therefore, now they shall be the first to go into exile,
    and their wanton revelry shall be done away with.

PSALM RESPONSE
Psalm 146:1b

Praise the Lord, my soul!

SECOND READING
1 Timothy 6: 11–16

But you, man of God, pursue righteousness, devotion, faith, love, patience, and gentleness. Compete well for the faith. Lay hold of eternal life, to which you were called when you made the noble confession in the presence of many witnesses. I charge you before God, who gives life to all things, and before Christ Jesus, who gave testimony under Pontius Pilate for the noble confession, to keep the commandment without stain or reproach until the appearance of our Lord Jesus Christ that the blessed and only ruler will make manifest at the proper time, the King of kings and Lord of lords, who alone has immortality, who dwells in unapproachable light, and whom no human being has seen or can see. To him be honor and eternal power. Amen.

GOSPEL
Luke 16:19–31

Jesus said to the Pharisees: "There was a rich man who dressed in purple garments and fine linen and dined sumptuously each day. And lying at his door was a poor man named Lazarus, covered with sores, who would gladly have eaten his fill of the scraps that fell from the rich man's table. Dogs even used to come and lick his sores. When the poor man died, he was carried away by angels to the bosom of Abraham. The rich man also died and was buried, and from the netherworld, where he was in torment, he raised his eyes and saw Abraham far off and Lazarus at his side. And he cried out, 'Father Abraham, have pity on me. Send Lazarus to dip the tip of his finger in water and cool my tongue, for I am suffering torment in these flames.' Abraham replied, 'My child, remember that you received what was good during your lifetime while Lazarus likewise received what was bad; but now he is comforted here, whereas you are tormented. Moreover, between us and you a great chasm is established to prevent anyone from crossing who might wish to go from our side to yours or from your side to ours.' He said, 'Then I beg you, father, send him to my father's house, for I have five brothers, so that he may warn them, lest they too come to this place of torment.' But Abraham replied, 'They have Moses and the prophets. Let them listen to them.' He said, 'Oh no, father Abraham, but if someone from the dead goes to them, they will repent.' Then Abraham said, 'If they will not listen to Moses and the prophets, neither will they be persuaded if someone should rise from the dead.' "

❖ Understanding the Word

Today's Gospel from Luke builds on the message of last week's Gospel to show how difficult it is to use our resources liberally for others, even if we believe that this will determine our future life.

Jesus tells them another parable. This one is about a "rich man" and a "poor man" named Lazarus. The first scene takes place at the door of the rich man's house, where the poor man is lying down (Luke 16:19–21). There is a brutal contrast between what is going on indoors and what is happening outdoors. The rich man "dined sumptuously each day" (16:19). The poor man would have liked to have even the scraps that fell from the table of the rich man; instead, dogs licked his sores (16:20–21).

Then the scene shifts to the postmortem existences of these two people. Now the poor man is comforted with Abraham while the rich man is in torment in the netherworld. Although the rich man asks that Lazarus be sent down to assuage a little bit of his torment, Abraham replies that "a great chasm" prevents any crossing from one side to the other (16:26).

Images can make abstract thought more viscerally compelling to us. The preceding images portray the great separation between the two men that existed on earth, the comforts of the one never meeting the needs of the other, and replicated but reversed in the next life. By his callousness toward the poor and his refusal to share, the rich man has sealed his own future and eliminated any chance of help for himself in this postmortem life.

188

The passage ends with a warning. People often become so set in their ways that not even someone rising from the dead—and thus showing that life extends far beyond death—can help them live according to the long view about what is good for everyone (16:27–31).

❖ Reflecting on the Word

If anyone is the prophet of the punch line, it is Amos. He travels up from the south to preach to the people of the northern kingdom of Israel and he pulls no punches. "Woe to the complacent," he begins, and then in a quick series of brush strokes lets them know how God sees them: lying upon their beds, stretched out on their couches, eating their tender lamb and calves, drinking fine wine while the music plays and they anoint themselves with the best oils. Then, the punch line: they shall be the first to go into exile. The party is over!

In a similar vein Jesus paints a portrait of "Richman"—tradition has named him Dives (Latin for "rich man")—dressed in the best, eating the best, insulated in his own little world, while at his door Lazarus lies starving, with only dogs coming to lick his sores. It is a scene of total indifference to the plight of the poor. God's response is clear. The wheel will turn. And when it does, so shall Lazarus and Richman. What was a gap between them becomes a chasm.

The Letter to Timothy today contains advice from a mentor to his beloved child in the faith. It offers a profile of how the baptized person is to live. It's a shame that the reading does not begin earlier (1 Timothy 6:9–10) and end later (6:17–19), because these verses directly warn about the dangers of money, offering advice for the wealthy so that they may "[l]ay hold of eternal life" (6:12).

❖ Consider/Discuss:

- Do you see yourself as living in a country often perceived as Dives by so many other nations who have such great poverty?
- Do we allow God's word to penetrate our hearts and hear God's call to care for the poor and the needy?

❖ Responding to the Word

Jesus became poor so that we might be rich in the grace and wisdom of the Lord. We can pray and meditate on the responsorial psalm for this week: Blessed is the one who keeps faith forever, secures justice for the oppressed, gives food to the hungry. The Lord sets captives free.

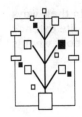

October 3, 2010

TWENTY-SEVENTH SUNDAY IN ORDINARY TIME

Today's Focus: The Trial of Faith

Faith is not always a smooth road. It is not a condition that is consistent, changeless, or free from trials or temptations. Faith often involves a struggle, sometimes an intense one. In all three readings today we meet people struggling with their faith.

FIRST READING
Habakkuk 1: 2–3; 2:2–4

How long, O LORD? I cry for help
    but you do not listen!
I cry out to you, "Violence!"
    but you do not intervene.
Why do you let me see ruin;
    why must I look at misery?
Destruction and violence are before me;
    there is strife, and clamorous discord.
Then the LORD answered me and said:
    Write down the vision clearly upon the tablets,
    so that one can read it readily.
For the vision still has its time,
    presses on to fulfillment, and will not disappoint;
if it delays, wait for it,
    it will surely come, it will not be late.
The rash one has no integrity;
    but the just one, because of his faith, shall live.

PSALM RESPONSE
Psalm 95:8

If today you hear his voice, harden not your hearts.

SECOND READING
2 Timothy 1: 6–8, 13–14

Beloved: I remind you to stir into flame the gift of God that you have through the imposition of my hands. For God did not give us a spirit of cowardice but rather of power and love and self-control. So do not be ashamed of your testimony to our Lord, nor of me, a prisoner for his sake; but bear your share of hardship for the gospel with the strength that comes from God.

Take as your norm the sound words that you heard from me, in the faith and love that are in Christ Jesus. Guard this rich trust with the help of the Holy Spirit that dwells within us.

The apostles said to the Lord, "Increase our faith." The Lord replied, "If you have faith the size of a mustard seed, you would say to this mulberry tree, 'Be uprooted and planted in the sea,' and it would obey you.

"Who among you would say to your servant who has just come in from plowing or tending sheep in the field, 'Come here immediately and take your place at table'? Would he not rather say to him, 'Prepare something for me to eat. Put on your apron and wait on me while I eat and drink. You may eat and drink when I am finished'? Is he grateful to that servant because he did what was commanded? So should it be with you. When you have done all you have been commanded, say, 'We are unprofitable servants; we have done what we were obliged to do.' "

❖ *Understanding the Word*

The disciples seem to be in tune at this time with the message Jesus has been giving. We saw that last week's Gospel stressed the difficulty of the transformed lifestyle to which Jesus calls people. In today's Gospel reading the disciples ask Jesus to increase their faith (Luke 17:5). This demonstrates their appreciation of the difficulty that Jesus said people will have believing in his message even when he rises from the dead (16:31). Jesus' reply to them appears to be dismissive. He says that if they had faith only as big as a mustard seed, a very small seed, they could cause a mulberry tree to transplant itself into the sea (17:6). At this time Jesus says nothing more explicitly about their faith. Rather, he speaks once again about the life of service that they should live (17:7–10). In doing so, however, he addresses their request to increase their faith.

He does so by stretching their temporal field of vision. They are not to look for reward right after they have served. Rather, their service must extend even beyond their daily duties. In the language of the parable, when they come in from their daily work they must be prepared to cook and serve at dinner (17:7–8). These words are intended to help the disciples to see that their faith should not be tested by an absence of immediate reward for their service.

The way that Jesus concludes his advice to the disciples provides another perspective to support their faith. He encourages the disciples to look at their service not as something deserving of reward but as something that they should be doing: "When you have done all you have been commanded, say, 'We are unprofitable servants; we have done what we were obliged to do' " (17:10). The idea is that we should not need to have our service to others buttressed by a faith that looks for a reward. Rather, we should see service as the way we ought to be living in the light of the human need all around us.

For many people it was a shock to read Mother Teresa of Calcutta's writings that indicated how much struggle she endured in her life as a believer. She wrote that for decades there was "this terrible sense of loss—this untold darkness—this loneliness—this continual longing for God—which gives me that pain deep down in my heart" (*Mother Teresa: Come Be My Light*. New York: Doubleday Books, 2007, p. 210).

We hear this same struggle from the prophet Habakkuk: "How long, O LORD? I cry for help / but you do not listen" (Habakkuk 1:2). We hear the apostles say to the Lord, "Increase our faith" (Luke 17:5). And Paul urges his "dear child" Timothy to "stir into flame the gift of God that you have through the imposition of my hands" (2 Timothy 1:2, 6).

How does one feed the fire when there seems to be little more than embers? While God offers Habakkuk a vision, the prophet is still called to live by faith. Paul encourages Timothy not to be ashamed of his testimony to our Lord, but to cling to what Paul has taught him. Jesus himself seems to indicate that the issue isn't the quantity of faith—a mustard-seed amount will get things to happen. Quality is what matters.

In short, endure, stick with it, work it through. Jesus himself knew the darkness. His cry from the cross is both shocking and consoling. He knew what it was to look into the darkness and find nothing, no one there. So we keep working in his name, sometimes waiting for the first light of dawn to break through the darkness of a long night, trusting as he trusted, in the One who once said, "Let there be light."

✦ Consider/Discuss:

- Have you ever experienced a "dark night of the soul"?
- Do you have the freedom of the prophet to lament, to cry out to the Lord for help, to ask to see God's face?

✦ Responding to the Word

Our prayer can be as simple as that of the apostles today: "Increase our faith." At other times we may be more like the man who brought his son to Jesus for release from an evil spirit. When Jesus said, "Everything is possible to one who has faith," he replied: "I do believe, help my unbelief!" (Mark 9:23, 24).

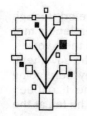

October 10, 2010

TWENTY-EIGHTH SUNDAY IN ORDINARY TIME

Today's Focus: Trusting and Acting on the Word

Leprosy was the great scourge in biblical times. If you had it, you were cast out of the community: no worship, no companionship, not much of anything, except other lepers—unless a prophet of the Lord came along. Today we hear two stories about lepers whose trust in the word of God's prophets leads to faith in God.

FIRST READING
2 Kings 5: 14–17

Naaman went down and plunged into the Jordan seven times at the word of Elisha, the man of God. His flesh became again like the flesh of a little child, and he was clean of his leprosy.

Naaman returned with his whole retinue to the man of God. On his arrival he stood before Elisha and said, "Now I know that there is no God in all the earth, except in Israel. Please accept a gift from your servant."

Elisha replied, "As the LORD lives whom I serve, I will not take it"; and despite Naaman's urging, he still refused. Naaman said: "If you will not accept, please let me, your servant, have two mule-loads of earth, for I will no longer offer holocaust or sacrifice to any other god except to the LORD."

PSALM RESPONSE
Psalm 98:2b

The Lord has revealed to the nations his saving power.

SECOND READING
2 Timothy 2: 8–13

Beloved: Remember Jesus Christ, raised from the dead, a descendant of David: such is my gospel, for which I am suffering, even to the point of chains, like a criminal. But the word of God is not chained. Therefore, I bear with everything for the sake of those who are chosen, so that they too may obtain the salvation that is in Christ Jesus, together with eternal glory. This saying is trustworthy:

If we have died with him
we shall also live with him;
if we persevere
we shall also reign with him.
But if we deny him
he will deny us.
If we are unfaithful
he remains faithful,
for he cannot deny himself.

193

GOSPEL
Luke 17:11–19

As Jesus continued his journey to Jerusalem, he traveled through Samaria and Galilee. As he was entering a village, ten lepers met him. They stood at a distance from him and raised their voices, saying, "Jesus, Master! Have pity on us!" And when he saw them, he said, "Go show yourselves to the priests." As they were going they were cleansed. And one of them, realizing he had been healed, returned, glorifying God in a loud voice; and he fell at the feet of Jesus and thanked him. He was a Samaritan. Jesus said in reply, "Ten were cleansed, were they not? Where are the other nine? Has none but this foreigner returned to give thanks to God?" Then he said to him, "Stand up and go; your faith has saved you."

❖ Understanding the Word

In last week's Gospel passage the disciples asked Jesus to increase their faith. This showed their understanding of Jesus' caution that it will be difficult for people to believe and change their ways even if someone were to rise from the dead (16:31). Jesus helped increase their faith by expanding their concept of how much service is required of them. This helps them not to despair over the long haul.

In this week's Gospel passage Jesus gives the disciples another way to increase their faith: by feeling and expressing gratitude. In a village Jesus encounters ten lepers who call to him to have pity on them. He sends them to the priests and on the way they are healed. Yet only one returns and thanks Jesus, who says to him, "your faith has saved you" (Luke 17:11–19). This is precisely what the disciples had been looking for when they asked Jesus to increase their faith: the faith that saves. Their request for an increase of faith was a reaction to the lesson in the parable that without the great faith that empowers service to others, people end up tormented (16:25–26).

Jesus links faith to gratitude. Gratitude increases faith. Gratitude expressed is faith nourished; gratitude expressed is the acknowledgment of daily gifts from God. These gifts are confirmations of our faith.

Two elements of this gratitude especially deserve attention. The first is that gratitude is not only felt but is consciously expressed. Feelings tend to slide quickly away as one supplants another. Expressing gratitude concretizes it and imprints it in our souls as a resource for faith. The second thing worth noting is that it is a Samaritan who declares his thanks. It was not one of the others healed whom one might have thought more likely to give thanks. This suggests that expression of gratitude to God may not come as naturally as we might think. Gratitude exercised is gratitude learned.

Today's stories deal not only with healing but with conversion. Two lepers find their lives transformed because they obey the word of God's prophets. The first one was an important general in the Syrian army named Naaman. His wife had a maid who told her about a prophet back home in Israel who cured leprosy. The wife goes to her husband-general, who goes to his king, who dashes off a letter "requesting" the king of Israel to do something to heal his top general. Israel's king is distraught until the prophet Elisha checks in: "Send him over to my place."

The best part is when the general shows up on the prophet's doorstep and the prophet won't even come to the door, but sends his servant with a message to wash seven times in the Jordan. At this point, Naaman becomes angry, muttering about the wonderful clean rivers back home and having to bathe in this instead. Fortunately, the general's servants calm him down; most importantly, they get him to listen and obey the word of the prophet. Today's reading begins as Naaman washes and is cured.

Thus, a happy ending, with the general requesting a gift of "two mule-loads of earth" (2 Kings 5:17) so he can worship the God of Israel when he gets home (the belief at the time being that all gods were geographically handicapped, only able to work on their own turf).

It's a story of an outsider, a Syrian, coming to faith in the God of Israel, just as today's Gospel is the story of another outsider, a nameless Samaritan, coming to faith in the son of the God of Israel. In both cases, faith reveals itself as obedience to God's word, which, as Paul reminds us, cannot be chained. It will work its way in the world.

❖ Consider/Discuss:

- Do you believe in the power of God's word to work miracles, if we both trust in it and act on it?
- Have you noticed how often the outsiders (Syrians, Samaritans, Gentiles) are more apt to trust in God's ability to do something for—and in—them than the insiders are?

❖ Responding to the Word

We pray that we might hear the word of God that can come to us in unlikely places and from unlikely people. If today we hear God's voice, let us not harden our hearts.

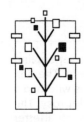

October 17, 2010

TWENTY-NINTH SUNDAY IN ORDINARY TIME

Today's Focus: The Rewards of Persistence

To persist is to stand firm, to stick with it, not giving in when "common sense" would suggest otherwise. Jesus tells a tale of a persistent widow that would both get a laugh and make a point. A powerless widow is able to change a corrupt judge through her persistence. Moses and Paul also weigh in on persistence.

FIRST READING
Exodus 17: 8–13

In those days, Amalek came and waged war against Israel. Moses, therefore, said to Joshua, "Pick out certain men, and tomorrow go out and engage Amalek in battle. I will be standing on top of the hill with the staff of God in my hand." So Joshua did as Moses told him: he engaged Amalek in battle after Moses had climbed to the top of the hill with Aaron and Hur. As long as Moses kept his hands raised up, Israel had the better of the fight, but when he let his hands rest, Amalek had the better of the fight. Moses' hands, however, grew tired; so they put a rock in place for him to sit on. Meanwhile Aaron and Hur supported his hands, one on one side and one on the other, so that his hands remained steady till sunset. And Joshua mowed down Amalek and his people with the edge of the sword.

PSALM RESPONSE
Psalm 121:2

Our help is from the Lord, who made heaven and earth.

SECOND READING
2 Timothy 3:14 — 4:2

Beloved: Remain faithful to what you have learned and believed, because you know from whom you learned it, and that from infancy you have known the sacred Scriptures, which are capable of giving you wisdom for salvation through faith in Christ Jesus. All Scripture is inspired by God and is useful for teaching, for refutation, for correction, and for training in righteousness, so that one who belongs to God may be competent, equipped for every good work.

I charge you in the presence of God and of Christ Jesus, who will judge the living and the dead, and by his appearing and his kingly power: proclaim the word; be persistent whether it is convenient or inconvenient; convince, reprimand, encourage through all patience and teaching.

GOSPEL
Luke 18:1–8

Jesus told his disciples a parable about the necessity for them to pray always without becoming weary. He said, "There was a judge in a certain town who neither feared God nor respected any human being. And a widow in that town used to come to him and say, 'Render a just decision for me against my adversary.' For a long time the judge was unwilling, but eventually he thought, 'While it is true that I neither fear God nor respect any human being, because this widow keeps bothering me I shall deliver a just decision for her lest she finally come and strike me.' " The Lord said, "Pay attention to what the dishonest judge says. Will not God then secure the rights of his chosen ones who call out to him day and night? Will he be slow to answer them? I tell you, he will see to it that justice is done for them speedily. But when the Son of Man comes, will he find faith on earth?"

❖ Understanding the Word

Luke has been articulating a vision of service to others and the faith that sustains and empowers it. In the meantime, however, the Pharisees have been concerned with when the kingdom of God will come (Luke 17:20). Jesus has responded that the kingdom is both a present (17:21) and future reality (17:22–37). It is not something that we should await passively but a reality toward which we should live. Clearly, Jesus has taught that service to others is the means by which we can live toward the fulfillment of the kingdom in the final coming of Christ.

In this Sunday's Gospel reading, the parable about prayer is Jesus' response to the impatience that is behind the Pharisees' question about when the fullness of God's kingdom will come. Luke says that the parable is "about the necessity . . . to pray always without becoming weary" (18:1). In it Jesus speaks about an insistent widow who by her persistence receives a just decision from an unjust judge, who acts simply to rid himself of the annoyance that she causes him (18:2–4). From this Jesus draws the lesson of how much the disciples can trust that God will judge rightly and quickly for those who call out to God. The concluding warning is, "But when the Son of Man comes, will he find faith on earth?" (18:8).

Faith, then, is nurtured by gratitude and frequent prayer. Faith is food for the journey whose length can sometimes clash with our hurried expectations. Faith is not only nurtured by prayer, it is expressed in the continual prayer that is rooted in our recognition of the justness and goodness of God.

During the last two weeks we have heard about faith: the disciples requesting an increase of faith, Jesus saying even a little will do, the Syrian general and
Samaritan leper whose faith delivers them. Today Jesus asks: "When the Son of
Man comes, will he find faith on earth?" (Luke 18:8). This question seems to hang
in mid-air, but not if we relate it to what Jesus has just said about persisting in
prayer.

Persistence in prayer lies at the heart of the parable of the widow and the
unjust judge. This parable must have gotten a laugh. Widows and orphans were
among the most powerless people in society in those days. That's why the prophets were always taking up their cause. But here you have a judge who neither
fears God nor respects anybody else cowering before a widow who won't go away.
He even goes so far to say that his only reason for deciding in her favor was the
fear that she would give him a black eye, a more accurate translation of "come
and strike me" (18:5).

Moses is also shown persisting in prayer with the help of Aaron and Hur, so
that the Israelite people will have access to land for their flocks and water for
humans and beasts. And Paul urges Timothy to be persistent in learning and
preaching from the scriptures, which would mean the Old Testament, since the
New Testament was a work in progress.

Will the Son of Man find faith? He will, if we persist both in prayer and learning
the word of God.

❖ *Consider/Discuss:*

- Do you see yourself as a persistent person? Do you persist in
  prayer?
- Do you persist in turning to scripture for its wisdom and to hear the
  voice of God?

❖ *Responding to the Word*

Like the apostles, we ask Jesus to teach us to pray and we turn to the Holy
Spirit to pray in us. St. Paul reminds us that "the Spirit too comes to the aid of
our weakness; for we do not know how to pray as we ought, but the Spirit itself
intercedes with inexpressible groanings" (Romans 8:26).

October 24, 2010

THIRTIETH SUNDAY IN ORDINARY TIME

Today's Focus: Prayer as Receiving, Not Achieving

The focus of the readings remains on prayer this week, with special attention to who gets God's ear and why. We don't have to be perfect to pray, or even say the perfect prayer. It is more important to allow some room for God to work in us. This is more likely to happen when we bow our heads in recognition of who God is and who we are.

FIRST READING
Sirach 35: 12–14, 16–18

The LORD is a God of justice,
  who knows no favorites.
Though not unduly partial toward the weak,
  yet he hears the cry of the oppressed.
The Lord is not deaf to the wail of the orphan,
  nor to the widow when she pours out her complaint.
The one who serves God willingly is heard;
  his petition reaches the heavens.
The prayer of the lowly pierces the clouds;
  it does not rest till it reaches its goal,
nor will it withdraw till the Most High responds,
  judges justly and affirms the right,
and the Lord will not delay.

PSALM RESPONSE
Psalm 34:7a

The Lord hears the cry of the poor.

SECOND READING
2 Timothy 4: 6–8, 16–18

Beloved: I am already being poured out like a libation, and the time of my departure is at hand. I have competed well; I have finished the race; I have kept the faith. From now on the crown of righteousness awaits me, which the Lord, the just judge, will award to me on that day, and not only to me, but to all who have longed for his appearance.

At my first defense no one appeared on my behalf, but everyone deserted me. May it not be held against them! But the Lord stood by me and gave me strength, so that through me the proclamation might be completed and all the Gentiles might hear it. And I was rescued from the lion's mouth. The Lord will rescue me from every evil threat and will bring me safe to his heavenly kingdom. To him be glory forever and ever. Amen.

Jesus addressed this parable to those who were convinced of their own righteousness and despised everyone else. "Two people went up to the temple area to pray; one was a Pharisee and the other was a tax collector. The Pharisee took up his position and spoke this prayer to himself, 'O God, I thank you that I am not like the rest of humanity—greedy, dishonest, adulterous—or even like this tax collector. I fast twice a week, and I pay tithes on my whole income.' But the tax collector stood off at a distance and would not even raise his eyes to heaven but beat his breast and prayed, 'O God, be merciful to me a sinner.' I tell you, the latter went home justified, not the former; for whoever exalts himself will be humbled, and the one who humbles himself will be exalted."

✦ Understanding the Word

There has been, in the readings over the last month and a half, an undercurrent of Pharisaic criticism of Jesus' radical message of service to those in need. Thus, after Jesus had spoken about the liberal use of money to help others, Luke writes: "The Pharisees, who loved money, heard all these things and sneered at him" (16:14). In response to Jesus telling the grateful Samaritan whose leprosy had been healed that his faith had saved him, the Pharisees asked when the kingdom of God would arrive (17:20). They had clearly not seen the "already" part of the "already and not yet fully" aspect of salvation.

In today's Gospel passage Luke shows Jesus directly confronting the underlying attitude of the Pharisees that is at the heart of their opposition to him. It is a parable about two men praying in the temple, one a Pharisee and the other a tax collector. The disparity in social prestige is glaring: the former had an extremely lofty religious reputation and the latter's position was held in scorn by people who saw tax collectors as Roman collaborators.

The prayers and self-concepts of each man are interwoven. The Pharisee thanks God for the good fellow that he is, contrasting himself in the process with the whole "rest of humanity" and with the tax collector near him in particular (Luke 18:11). In contrast, the tax collector can't even raise his eyes and asks for God's mercy on the sinner that he is (18:13). The Pharisee may be correct when he says that he is not "greedy, dishonest, adulterous" and that he fasts twice a week and tithes (18:12). It has already been shown, however, in their previous reactions to Jesus' message, that the Pharisees lack the extra degree of personal generosity that Jesus requires of his disciples. For this reason, the tax collector's self-reflection and prayer are on target. In relation to how much Jesus asks of us we are all in need of mercy.

Luke's message is that prayer should express the realization that we can give even more; in our prayer we plead for the divine mercy that powers all giving.

It's not that the Pharisee's prayer is a bad prayer. It starts out well: "O God, I thank you . . ." Gratitude is good. But then it gets into boasting: "I am not like the rest of humanity . . . I fast . . . I pay tithes" (Luke 18:11, 12). It's a Little Jack Horner prayer. Remember the old nursery rhyme that ends with Jack saying, "What a good boy am I!"? The Pharisee's prayer is all about him and what he does, all the while gauging the distance between himself and the rest of humankind.

In contrast, the tax collector "stood off at a distance" with bowed head, beating his breast and saying, "O God, be merciful to me a sinner" (18:13). He knows who he is and who God is and what God alone can do for him. No repetitive "I," no swelling ego there, just a repentant figure, one who asks to receive what only God can give: mercy.

Jesus tells this story "to those who were convinced of their own righteousness and despised everyone else" (18:9). How do we hear it? It acknowledges God who makes us "just," that is, who helps us to be in proper relationship with God, with each other, and with all creation.

Sirach reminds us that our just God hears the cry of the oppressed, the wail of the orphan, the complaint of the widow, the petition of those who serve God willingly, and the prayer of the lowly. These folk allow room for God to enter their minds and hearts, and then all kind of things can begin to happen, both within and all around them.

❖ Consider/Discuss:

- Does this parable let the tax collector off the hook too easily—with bowed head and short prayer, all is well?
- How God can be both just judge and merciful Lord? Wouldn't justice call for appropriate punishment, while mercy simply wipes the slate clean?

❖ Responding to the Word

We pray that God will give us the grace of humility when we pray, the ability to recognize who God is and who we are, to trust that God will give us what we most need, to be thankful for what we have received more than for what we have achieved.

October 31, 2010

THIRTY-FIRST SUNDAY IN ORDINARY TIME

Today's Focus: The Man Who Was Up a Tree

Luke provides us with some wonderful characters. Their stories embrace human situations that we all know and show how God's grace can transform them into new ways of living. Zacchaeus was a man who was "up a tree" in more ways than one, but the power of God's mercy was able to transform him and his situation.

FIRST READING
Wisdom
11:22 — 12:2

Before the LORD the whole universe is as a grain
      from a balance
   or a drop of morning dew come down upon the earth.
But you have mercy on all, because you can do all things;
   and you overlook people's sins that they may repent.
For you love all things that are
   and loathe nothing that you have made;
      for what you hated, you would not have fashioned.
And how could a thing remain, unless you willed it;
   or be preserved, had it not been called forth by you?
But you spare all things, because they are yours,
   O LORD and lover of souls,
      for your imperishable spirit is in all things!
Therefore you rebuke offenders little by little,
   warn them and remind them of the sins
      they are committing,
   that they may abandon their wickedness
      and believe in you, O LORD!

PSALM RESPONSE
Psalm 145:1

I will praise your name for ever, my king and my God.

SECOND READING
2 Thessalonians
1:11 — 2:2

Brothers and sisters: We always pray for you, that our God may make you worthy of his calling and powerfully bring to fulfillment every good purpose and every effort of faith, that the name of our Lord Jesus may be glorified in you, and you in him, in accord with the grace of our God and Lord Jesus Christ.

We ask you, brothers and sisters, with regard to the coming of our Lord Jesus Christ and our assembling with him, not to be shaken out of your minds suddenly, or to be alarmed either by a "spirit," or by an oral statement, or by a letter allegedly from us to the effect that the day of the Lord is at hand.

202

GOSPEL
Luke 19:1–10

At that time, Jesus came to Jericho and intended to pass through the town. Now a man there named Zacchaeus, who was a chief tax collector and also a wealthy man, was seeking to see who Jesus was; but he could not see him because of the crowd, for he was short in stature. So he ran ahead and climbed a sycamore tree in order to see Jesus, who was about to pass that way. When he reached the place, Jesus looked up and said, "Zacchaeus, come down quickly, for today I must stay at your house." And he came down quickly and received him with joy. When they all saw this, they began to grumble, saying, "He has gone to stay at the house of a sinner." But Zacchaeus stood there and said to the Lord, "Behold, half of my possessions, Lord, I shall give to the poor, and if I have extorted anything from anyone I shall repay it four times over." And Jesus said to him, "Today salvation has come to this house because this man too is a descendant of Abraham. For the Son of Man has come to seek and to save what was lost."

✤ Understanding the Word

Today Luke presents the entertaining passage about Jesus' meeting with Zacchaeus. What we probably remember is Zacchaeus' climbing the tree to look at Jesus (19:4). The passage is, however, a continuation of the theme found in last week's Gospel. The connections are clear. Zacchaeus is a tax collector like one of the men in the story we heard last week (18:11; 19:2). The crowd considers Zacchaeus to be a sinner just as the Pharisee who prayed in the temple looked down on the tax collector there (18:11; 19:7). The Pharisee points out that he gave money to others, and so does Zacchaeus (18:12; 19:8).

The contrast is also clear. The Pharisee gives what he is expected to give: a tithe of his income. Zacchaeus offers, however, to give to the poor not only part of his income but half his possessions. Moreover, he says that if he has wronged anyone he will repay them "four times over" (19:8).

Zacchaeus has shown the generous heart that we have seen Jesus calling his disciples to have in their service of others. Between last week's Gospel reading (18:9–14) and this week's, Jesus continued this call to magnanimity. He said first that the kingdom must be received like a child in order to "enter it" (18:17). Then he explained this image by claiming that "it is easier for a camel to pass through the eye of a needle than for a rich person to enter the kingdom of God" (18:25). This he said because a rich official was unwilling to "sell all that [he had] and distribute it to the poor" (18:22).

From these earlier passages it becomes clear why Jesus says to Zacchaeus, "Today salvation has come to this house because this man too is a descendant of Abraham" (19:9). Zacchaeus has shown the interior disposition that is required whenever there is great human need.

Luke sketches his characters quickly but with precision, telling us all we need to know to appreciate the situation. Zacchaeus was chief tax collector, a wealthy man, and short. Most important, he a seeker, trying to catch sight of Jesus. Because of the crowd Jesus attracted as he was passing through town and because of his height, Zacchaeus had to climb a tree. His stature might not have been the only reason why. Tax collectors were nobody's favorite: they collaborated with the Roman occupiers and became rich to the detriment of their own people. Up a tree would have been the safest location for a tax collector in a crowd.

What makes this story so appealing is the joy that both Jesus and Zacchaeus show in meeting each other. "[C]ome down quickly," Jesus says, "for today I must stay at your house" (Luke 19:50). Zacchaeus drops quickly and receives Jesus with joy. The crowd, however, does not share in their joy. They grumble about a prophet eating with a sinner! But Zacchaeus holds his ground, saying that if—notice the "if"—he has defrauded anyone, he will make amends four-fold, keeping to the strictest restitution demanded by the law. Jesus, not to be over-done in generosity, proclaims: "Today salvation has come to this house" (19:9), adding that this is why he come in the first place: "to seek and save what was lost" (19:10).

Sometimes we can find ourselves "up a tree," even in our relationship with God. Remember Zacchaeus. Jesus brought him down safely, and restored him to the community. This is why he still comes into our lives: to bring salvation to our own house.

❖ Consider/Discuss:

- Have you been—or are you now—"up a tree" in your relationship with God, wishing to know God better but feeling at a distance or even trapped by circumstances?
- Are you aware that Jesus comes into our lives today?

❖ Responding to the Word

Pray that you may know the God of whom Wisdom speaks today, a God who has mercy on all, who loves all things that are, who is a lover of souls, who has placed the divine imperishable spirit in us, and who patiently waits for us to believe.

November 1, 2010

THE SOLEMNITY OF ALL SAINTS

Today's Focus: Give Thanks for the Saints

In the church year of the Eastern church, this feast occurs the Sunday after Pentecost, reminding worshipers that the saints are those who have opened their lives to the gift of the Spirit. The saints embrace this gift of the risen Christ and the Father and do not imprison it, but allow it to move them to act in the world.

FIRST READING
Revelation 7: 2–4, 9–14

I, John, saw another angel come up from the East, holding the seal of the living God. He cried out in a loud voice to the four angels who were given power to damage the land and the sea, "Do not damage the land or the sea or the trees until we put the seal on the foreheads of the servants of our God." I heard the number of those who had been marked with the seal, one hundred and forty-four thousand marked from every tribe of the Israelites.

After this I had a vision of a great multitude, which no one could count, from every nation, race, people, and tongue. They stood before the throne and before the Lamb, wearing white robes and holding palm branches in their hands. They cried out in a loud voice:
"Salvation comes from our God, who is seated on the throne,
and from the Lamb."
All the angels stood around the throne and around the elders and the four living creatures. They prostrated themselves before the throne, worshiped God, and exclaimed:
"Amen. Blessing and glory, wisdom and thanksgiving,
honor, power, and might
be to our God forever and ever. Amen."
Then one of the elders spoke up and said to me, "Who are these wearing white robes, and where did they come from?" I said to him, "My lord, you are the one who knows." He said to me, "These are the ones who have survived the time of great distress; they have washed their robes and made them white in the blood of the Lamb."

PSALM RESPONSE
Psalm 24:6

Lord, this is the people that longs to see your face.

SECOND READING
1 John 3:1–3

Beloved: See what love the Father has bestowed on us that we may be called the children of God. Yet so we are. The reason the world does not know us is that it did not know him. Beloved, we are God's children now; what we shall be has not yet been revealed. We do know that when it is revealed we shall be like him, for we shall see him as he is. Everyone who has this hope based on him makes himself pure, as he is pure.

205

GOSPEL
Matthew 5:1–12a

When Jesus saw the crowds, he went up the mountain, and after he had sat down, his disciples came to him. He began to teach them, saying:

"Blessed are the poor in spirit,
for theirs is the kingdom of heaven.
Blessed are they who mourn,
for they will be comforted.
Blessed are the meek,
for they will inherit the land.
Blessed are they who hunger and thirst for righteousness,
for they will be satisfied.
Blessed are the merciful,
for they will be shown mercy.
Blessed are the clean of heart,
for they will see God.
Blessed are the peacemakers,
for they will be called children of God.
Blessed are they who are persecuted for the sake of righteousness,
for theirs is the kingdom of heaven.
Blessed are you when they insult you and persecute you
and utter every kind of evil against you falsely because of me.
Rejoice and be glad,
for your reward will be great in heaven."

✛ *Understanding the Word*

What is the basis of sanctity? The First Letter of John provides a rich image that strengthens our will to live holy lives.

The image is that of Christians as children of God; this relationship with God has implications both for our present and our future. First John tells us that the Father has shown great love in "that we may be called the children of God" (1 John 3:1a). A family is one of the richest gifts that anyone can be given. It is a group that should provide support for one as long as it exists: a support guaranteed by the close relationships that exist among family members. The quality of family life is the basis of the quality of support that is extended to each of its members. Being a part of God's family assures one of maximum support.

How foolish that the idea of belonging to a royal family has such great appeal among the general public! For all the privilege and wealth associated with such lofty stature, royalty guarantees no greater quality of life. The true privilege comes from being a member of God's family. This realization should encourage people to act like members of this family.

The second major motivation in this passage for living godly lives is the promise that we will become like God when God is revealed (3:2). The primary image of God that the author of First John provides throughout this letter is that "God is love." Therefore, in 3:2 First John says that in the future our nature will be transformed into love. This is a poetic way of speaking about the holiness that is always focused on love.

First John is convinced that these twin aspects of the image of ourselves can empower change in our lives: "Everyone who has this hope based on [God] makes himself pure, as [God] is pure" (3:3).

✢ Reflecting on the Word

As a boy of ten, I remember buying a comic book from the rack at the back of church. It featured the stories of five saints for young people. It brought a boy close to my own age into my life. His name was Dominic Savio. I no longer remember much about him and what he did to become a saint, but for several years he was part of my life. I would pray to him, talk to him, think about how he might handle this or that situation I was facing. I guess you could say I befriended him. Or perhaps he befriended me. He brought the presence of God into my life in a concrete way.

Today's solemnity especially honors those holy ones who have not made it into the main listing of saints whom the universal Church celebrates each year with a special feast day. These saints of all ages, times, and cultures have gone before us, faithful to their baptismal commitment to live out the dying and rising of Jesus Christ. Some were martyred, but many simply lived good lives, trying to bring God into the world as people who were poor in spirit, merciful, peacemakers, humble, seekers of justice—those characteristics that witness to the Holy Spirit at work in transforming not just bread and wine but people into the body of Christ.

Today is a great feast because it reminds us that, even though we can feel very alone on occasions when we say or do something that the Spirit prods us to do but that does not get much approval from those around us, we know that we are part of a great family, one joined together by the Spirit under the lordship of Jesus Christ.

✢ Consider/Discuss:

- Read today's Gospel of the Beatitudes and see how they "fit" into your life.
- Which Beatitude are you most drawn to and which is the most difficult for you?

✢ Responding to the Word

Take a moment to thank God for the saints who have touched your life. Think about those members of your family who handed on the faith to you and those friends who have supported you in your faith. Try also to remember people who may have crossed your path only once but whose presence was invaluable in bringing God to you.

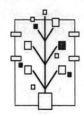

November 7, 2010

THIRTY-SECOND SUNDAY IN ORDINARY TIME

Today's Focus: God of the Living

November is a month when we remember our loved ones, family and friends who have gone on ahead of us. Remembering can bring a certain sadness at our loss and even evoke fear as we ourselves move closer to death. Today's readings clearly sound the hope that we have in resurrection, hope rooted in both the Jewish and Christian scriptures.

FIRST READING
2 Maccabees 7: 1–2, 9–14

It happened that seven brothers with their mother were arrested and tortured with whips and scourges by the king, to force them to eat pork in violation of God's law. One of the brothers, speaking for the others, said: "What do you expect to achieve by questioning us? We are ready to die rather than transgress the laws of our ancestors."

At the point of death he said: "You accursed fiend, you are depriving us of this present life, but the King of the world will raise us up to live again forever. It is for his laws that we are dying."

After him the third suffered their cruel sport. He put out his tongue at once when told to do so, and bravely held out his hands, as he spoke these noble words: "It was from Heaven that I received these; for the sake of his laws I disdain them; from him I hope to receive them again." Even the king and his attendants marveled at the young man's courage, because he regarded his sufferings as nothing.

After he had died, they tortured and maltreated the fourth brother in the same way. When he was near death, he said, "It is my choice to die at the hands of men with the hope God gives of being raised up by him; but for you, there will be no resurrection to life."

PSALM RESPONSE
Psalm 17:15b

Lord, when your glory appears, my joy will be full.

SECOND READING
2 Thessalonians 2:16 – 3:5

Brothers and sisters: May our Lord Jesus Christ himself and God our Father, who has loved us and given us everlasting encouragement and good hope through his grace, encourage your hearts and strengthen them in every good deed and word.

Finally, brothers and sisters, pray for us, so that the word of the Lord may speed forward and be glorified, as it did among you, and that we may be delivered from perverse and wicked people, for not all have faith. But the Lord is faithful; he will strengthen you and guard you from the evil one. We are confident of you in the Lord that what we instruct you, you are doing and will continue to do. May the Lord direct your hearts to the love of God and to the endurance of Christ.

GOSPEL
Luke 20:27–38
or 20:27, 34–38

Some Sadducees, those who deny that there is a resurrection, came forward | and put this question to Jesus, saying, "Teacher, Moses wrote for us,

> *If someone's brother dies leaving a wife but no child,*
> *his brother must take the wife*
> *and raise up descendants for his brother.*

Now there were seven brothers; the first married a woman but died childless. Then the second and the third married her, and likewise all the seven died childless. Finally the woman also died. Now at the resurrection whose wife will that woman be? For all seven had been married to her." | Jesus said to them, "The children of this age marry and remarry; but those who are deemed worthy to attain to the coming age and to the resurrection of the dead neither marry nor are given in marriage. They can no longer die, for they are like angels; and they are the children of God because they are the ones who will rise. That the dead will rise even Moses made known in the passage about the bush, when he called out 'Lord,' the God of Abraham, the God of Isaac, and the God of Jacob; and he is not God of the dead, but of the living, for to him all are alive."

❖ Understanding the Word

In today's Gospel we hear an attempt by the Sadducees to best Jesus in a debate. This religious group did not believe in a resurrection, so they posed a hypothetical situation to Jesus that they thought showed how ridiculous was of the concept of resurrection.

Their case is based on the levirate law that states that if a brother who is married dies before he has any children, it is the duty of his brother to marry the deceased brother's wife and raise their first child as the child of the deceased brother. The Sadducees tell of a situation in which a man died childless after having married a woman. Six of his other brothers also died childless after marrying her. Therefore, they ask Jesus, whose wife will she be at the resurrection? Their intent is to try to show that no couple can be considered closer to each other than any other couple, and therefore resurrection would make a mockery of the closeness of each by privileging one over the others.

Jesus circumvents this obstacle by saying that intimacy is not diminished by the resurrection. Rather, the resurrection keeps people in touch with God and, by so doing, in touch with each other. The guiding image for Jesus is that of "children." It is "the children of this age" who "marry and remarry" (20:34). But they will rise as "children of God" (20:36). In other words, their closeness as God's children grounds their intimacy with each other. The resurrection occurs because God will not be separated from the children of God, and it is this closeness that will enable the intimacy of all other relationships.

The Sadducees claim that the resurrection makes a mockery out of closeness. Jesus responds that the resurrection is God's confirmation and continuation of the closeness that exists between God and the children of God. To try to say that the resurrection logically would not be able to restore the closeness that existed in some situations is to fail to realize that all true intimacy is rooted in our primary closeness of being the children of God.

✤ Reflecting on the Word

Belief in the resurrection was one area where Jesus agreed with the Pharisees. The Sadducees, however, the power people of Jesus' time, from whose ranks came members of the Sanhedrin and the high priest, did not hold to any possibility of a bodily resurrection. They believed only what was written in the first five books of the Bible, called the Pentateuch or the Torah. No mention of bodily resurrection was to be found there. So, to make Jesus look foolish, they posed this story of a woman who marries seven brothers, asking whose wife she would be at the resurrection.

But Jesus is not so easily cornered. Your vision is poor and your hearing isn't much better, he tells them. First, there will no longer be need for marriage; it's a different world in heaven. We will be like angels then, God's very own children. Furthermore, if you open the book of Exodus, which is part of the Torah, you will find God introducing himself to Moses as the God of Abraham, Isaac, and Jacob, patriarchs long dead, but about whom God speaks as though they are living. Indeed, they are living—in God! So open your ears and your eyes.

To complete this message we also hear the story of the mother of seven sons whose belief in the resurrection carried them through terrible torture into the arms of God. Read the whole story in 2 Maccabees 7; it is very moving and brings home how this mystery of faith in a bodily resurrection goes back even to the time before Jesus.

✤ Consider/Discuss:

- What does it mean to say in the Creed, "I believe in the resurrection of the body and life everlasting"? How do you understand this mystery of our faith?
- Have you had any experience of the risen Lord that helps you to believe in the resurrection of the body?

✤ Responding to the Word

We can name in our prayers all those who have gone before us, especially those who were most influential in our lives in handing on the faith to us, those who have died recently, and those who left us with "unfinished business" in our relationships with them.

210

THIRTY-THIRD SUNDAY IN ORDINARY TIME

Today's Focus: The Day Is Coming

Today's scriptures focus on the "end time," when God will come in power, when Christ will come to judge the living and the dead. The Old Testament prophet Malachi referred to it as the day of the Lord; Jesus called it the day when we will see "the Son of Man coming in a cloud" (Luke 21:27).

FIRST READING
Malachi 3: 19–20a

Lo, the day is coming, blazing like an oven,
    when all the proud and all evildoers will be stubble,
and the day that is coming will set them on fire,
    leaving them neither root nor branch,
    says the LORD of hosts.
But for you who fear my name, there will arise
    the sun of justice with its healing rays.

PSALM RESPONSE
Psalm 98:9

The Lord comes to rule the earth with justice.

SECOND READING
2 Thessalonians 3: 7–12

Brothers and sisters: You know how one must imitate us. For we did not act in a disorderly way among you, nor did we eat food received free from anyone. On the contrary, in toil and drudgery, night and day we worked, so as not to burden any of you. Not that we do not have the right. Rather, we wanted to present ourselves as a model for you, so that you might imitate us. In fact, when we were with you, we instructed you that if anyone was unwilling to work, neither should that one eat. We hear that some are conducting themselves among you in a disorderly way, by not keeping busy but minding the business of others. Such people we instruct and urge in the Lord Jesus Christ to work quietly and to eat their own food.

GOSPEL
Luke 21:5–19

While some people were speaking about how the temple was adorned with costly stones and votive offerings, Jesus said, "All that you see here—the days will come when there will not be left a stone upon another stone that will not be thrown down."

Then they asked him, "Teacher, when will this happen? And what sign will there be when all these things are about to happen?" He answered, "See that you not be deceived, for many will come in my name, saying, 'I am he,' and 'The time has come.' Do not follow them! When you hear of wars and insurrections, do not be terrified; for such things must happen first, but it will not immediately be the end." Then he said to them, "Nation will rise against nation, and kingdom against kingdom. There will be powerful earthquakes, famines, and plagues from place to place; and awesome sights and mighty signs will come from the sky.

"Before all this happens, however, they will seize and persecute you, they will hand you over to the synagogues and to prisons, and they will have you led before kings and governors because of my name. It will lead to your giving testimony. Remember, you are not to prepare your defense beforehand, for I myself shall give you a wisdom in speaking that all your adversaries will be powerless to resist or refute. You will even be handed over by parents, brothers, relatives, and friends, and they will put some of you to death. You will be hated by all because of my name, but not a hair on your head will be destroyed. By your perseverance you will secure your lives."

❖❖ *Understanding the Word*

What lasts? What is worth our attention? Luke treats these fundamental questions in his discourse on the last days.

As a prelude to this discourse Luke presents two brief accounts on wealth and its uses. In the first, Jesus commends a poor widow for having contributed to the temple treasury by her "two small coins" more than all the rest have. This is so because she "has offered her whole livelihood" (Luke 21:4). Once again we see the Lukan stress on giving unstintingly of yourself and of your resources. In the second account, some people marvel at the "costly stones and votive offerings" that adorn the temple (21:5). They focus on the externals of how wealth is aggregated, whereas Jesus focuses on the internals of how wealth is spent.

This dichotomy of perspectives leads Jesus to declare that the whole wealthy temple will be destroyed. People ask him when this will occur (21:6–7). Jesus responds by focusing on two elements: the sufferings at the end of time and the need for perseverance in the face of them. The last days are times when commitment is called for in order to remain faithful. In other words, the last days are times that will require the inner resources exemplified by the poor widow who was willing to give till it hurt.

Great transformations require radical upheavals that can be unnerving and very difficult. The discourse on the last days presents these upheavals as prepatory to Jesus' second coming and the fulfillment of the kingdom of God (21:27–28). We bring to periods of trial the resources that we have developed at other times.

What lasts? Habits cultivated over a lifetime. The generous giving of ourselves and what we have been given enables us to persevere through the radical transition necessary for the coming of God's reign.

Some time ago, I read that many believers have lost "a sense of an ending" to all things. In the past preachers spoke about the "four last things," that is, death, judgment, heaven, and hell. But today churchgoers rarely hear anything about them; as a matter of fact preachers often seem a bit embarrassed to address these realities.

The prophet Malachi (whose name means "my messenger") had no such hesitation. There will be an end, a day blazing like an oven, burning up all evildoers like stubble; no roots or branches will be found. This will not be everyone's experience of that day. The just, who reverence and honor God, will experience not a blazing firestorm but the sun of justice with its healing rays.

Jesus is also referring to an end time in today's Gospel, most likely one that has already occurred by the time that Luke's Gospel is recorded. Luke's hearers had already seen the destruction of the city of Jerusalem and its temple, accompanied by the persecution of the church. Jesus' words here were a call to encouragement, to persevere, that God will be there and "you will secure your lives" (Luke 21:19).

We believe the end time has begun with the death and resurrection of Jesus, but we live between what theologians call "the already and the not yet." Already God has acted in a definitive way by raising Jesus from the dead, but the total results of this action have yet to be realized in the world. God's word today is meant to give us hope that God will be faithful to the divine promises, and we will see the Lord face to face. We can count on this.

❖ *Consider/Discuss*:

- Do you live with "a sense of an ending" that will open up to a new life?
- Do you believe that Christ will come in power and glory to judge the living and the dead?

❖ *Responding to the Word*

The book of Revelation offers to believers the simplest of prayers in this regard: *Maranatha*, that is, Come, Lord Jesus. We can make that prayer our own, a daily prayer that turns to the Lord believing that in the end God is to be found. Let us pray: *Maranatha*. Come, Lord Jesus.

November 21, 2010

THE SOLEMNITY OF OUR LORD JESUS CHRIST THE KING

Today's Focus: The Thief Who Stole Paradise

Only Luke gives us the story of the "good thief" at Calvary, emphasizing that, up to the very end, Jesus remained the "Son of man who came to seek and save what was lost" (Luke 19:10). In Jesus we see the compassion of God at work in his final moments and in the most extreme agony.

FIRST READING
2 Samuel 5:1–3

In those days, all the tribes of Israel came to David in Hebron and said: "Here we are, your bone and your flesh. In days past, when Saul was our king, it was you who led the Israelites out and brought them back. And the LORD said to you, 'You shall shepherd my people Israel and shall be commander of Israel.' " When all the elders of Israel came to David in Hebron, King David made an agreement with them there before the LORD, and they anointed him king of Israel.

PSALM RESPONSE
Psalm 122:1

Let us go rejoicing to the house of the Lord.

SECOND READING
Colossians 1: 12–20

Brothers and sisters: Let us give thanks to the Father, who has made you fit to share in the inheritance of the holy ones in light. He delivered us from the power of darkness and transferred us to the kingdom of his beloved Son, in whom we have redemption, the forgiveness of sins.

He is the image of the invisible God,
    the firstborn of all creation.
For in him were created all things in heaven and on earth,
    the visible and the invisible,
    whether thrones or dominions or principalities or powers;
    all things were created through him and for him.
He is before all things,
    and in him all things hold together.
He is the head of the body, the church.
He is the beginning, the firstborn from the dead,
    that in all things he himself might be preeminent.
For in him all the fullness was pleased to dwell,
    and through him to reconcile all things for him,
    making peace by the blood of his cross
    through him, whether those on earth or those in heaven.

GOSPEL
Luke 23:35–43

The rulers sneered at Jesus and said, "He saved others, let him save himself if he is the chosen one, the Christ of God." Even the soldiers jeered at him. As they approached to offer him wine they called out, "If you are King of the Jews, save yourself." Above him there was an inscription that read, "This is the King of the Jews."

Now one of the criminals hanging there reviled Jesus, saying, "Are you not the Christ? Save yourself and us." The other, however, rebuking him, said in reply, "Have you no fear of God, for you are subject to the same condemnation? And indeed, we have been condemned justly, for the sentence we received corresponds to our crimes, but this man has done nothing criminal." Then he said, "Jesus, remember me when you come into your kingdom." He replied to him, "Amen, I say to you, today you will be with me in Paradise."

✦ Understanding the Word

How can a person determine what is the most powerful force in life? This is the issue that Luke sees being contested while Jesus is crucified.

Like Matthew and Mark, Luke writes about two other people being crucified with Jesus. Matthew and Mark call them "revolutionaries" (Matthew 27:38; Mark 15:27). Luke says they were "criminals" (Luke 23:32–33). This Lukan designation will be important as the scene develops. Only Luke will have these two people talk to Jesus while they are crucified. Their words are themselves a response to what others have been saying about and to Jesus at this time. The rulers of the people have been mocking him, saying that although he could save others he apparently cannot save himself. They see in this "failure" a clear indication that he is not the Messiah of God (23:35b). The soldiers, too, see in this failure to save himself that he is not the "King of the Jews" (23:37–38).

At issue is how the divine power is expressed in this world. Is God self-directed or other-oriented? The two criminals pick up this line of thought. The first tells Jesus to "save yourself and us" if he is the Messiah (23:39). His words show how he thinks that if you have the power you should use it for your benefit. The second criminal has a different perspective. He says to the first that they are both guilty and receiving their just deserts. But Jesus, he continues, did "nothing criminal" (23:40–42). He also asks Jesus to save him, as does the other criminal. His request is, however, significantly different: "Jesus, remember me when you come into your kingdom" (23:42). This request is not, like all the taunts that preceded it, a request for instant deliverance as proof of God's presence in Jesus. Rather, it is a request stemming from a faith in this presence. It is met by Jesus with assurance of the instantaneous deliverance that all the others were looking for: "Amen, I say to you, today you will be with me in Paradise" (23:43).

The most powerful force in life, God's reign, expresses itself for others. We are open to it when we recognize God in this other-oriented attitude.

215

When we think of Christ the King, we usually do not think of Jesus hanging on the cross, but rather the risen Christ, seated at the right hand of the Father, wearing the crown bestowed upon him by the Father. But Luke presents us with an image of Christ whose reign begins on the cross with his promise of Paradise to a thief hanging at his side.

Jesus brings about the kingdom even in the last moment of his life, extending the mercy of God to yet another nameless outsider, a thief "condemned justly" to death (Luke 23:41). This man recognizes Jesus both as a man who "has done nothing criminal," but also one who is about to "come into [his] kingdom" (23:41, 42).

The kingdom of God that Jesus proclaimed as being "already in your midst" is present in Jesus on the cross, extending mercy by asking God to forgive those who have crucified him, for "they know not what they do" (23:34). To the thief who asks Jesus to remember him when he comes into his kingdom, Jesus promises, "Today you will be with me in Paradise" (23:43). What wonderful words to bring the church year to a close.

We might think of this dying thief as one who stole heaven at the last moment, but perhaps that is inaccurate. How could it be a theft when Paradise was there for the taking? The crucified One himself, being the king of hearts, the shepherd king lifted up one last time a beloved sheep who had wandered far astray but unexpectedly found himself at heaven's door. If we call him king, it is because he was faithful to his calling, not to save himself but to save us.

❖ *Consider/Discuss:*

- Why do you think this story was chosen for the solemnity of Christ the King?
- Does this story address anything in your life or is it simply just another "heartwarming story" about the compassion of Jesus to outcasts and those most abandoned?

❖ *Responding to the Word*

Let your heart speak to the thief in this story. Do you have anything to say to or ask him? Then, talk to Jesus about what you want most to ask from him, what you experience as your greatest need at this time in your life.

Twenty-five Years and Counting

This year's edition of *Living the Word* marks the twenty-fifth anniversary of its first publication. It was the brainchild of Rod Brownfield, its first author, and Dolores Orzel, its first editor, together with managing editor Pat McGeary. *Living the Word—Not Only on Sunday* first saw the light of day in 1986 as a more or less bi-monthly periodical, accommodated to the seasons of the liturgical year as necessary. It continued in that format until its fifteenth year, when its title was shortened and it took its present form as an annual publication.

While authors, editors, and formats have changed over the years, *Living the Word* remains true to its original vision of providing thoughtful scripture commentary and challenging reflection leading to a life more closely conformed to God's word. For that, I would like to express my profound gratitude to all the authors and editors whose faith and work has shaped *Living the Word* for the past twenty-five years and will continue to inspire us for at least twenty-five more!

—*Michael Novak, editor*

Authors

Rod Brownfield

Helen Kenik Mainelli

Eugene Mainelli

Jim Bitney

Yvette Nelson

Marianne Slattery

Rev. Robert Duggan

Rev. Richard Zajac

Virginia Stillwell

Msgr. Ralph Kuehner

Rev. Joseph Juknialis

Rev. James Wallace, C.Ss.R.

Dennis Sylva

Editors

Dolores J. Orzel

Ron Pazola

J. Tyrrell Keller

Dennis Sylva is Director of Lifelong Faith Formation at St. Jerome Parish in Oconomowoc, Wisconsin and an adjunct professor of biblical studies at Stritch University in Milwaukee, Wisconsin. Dr. Sylva has authored books and articles on the Old and New Testaments that have appeared in American, British, French, and German publications. He is currently working on commentaries on the book of Wisdom and the Pentateuch, and developing a series of books about discipleship in the Gospel of John. Recent publications include articles on 2 Peter and about the portrayal of Isaac in Genesis. Dr. Sylva specializes in addressing the human concerns that undergird biblical texts, and the ways that the biblical authors portray God's response to these concerns in order to help people live to their full potential. He is a member of the Society of Biblical Literature, the Catholic Biblical Association of America, and the Rhetoric of Religious Antiquity group.

James A. Wallace, C.Ss.R., is professor of homiletics at the Washington Theological Union, Washington, D.C. He is the author of *Preaching to the Hungers of the Heart* (Liturgical Press, 2002) and co-author of three books of homilies, *Lift Up Your Hearts: Homilies for the A, B, and C Cycles* (Paulist Press 2004, 2005, and 2006). He has served as president of the Academy of Homiletics, the Catholic Association of Teachers of Homiletics, and the Religious Speech Communication Association. His articles have appeared in various journals, and he has lectured on preaching in this country, Europe, and Asia.

Notes

Notes

Notes

Notes

Notes